WITHDRAWN BY THE
UNIVERSITY OF MICHIGAN

Wojciech Cwalina, PhD
Andrzej Falkowski, PhD
Bruce I. Newman, PhD

A Cross-Cultural Theory of Voter Behavior

Pre-publication
REVIEWS,
COMMENTARIES,
EVALUATIONS . . .

"Offers up-to-date, scientifically based models. . . . extremely wide-ranging. . . . A comprehensive, interdisciplinary account of intercultural approach of voter behavior as it has evolved over the past years. . . . invigorating. . . . provocative. . . . opens up pathways for others . . . challenges many of our ingrained assumptions about the direction of political imagery and offers valuable treatments as well as perspectives that provide an ideal baseline for teaching and research in disciplines pertinent to political marketing and communication."

Kosta Gouliamos, PhD,
Vice Rector, Cyprus College

"Covers important aspects of how marketing techniques in politics influence the formation of voters' attitudes. . . . Contributes significantly to our understanding of voter behavior. Cwalina, Falkowski, and Newman present new research insights and their work enhances our understanding of political marketing on the one hand, and of determinants of decision making by voters on the other. The reinterpretation of existing models of voting behavior especially represents a significant contribution to psephology."

Dr. Stephan C. Henneberg,
Senior Lecturer
(Associate Professor) in Marketing,
Manchester Business School, Manchester, UK

More pre-publication
REVIEWS, COMMENTARIES, EVALUATIONS . . .

"This book pulls together some of the best thinking and leading research in the world on psychology, voter choice, and consumption and applies it to the political market perfectly. For anybody wishing to study the best in cutting-edge research on political campaigning and voter choice this is the book. Well done Cwalina, Falkowski, and Newman for pulling this off."

Professor Phil Harris,
Head of the Department of Marketing, School of Business, University of Otago

"A thorough exposition of political marketing. . . . Provides robust statistical evidence for the conclusions. The next stage might be to explore some of the issues in greater depth through insightful qualitative research. . . . Should not only be read by scholars of political marketing but also by policy makers and anti 'spin' pressure groups."

Martin Evans, Senior Fellow,
Cardiff Business School, UK

The Haworth Press
Taylor & Francis Group
New York • London

NOTES FOR PROFESSIONAL LIBRARIANS AND LIBRARY USERS

This is an original book title published by The Haworth Press, Taylor & Francis Group. Unless otherwise noted in specific chapters with attribution, materials in this book have not been previously published elsewhere in any format or language.

CONSERVATION AND PRESERVATION NOTES

All books published by The Haworth Press and its imprints are printed on certified pH neutral, acid-free book grade paper. This paper meets the minimum requirements of American National Standard for Information Sciences-Permanence of Paper for Printed Material, ANSI Z39.48-1984.

DIGITAL OBJECT IDENTIFIER (DOI) LINKING

The Haworth Press is participating in reference linking for elements of our original books. (For more information on reference linking initiatives, please consult the CrossRef Web site at www.crossref.org.) When citing an element of this book such as a chapter, include the element's Digital Object Identifier (DOI) as the last item of the reference. A Digital Object Identifier is a persistent, authoritative, and unique identifier that a publisher assigns to each element of a book. Because of its persistence, DOIs will enable The Haworth Press and other publishers to link to the element referenced, and the link will not break over time. This will be a great resource in scholarly research.

A Cross-Cultural Theory of Voter Behavior

THE HAWORTH PRESS
New, recent, and forthcoming titles of related interest

Campaigns and Political Marketing edited by Wayne P. Steger and Sean Q. Kelly

Communication of Politics: Cross-Cultural Theory Building in the Practice of Public Relations and Political Marketing: 8th International Public Relations Research Conference, Vila Bled, Slovenia, July 2001 edited by Bruce I. Newman and Dejan Veric

Women and Congress: Running, Winning, and Ruling edited by Karen O'Connor

Euromarketing and the Future edited by Lynn R. Kahle

Gendering Politics and Policy: Recent Developments in Europe, Latin America, and the United States by Heidi Hartmann

The Politics of Youth, Sex, and Health Care in American Schools by James W. Button and Barbara A. Rienzo

Race, Politics, and Community Development Funding: The Discolor of Money by Michael Bonds

Political Violence and the Palestinian Family: Implications for Mental Health and Well-Being by Vivian Khamis

A Cross-Cultural Theory of Voter Behavior

Wojciech Cwalina, PhD
Andrzej Falkowski, PhD
Bruce I. Newman, PhD

The Haworth Press
Taylor & Francis Group
New York • London

For more information on this book or to order, visit
http://www.haworthpress.com/store/product.asp?sku=5478

or call 1-800-HAWORTH (800-429-6784) in the United States and Canada
or (607) 722-5857 outside the United States and Canada

or contact orders@HaworthPress.com

© 2008 by The Haworth Press, Taylor & Francis Group. All rights reserved. No part of this work may be reproduced or utilized in any form or by any means, electronic or mechanical, including photocopying, microfilm, and recording, or by any information storage and retrieval system, without permission in writing from the publisher. Printed in the United States of America.

The Haworth Press, Taylor & Francis Group, 270 Madison Avenue, New York, NY 10016.

PUBLISHER'S NOTE
The development, preparation, and publication of this work has been undertaken with great care. However, the Publisher, employees, editors, and agents of The Haworth Press are not responsible for any errors contained herein or for consequences that may ensue from use of materials or information contained in this work. The Haworth Press is committed to the dissemination of ideas and information according to the highest standards of intellectual freedom and the free exchange of ideas. Statements made and opinions expressed in this publication do not necessarily reflect the views of the Publisher, Directors, management, or staff of The Haworth Press, or an endorsement by them.

Library of Congress Cataloging-in-Publication Data

Cwalina, Wojciech.
  A cross-cultural theory of voter behavior / Wojciech Cwalina, Andrzej Falkowski, Bruce I. Newman.
      p. cm.
  Includes bibliographical references.
  ISBN: 978-0-7890-2735-1 (hard : alk. paper)
  ISBN: 978-0-7890-2736-8 (soft : alk. paper)
  1. Voting research—Cross-cultural studies. 2. Voting—Social aspects—Cross-cultural studies. 3. Political participation—Cross-cultural studies. 4. Politics, Practical—Cross-cultural studies. 5. New democracies. 6. Democratization. I. Falkowski, Andrzej. II. Newman, Bruce I. III. Title.

  JF1001.C83 2007
  324.9—dc22

                                                                      2007000550

This book is dedicated to our families

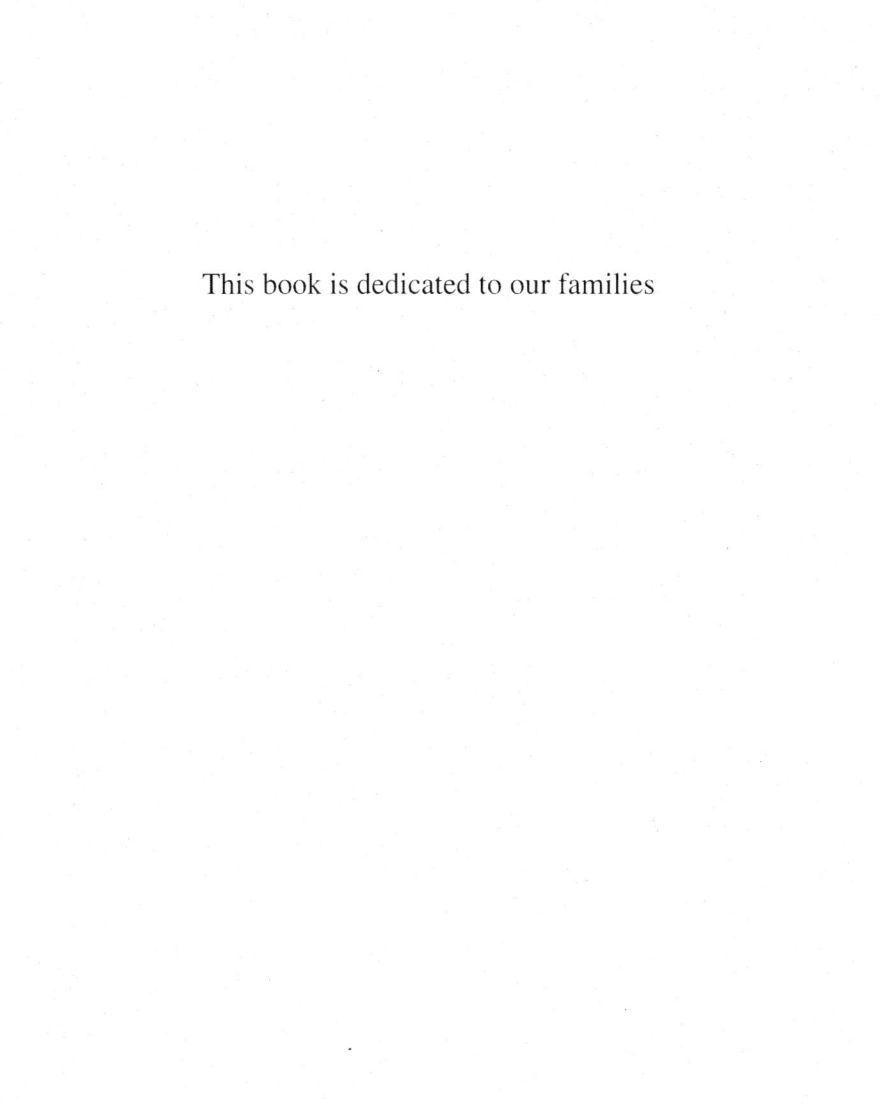

CONTENTS

Acknowledgments ix

About the Authors x

Introduction 1

Chapter 1. Politics in an Age of Manufactured Images 7
    Decline of Social Cleavage Voting 9
    Decline of Partisanship and Party Identification 11
    Candidate-Centered Politics 16
    How Are Political Images Manufactured? 18

Chapter 2. Political Cognition 25
    Constructivism and Realism 25
    Social Categorization of Politicians 34
    The Role of Emotion in Politics 54

Chapter 3. Political Marketing 57
    Economic versus Political Marketing 59
    Marketing Orientation in Political Campaigns 63
    The Process of Political Marketing according to Phillip B. Niffenegger 65
    A Model of Political Marketing according to Bruce I. Newman 71

Chapter 4. Traditional Models of Voter Behavior 85
    Sociological Approach 85
    Social Psychological Approach 90
    Economic Approach 95
    Multidimensional Models of Voter Behavior 104

Chapter 5. A Model of Voter's Choice Behavior: A Newman and Sheth Approach   **113**

Model Description   113
Primary Election in Illinois (U.S.) in 1980: Reagan versus Anderson   117
U.S. Presidential Election in 1996: Clinton versus Dole   120
U.S. Presidential Election in 2000: Bush versus Gore   125
Parliamentary Election in Slovenia in 2000   129
Presidential Election in Poland in 2000: Kwaśniewski versus Olechowski   134
Comparative Analysis of Predictive Model of Voter's Choice Behavior and Traditional Models   142

Chapter 6. Predictive Models of Voter Behavior: A Reinterpretation of Newman's Approach   **147**

Emotional Feelings as a Predictor of Voter Behavior   148
Media in Election   149
Sequential Model of the Influence of Political Advertisements   153
Structural Equation Models of Voter Behavior: A Constructivist Approach   156
Structural Equation Models of Voter Behavior: A Realistic Approach   177
Comparative Analysis of Models of Voter Behavior in Established and Developing Democracies   185
Practical Implications for Marketing Strategy   192

Chapter 7. Constructive Mind: Political Marketing, Freedom, and Democracy   **195**

Constructive Information Society   195
"Laboratory World" of Cognitive Psychology and Political Marketing   197
Resistance to Voting Manipulation   205
Freedom in Democratic Nations: A Paradox   212

References   **219**

Index   **233**

Acknowledgments

This book could not have been completed without the help of our colleagues and assistants. We would like to first thank Andrzej Antoszek from the Catholic University of Lublin in Poland and Kate Delaney from the Massachusetts Institute of Technology for their careful reading of the manuscript. Their helpful suggestions clarified the text, and their vigorous and dedicated effort was invaluable. We want to thank Lynda Lee Kaid from the University of Florida for her continued inspiration. We also want to thank the administration of the Warsaw School of Social Psychology for their financial research support. We want to acknowledge the assistance from DePaul University's Judith Rae Ross for help with data collection in the United States and Danuta Dzierzanowska for help with the editing of an earlier draft of the book. We want to also thank the administrative and editorial staff at The Haworth Press for their support of this project. Finally, we want to thank our families for their continued support and love.

A Cross-Cultural Theory of Voter Behavior
© 2008 by The Haworth Press, Taylor & Francis Group. All rights reserved.
doi:10.1300/5478_a

ABOUT THE AUTHORS

Wojciech Cwalina, PhD, is a Professor in the Department of Marketing Psychology at the Warsaw School of Social Psychology in Poland and a marketing specialist and media advisor in Polish political campaigns. He is the author of *Television Political Advertising and Political Marketing* (with A. Falkowski), and numerous articles and book chapters. Dr Cwalina was awarded the Domestic Grant for Young Beneficiaries by the Foundation for Polish Science and is a member of the Polish Association of Social Psychology and the Polish Political Marketing Association. He is also a member of the editorial board of *Journal of Political Marketing*.

Andrzej Falkowski, PhD, is a Professor in and Chairman of the Department of Marketing Psychology at the Warsaw School of Social Psychology in Poland. The author of many books, articles, and chapters—including *Branding and Advertising* and *Cognitive Applied Psychology: Marketing and Advertising*—Dr. Falkowski is a Fulbright Scholar and Ministry of Education Award recipient. A member of the International Society for Ecological Psychology and the Association of Consumer Research, he is also Advisory Editor for the *Handbook of Political Marketing* and the *Handbook of Psychology*.

Bruce I. Newman, PhD, is a leading expert in Political Marketing. The author of *Marketing the President*, seven other books, and numerous scholarly and popular articles on political marketing and consumer psychology, he is the Founding Editor-in-Chief of the *Journal of Political Marketing*. A former advisor to the White House and recipient of the Ehrenring from the Austrian Advertising Research association, Dr. Newman is Professor of Marketing at DePaul University.

Introduction

Efficient political systems in democratic countries are based on the same free-market principles utilized in large economic corporations as well as small companies. In recent years, understanding the importance of these principles has led politicians to become more and more pragmatic and sensitive to voters' needs and to the social atmosphere, and to put less emphasis on their own political views. It is the voters who decide whether a politician will remain on the political stage and whether a new political star will be born. Politicians have realized that winning parliamentary or presidential elections without marketing is nearly impossible. Although initially voter and political behavior methodology was adopted from such areas as consumer behavior and marketing strategies, at present, an independent discipline seems to be emerging, namely political marketing.

The development of democracy and political freedom facilitates the fast development of marketing techniques that intend to influence human behavior. In political marketing, marketing techniques are used to form voters' attitudes in order to make them support a given candidate or political party. Therefore, new and sophisticated methods of influencing voter behavior are created that are often based on psychological knowledge and principles.

The purpose of this study is to present theoretical and practical knowledge from the field of political marketing, stressing in particular the importance of psychological mechanisms for forming voter behavior. The results from psychological research on evoking emotions and creating perceptions through perceived objects are commonly used to construct persuasion messages employed in political campaigns. Such methods are based on manipulating people's attitudes and preferences beyond their conscious control, on the "automatic" level. Often, the voter does not realize that his or her behavior is formed by those who purposefully use complex marketing technology.

Such forming of voter behavior is strongly supported by the media, which reaches each person with information encouraging them to construct a certain way of perceiving the surrounding reality in his or her mind.

Who would be interested in such constructing? Managers responsible for marketing strategies in business as well as political marketing consultants would be two captivated entities. The first group uses the achievements of modern social science for influencing customer behavior, whereas the second group uses them for influencing voter behavior. Their increasingly sophisticated promotional campaigns influence the cognitive and emotional spheres of the voters, creating a certain image of reality in their minds. In this way, the customer or the voter becomes a puppet in the hands of the manager, who by controlling their behavior, is limiting their freedom.

In the development of democratic societies, in which freedom is particularly valued, this situation is a bit of a paradox. The very foundation of the development of such societies is the freedom of their citizens. This freedom, however, permits the development of advanced marketing strategies, whose purpose is to convince the customer to buy a given product or vote for a particular political option. The side effect of such strategies in turn limits customer's and voter's freedom of behavior.

Such a situation may take place in well-developed democracies as well as in countries where democracy is just developing (see Cwalina, Falkowski, Kaid, 2000, 2005; Dalton, Wattenberg, 1993). The main difference is that marketing techniques in this first group of countries are much more advanced because the citizens of these countries are more familiar with the techniques that have been used for decades. On the other hand, the experiences of people in developing democracies in postcommunist countries are not as rich due to the later emergence of professional voter marketing in the 1990s (Cwalina, Falkowski, Roznowski, 1999; Kaid, 1999).

One should also note that the character of limiting freedom is different in democratic states than it is in totalitarian states. In the latter group, the limits are imposed on the individual from the outside. Legal acts, state laws, and other official rulings limit the freedom of ordinary citizens' actions, as was the case in the communist states of Central and Eastern Europe. To a great extent, these citizens were aware of the limitations on their freedom imposed on them by the state. In democratic countries, this limitation is imposed from the inside. The individual is its source, because he or she has a certain picture of a certain fragment of reality in his or her mind, which provokes certain actions. The character of such an internal limitation is significantly more dangerous than that of externally imposed restrictions. Normally, one does not realize that he or she is not fully free, and that no formal ways to resist this state of affairs exist. It is possible, however, to discover how social and psychological mechanisms controlling humankind's behavior operate. These mechanisms are the basis of the applied marketing strategies.

The chapters included in this study are based on theoretical foundations of cognitive psychology with a particular emphasis on emotional-cognitive processes. The particular importance of this knowledge lies in its developing of the flexibility of the practitioner—the political campaign consultant—not only in using the market research tools discussed in detail in the book, but also in creating and controlling the surrounding social reality.

This book presents (in the context of cognitive psychology) Newman's model of voter's choice behavior and its reconstruction using structural equation methodology. The reinterpretation of Newman's model allowed us to develop a number of cause-and-effect models related to the nature of human cognition of the surrounding social and political reality. Many philosophical debates are still had as to whether we experience the surrounding reality the way it actually is or whether what we see is a cognitive construct created in our minds.

In the context of political marketing, the nature of cognition comes down to the following question: Do voters recognize the social reality on an affective basis, or is the affect a consequence of social cognition and do the images of a particular social phenomena have little in common with the real world?

This problem was presented on the basis of empirical testing of two approaches to causal relationships of cognitive and affective elements and their influence on voting behavior. The first approach, called constructivist, stresses the role of a politician's image on the affective attitude towards him or her. The other, called the realist approach, points to the relevance of affects in the formation of the image itself. Thus, taking into account the following simple sequences: cognition → affect or affect → cognition, we are using either a constructivist or realist approach to perceive the social environment. The primary criterion to differentiate between these approaches is whether perception of affect is direct or not. According to the constructivist approach, the affect is the result of stimuli processed in cognitive structures. According to the realist approach, the affect is the result of direct perception and is independent of information processing (Buck, 1988; Lazarus, 1991a; Zajonc, 1980).

A presentation of such often contradictory approaches to recognizing reality is particularly important, as its goal is to evoke a sense of criticism and methodological awareness in the reader. Adjusting research methods to the changing social and political reality is very important. Such criticism and awareness helps one to develop sensitivity to the ethical side of the marketing effort. The sophisticated methods of forming voter behavior are an efficient control tool that people in business and politics can use in unfair competition. Therefore, in addition to increasing the level of ethical culture and requiring managers to be honest in developing promotion strategies or preparing legislatures to put some limits on the activities of the mass media, one should also think about increasing voters' awareness of the modern form of information control, including political advertising. The best way to achieve this goal is through education. People's knowledge about the different techniques of persuasion, supported by the laws of psychology, increases awareness and allows people to control their emotions and develop an intellectual distance between themselves and what they receive. This book is therefore to serve as a foundation for such an education, teaching the reader how to use research tools from the field of political marketing and how to understand and form social and political reality.

One should say that many efforts in the modern world are dedicated to creating a new information society, in which the media plays a very important role in creating reality in voters' minds in accordance to the methods developed a long time ago via laboratory research conducted within the constructivist paradigm of cognitive psychology (Neisser, 1967; Bruner, 1973). Business and political marketing strategies that use the power of the media's influence have expanded, metaphorically speaking, from the "constructive oriented laboratory of cognitive psychology" to the "natural social environment" in democratic countries. This is very well demonstrated by Bruce I. Newman's book, *The Mass Marketing of Politics: Democracy in An Age of Manufactured Images* (1999a), whose very title points to the process of creating politicians' images becoming increasingly important in modern democracies.

After 1989, many countries in Eastern and Central Europe left the Soviet Bloc and started the process of democratization. They followed various institutional patterns from established democracies. Economic marketing along with political marketing began to develop rapidly. Mass media began to be used to create economic and political realities in the minds of customers and voters. The reality constructed in such a way is reinforced by so-called brand images, in which the identities of political and economic objects are "recorded." It is precisely these images that are loaded with powerful emotions that control the behavior of the customer and voter. It can be said then, that the development of democracy in the former Soviet Bloc countries is heading in the same direction that the United States and Western Europe are heading.

Chapter 1

Politics in an Age of Manufactured Images

In his *Politics* (1995), Aristotle wrote that humankind is created to live in the political state. Despite the many years that have since passed, this statement is still valid and has inspired many theoreticians and practitioners studying the life of people under many social systems. However, it has been modified many times in order to keep it up to date with the changing picture of humankind's conditions. In social psychology, the statement was popularized by Elliot Aronson (1992), who coined the notion of man as a *social animal*. Sociology, and particularly sociology of politics, treats an individual as, to use Seymour M. Lipset's (1981) term, *homo politicus*. These concepts point to a person fulfilling his or her goals and desires only when he or she belongs to a group, namely society. Therefore, by belonging to such a group, he or she should also obey the rules and standards that exist there.

Democracy is currently the main form of people's organization of themselves within state structures in the world. Despite its common criticism, this system is spreading across the world and is becoming the final destination for many societies under authoritarian power (see Huntington, 1991). According to Robert A. Dahl (2000), in order to exist and develop, every modern democracy needs the following six institutions:

1. *Elected representatives.* They constitute the parliament elected by citizens, and their major task is to control the government's decisions.
2. *Free, honest, and frequent elections.* People are neither forced to participate in such elections nor are they forced to elect a given person or political party.

A Cross-Cultural Theory of Voter Behavior
© 2008 by The Haworth Press, Taylor & Francis Group. All rights reserved.
doi:10.1300/5478_02

3. *Freedom of speech.* Citizens have the right and absolute freedom to express their political views without fear of punishment. They can criticize their representatives, government, or system.
4. *Access to various sources of information.* Citizens have the right to seek political information from many different sources, independent of the power or other monopolies present.
5. *Freedom of association.* Citizens, if they wish, should have a chance to establish independent associations and organizations, including political parties and interest groups.
6. *Inclusive citizenship.* This means that no adult having the citizenship of a given country may be deprived of the rights that others enjoy and that are essential for democratic institutions.

Participants in political life are most interested in the first two democratic institutions mentioned by Dahl (2000): elected representatives and free, frequent, and honest elections. These two elements of democracy are the main areas of research involving citizens' voting behaviors and ways of influencing these behaviors through political marketing.

The interest in citizens' voting behaviors is influenced by very practical motives: What do I need to do to win in the elections? How do I speak so that people can understand me and support me? What do I say in order to make people vote for me? To whom should I speak—to everybody or only to "selected" groups? Why do people vote the way they do? Why do they support this particular party? Many questions can be asked, but getting convincing answers to them is much harder.

An interesting phenomenon of modern civilization is the development of marketing methods for influencing voting behaviors, which stress the importance of creating a particular image of a fragment of political reality in voters' minds in order to shape it as freely as possible. The evolution of this branch of science has been quite long and has required the development of a viewpoint that would embrace an idealistic philosophy. The philosophical roots of modern political marketing can then be found in the Kantian epistemological theory, from which the currently used term *cognitive sciences* is derived.

The most important element of this practice is cognitive psychology, through which one can understand the techniques of influencing voter behavior. Therefore, before presenting the cognitive foundations of modern methods of political persuasions, one should take a brief look at the evolution of the views leading to modern research on forming politicians' and political parties' images.

DECLINE OF SOCIAL CLEAVAGE VOTING

The oldest studies on voting behaviors are represented by the sociological approach also called the sociostructural method. As its starting point, it takes the assumption that one's main reason for voting is one's sense of belonging to a social community. Examples of such communities may include ethnic, religious, or professional groups, or a social class, all of which point to the collective character of voting behaviors. In other words, it is individuals who vote, but their preferences are determined by their belonging to a given group.

The pioneer studies in this area are represented by panel discussions conducted by American academics from the Bureau of Applied Social Research at Columbia University and directed by Paul F. Lazarsfeld (Lazarsfeld, Berelson, Gaudet, 1944; Berelson, Lazarsfeld, McPhee, 1954). The first study was conducted in Erie County (Ohio) during the presidential elections in 1940, when Franklin D. Roosevelt (Democratic Party) and Wendell Wilkie (Republican Party) were competing. A second series of the studies was conducted during the presidential elections in 1948 in the town of Elmira (New York), when Harry Truman (Democratic Party) and Thomas Dewey (Republican Party) were competing. Despite the fact that Lazarsfeld is known as a sociologist, his main academic interest was the field of political marketing (see Chaffee, Hochheimer, 1985). Such interests determined his approach to analyzing voting behaviors as a specific type of consumer decision. However, the major conclusions that Lazarsfeld's team reached was that supporting a given presidential candidate is a group process, consisting of the following: common preferences in families; similar voting decisions among friends, colleagues, and neighbors; the strong influence of opinion leaders; and little influence of the mass media.

The sociostructural model of voting behaviors therefore assumes that an act of a citizen's voting is conditioned by their place in social structures. Sociological variables show a united set of interests shaping political coalitions and defining the level of a party's fit to the needs of various groups of people. The voters are treated not as individuals but as a community of views determined by their social position (social stratification) and acceptance of the same values. Following such assumptions, researchers consider the broadly understood demographic and sociological variables as the main voting-decision determinants (see for example Agnew, 1996; Pattie, Johnston, 1998; Lipset, 1981).

According to the sociostructural perspectives, the goal of each citizen is to recognize their social status. Generally speaking, it may then be said that one's political activities are to some extent determined the day he or she is born. For example, if a boy is born into a working-class family living in the suburbs of a large industrial town, it is most likely that he will support left-wing programs and parties.

Despite that sociological analyses still play an important role in explaining voting behaviors, it is believed that the assumptions they created were not valid at the moment in which they were formulated. Models based on demographic variables put an emphasis on the continuity and stability of voters' behaviors. However, they are still unable to explain changes in voters' preferences (Dalton, Wattenberg, 1993). Many researchers from different countries speak about the end of class divisions and the collapse of the class voting model (Dalton, Wattenberg, 1993; Johnston, Pattie, Allsopp, 1988; Riley, 1988). This model suggests that the working class supports left-wing parties and the middle class supports right-wing parties. However, this trend seems to be disappearing in all democratic party systems, though it can, to some extent, be helpful in predicting citizens' voting behaviors.

Many scholars directly linked the decline of social cleavage voting to ongoing changes in the nature of Western societies (e.g. Inglehart, 1977; McAllister, Studlar, 1995). Virtually all industrial democracies have shared in the increasing affluence of the postwar economic boom. The embourgeoisement of the working class narrowed the differences in living conditions between class strata and attenuated the importance of class-based political conflict. The growth of the service sector and government employment further reshaped the structure of labor forces, creating new-postindustrial societies. These changes were paralleled by other shifts in the social structure. Modern societies require a more educated labor force and possess the resources to dramatically expand educational access. Changing employment patterns also stimulate increased geographic mobility and urbanization. The traditional closed community life was gradually supplanted by more open and cosmopolitan lifestyles.

Russell J. Dalton and Martin P. Wattenberg (1993) believe that these and other social forces transformed the social composition of the contemporary public from those of the electorates on which sociological models of voting behavior were based. The social class, religious, and community bases of social structure have been altered in equally profound ways.

A detailed analysis of the sociological approach will be presented in Chapter 4.

DECLINE OF PARTISANSHIP AND PARTY IDENTIFICATION

Until recently, partisanship was considered an important element of voting in democratic parties, and the only one in totalitarian countries. However, a number of modern studies on voting preferences conducted in the United States and Europe prove that the importance of voters' partisanship for voting for a given candidate is systematically decreasing.

In the second half of the twentieth century, researchers studying political behaviors believed that the majority of voters knew whom they were going to support in political elections from the beginning of the campaign. Therefore, they would not be open to any persuasion during the political campaign. The small group of undecided voters turned out to be so minute that, despite their susceptibility to a party's and candidate's information policy, their significance was very low. This position, also accepted by party leaders, helped them to determine the concept of the party and of the product in planning their campaign. The concept changed only when the number of undecided voters and those changing their decisions during the campaign increased (see Wattenberg, 1995; Chaffee, Rimal, 1996).

Due to the increasingly visible polarization of the voting market into those decided and undecided, Stephen Chaffee and Rajiv Rimal (1996) presented their *dichotomous model,* which divides the voters into two major groups: (1) a large segment of those decided, and (2) a smaller but increasing segment of those undecided.

Taking into consideration people's timing in making their decision to support a particular candidate, one may say that the voters in the first segment made these decisions a long time ago. They have a sense of belonging to a given party, agree with its views, and are therefore resistant to the actions of other parties, although they follow the campaign closely. The voters from the second segment have not made their decisions yet and are therefore more open and susceptible to voting communication. However, one may suspect that their indecisiveness results from their lack of interest in the election, which leads to *media voting paradox*. It means that even though undecided voters are more prone to the influence of the media, they are not in fact influenced by the media because they either pay no attention to it or disregard political news (Chaffee, Choe, 1980).

Chaffee and his colleagues believe that since 1950 the power of partisanship has been systematically decreasing and the number of voters making decisions during the campaign has been increasing. This is confirmed by Thomas M. Holbrook's analyses (1996), presenting in detail the changes in partisanship on the American voting market between 1952 and 1992. They show a systematic decrease in the number of voters identifying themselves with the Democratic or Republican Party and an increase in the number of independent voters. (See Figure 1.1.)

A more detailed study on the formation of the undecided voters segment over several decades was presented by Bernadette Hayes and Ian McAllister (1996) for the voting market in Britain. The authors observe a systematic decrease in voters affiliating themselves with any political party since 1960. Indeed, the loyalty toward the two major British parties, the Conservative Party and the Labour Party, is decreasing. One of the reasons for this is a noticeable increase in domestic and foreign policies' independence from party ideology. This leads to consistently fewer differences between the opposing parties in key issues of economic policy.

As time goes on, the segment of undecided voters is beginning to be more and more visible. According to Hayes and McAllister (1996), they are called "floating voters," and are not connected with any party. In order to achieve election success, parties should pay particular attention to such voters and concentrate less on their "permanent," loyal voters. The dynamics of the formation of voting segments, rela-

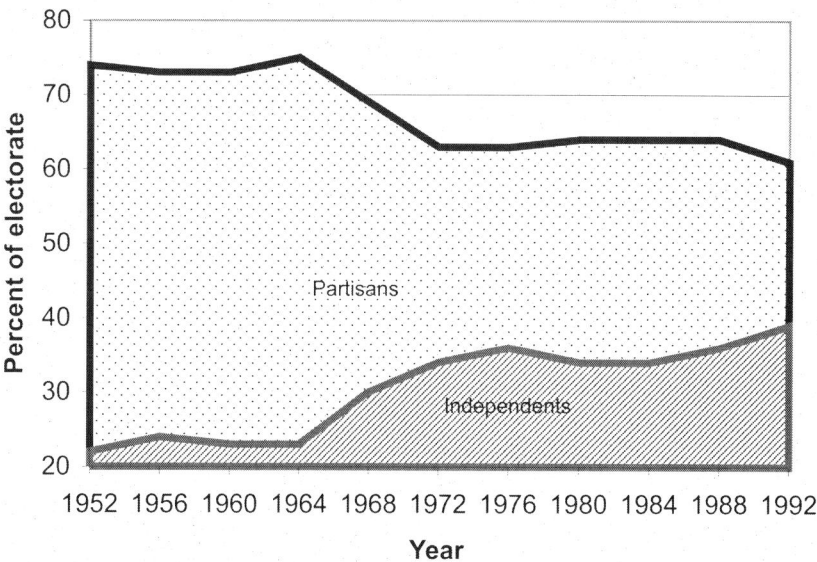

FIGURE 1.1. Changes in partisanship 1952-1992. *Source:* Adapted from Miller W.E. and the National Election Studies (1994). *American National Election Studies Cumulative Data File 1952-1992* [Computer File]. Sixth release. University of Michigan, Center for Political Studies [producer]. Ann Arbor, MI: Inter-University Consortium for Political and Social Research [distributor], 1991.

tive to the decision-making time between 1964 and 1992, is presented in Figure 1.2.

The figure shows three segments of voters: (1) voters loyal to a given party who made their decision quite early, (2) voters making decisions between general elections over the course of two years, and (3) campaign voters making their decisions only days before the elections.

One can clearly see that the number of loyal voters decreased from 77 percent in 1964 to 60 percent in 1992. On the other hand, the segment of undecided voters is growing very quickly. By 1992, it was already 24 percent of the individuals voting. This figure is important in light of the results of voting competition. One can then understand why, in recent years, so much investment has been made in the development of marketing techniques used during political campaigns. Private advertising agencies also participate in it, focusing on unde-

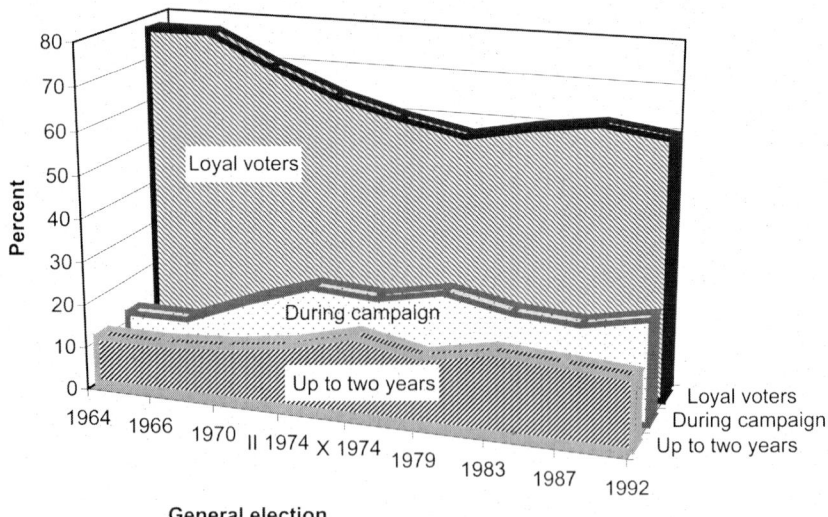

FIGURE 1.2. The time at which voters decide how to vote, 1964-1992. *Source:* Adapted from Hayes and McAllister (1996).

cided voters. Such investments rapidly increase campaign costs. An estimated nine million pounds was spent on the Conservatives' campaign in 1987, and although the record seemed unlikely to be broken, five years later it was ten million. A similar situation can be observed with the Labour Party, which in 1987 invested slightly more than four million pounds in its campaign. However, in 1992, its expenses almost tripled, exceeding seven million pounds.

One should note that Figure 1.2 illustrates changes strikingly similar to the changes one can observe in the United States (see Figure 1.1). It should therefore be stated that the decreasing number of loyal voters is not only the characteristic of the British voting market, but also applies to other democratic states.

Analyzing the research on voting behaviors in different countries, Russell J. Dalton and Martin P. Wattenberg (1993) conclude that partisan ties are disappearing in most modern democracies. They are more and more often accompanied by people voting for a particular person, no matter what party he or she represents. A clear example illustrating these two trends is split-ticket voting, which is taking place more frequently as well. Split-ticket voting occurs when parliamentary elections take place simultaneously, and a given person votes for a candidate from one party in the lower chamber (e.g. House of Representatives in the United States and Sejm in Poland), and for a representative of a competing party in the higher chamber (e.g. Senate in the United States and Poland). Wattenberg's studies (1995) suggest that about a quarter of all American voters in 1984 and 1988 split their ticket between presidential and House candidates. This is roughly twice as many as in the 1950s. These trends are shown in Table 1.1.

The emergence and the growth of the sector of voters who are uncertain of their decision at the beginning of political campaigns is a key argument for the use of political marketing in the election process. Therefore, current marketing efforts concentrate less on a candidate's party affiliation and more on the candidate him/herself.

The transformations in the setup of democratic institutions and the analyses of citizens' voting behaviors conducted within various paradigms support the thesis Dalton and Wattenberg (1993) put forward

TABLE 1.1. Key indicators of dealignment, 1952-1988.

	1952	1956	1960	1964	1968	1972	1976	1980	1984	1988
Percentage identifying with a party	75	73	75	77	70	64	63	64	64	63
Percentage splitting their ticket between president and House	12	16	14	15	26	30	25	34	25	25
Percentage splitting their ticket between Senate and House	9	10	9	18	22	23	23	31	20	27
Percentage neutral toward both parties	13	16	17	20	19	30	31	37	36	30
Percentage positive toward one party and negative toward the other	50	40	41	38	38	30	31	27	31	34

Source: Adapted from SRC/CPS National Election Studies; see also Wattenberg (1995).

about individualization of contemporary politics. One can see a clear shift from the earlier methods of making voting decisions based on directions given by social groups to more individualized and psychologically oriented ways of voting. Instead of being dependent on party elites and reference groups, more and more citizens try to cope on their own with the complexity of politics and make their decisions based on their individual, independent preferences. Besides, more and more often, voters begin to follow individual and well-known political candidates rather than parties. It is also becoming more frequent to see those who are not politically involved and do not have a traditional political background running for state offices (for example, Ross Perot in the American presidential elections in 1992 and 1996 and Stanisław Tymiński and Andrzej Olechowski in Poland in 2000).

CANDIDATE-CENTERED POLITICS

"Marketing" and "mediatization" have become important elements of such democratic institutions as general elections. Each candidate running for any state office surrounds himself or herself with an image-creation specialist, strategists planning his or her campaign, public opinion pollsters, etc. (Butler, Kavanagh, 1992; Kinsey, 1999; Newman, 1999a; Plasser, Scheucher, Senft, 1999). Only when properly "packaged" does a candidate stand a chance of election success. Sometimes it is at the expense of the temporary loss of his or her identity or of lying. Paul Ekman (1992) claims that every politician who gains power, who has the ability to speak in public and a good television image has a communicational predisposition to be a natural liar. And even though, according to Konrad Lorenz (1987), a lie can also be encountered in the world of animals and flowers, there it is always directed at representatives of preying species in order to improve chances of survival. People, however, break this evolutionary prohibition by providing their fellow human beings with untrue information. According to Lorenz, in the long run, it is a suicidal practice that is an example of "the waning of humaneness."

The constant interweaving of fiction and reality in the world of politics leads to politics being commonly referred to as the "political scene" and politicians as "actors." They perform a certain "play" in front of their audience, the voters, in order to win their support, which bestows power on them. Everybody, including politicians and voters, is immersed in what Erving Goffman (1959) called "the theater of everyday life." This situation bears out Guy Debord's (1994) bitter reflections that this kind of social performance is a reconstruction of collective illusions, a dream, a bad dream of the enslaved modern society whose only desire is to dream on.

Analyzing presidential elections in the 1980s in the United States, Martin P. Wattenberg (1995) actually announces the beginning of a new era in voting politics, referring to it as *candidate-centered politics*. It is characterized by the electorate's attention shift from political parties to specific candidates running for various offices, and, particularly, for president. The shift is accompanied by the growing importance of a candidate's individual characteristics of which his or her image is made up.

In this way, politicians are in the business of selling hope to people. The challenge to the political marketer is the ability to connect a politician's words, actions, and vision into a realistic transformation of the electorate's dreams and aspirations. That transformation takes the form of an image of the politician in the minds of the citizens, one that is carefully developed and fine-tuned over a long period of time. Consequently, as Bruce I. Newman (1999a,b) put it, politics enters the *age of manufactured images*.

This phenomenon is not limited to the United States. Efforts undertaken by image-creation specialists have become common practice in countries of Western Europe (for example, creating the image of Tony Blair in Britain: see McGuire, 1997b; Ingram, Lees-Marshment, 2002; Lionel Jospin in France: see Warner, 1997; Benjamin Netanyahu in Israel: see Beyer, 1996). The countries of the former communist bloc also follow this trend. Hans-Dieter Klingemann and Martin P. Wattenberg (1992) even suggest that the new democracies of Eastern Europe may resemble the United States even more than other European countries due to their greater focus on candidates relative to parties and their programs. It is more likely to have parties form around their leaders, as is often the case in Eastern Europe, than to have leaders selected from party organizations (see also Cwalina, Falkowski, Kaid, 2000).

An example supporting Klingemann's and Wattenberg's thesis is Stanisław Tymiński's presidential campaign in 1990. It was the first fully professional campaign in Poland that used television and other media in order to gain political support. And although it did not lead to Tymiński's victory, it was a huge success for its authors. From the beginning, Tymiński's aides cooperated closely with the advertising agency Golik & Dabrowski. Together they set the campaign plan and decided what its image should be (Bazylko, Fafara, Wysocki, 1991). Tymiński was running for the Polish presidency as a newcomer from abroad, unknown to the electorate. As a rich businessman and citizen of three countries (Poland, Canada, and Peru) he was a successful man who managed to avoid the dangers and traps of the capitalist world on his own (Krzemiński, 1991). In his election program, he stressed that Poland should follow its own, national way in the world. Although he perceived and showed the threats of capitalism, by using his own story, he claimed that these dangers can be avoided by Poles' creating a modern market economy. Ireneusz Krzemiński (1991) stresses that Tymiński's second attribute was his "foreignness." Building his image as an "external" candidate who is able to see the divisions in the Solidarity union and the people's embitterment with market reforms helped him gain support among many social strata. Besides, as noted by Jan Purzycki (1991), director, scriptwriter, and head of Lech Wałęsa's televison campaign, Tymiński's case proves that within two hours of a television election spectacle an outsider can defeat any candidate.

However, the most spectacular example supporting the thesis about the many similarities between the United States and Europe in concentrating on politicians' images is the Russian presidential campaign of 1996. Four "secret" marketing advisors from the United States helped Boris Yeltsin, who was both ill and losing popularity, win the elections. As Michael Kramer (1996) describes it, they used all the available marketing techniques (polls, focus groups, negative campaigning, etc.) to present Yeltsin as a candidate enjoying good health, and as one who is aware of the country's suffering and who knows how to handle it. Yeltsin's voting success was an important signal for the politicians from East-Central Europe. The door to political salons was already open.

HOW ARE POLITICAL IMAGES MANUFACTURED?

A citizen's image of a politician consists of the person's subjectivity, or what that person likes and dislikes about the politician. Similar to brand images, political images do not exist apart from the political objects (or the surrounding symbolism) that impact a person's feelings and attitudes about the politician. For example, in the United States, President Bill Clinton's image in the minds of the American people was impacted by charges that he did something unethical in the Whitewater situation, or that he sexually harassed women in the Oval Office. In sum, a politician's image consists of how people perceive him or her based on his or her characteristics, leadership potential, and surrounding messages that are conveyed through the mass media and by word-of-mouth in everyday communication with friends and family.

The term *candidate image* means creating a particular type of representation for a particular purpose (e.g., voting), which, by evoking associations, provides the object with additional values (e.g. social-psychological, ethical, or personality) and thus contributes to the emotional reception of the object (Falkowski, Cwalina, 1999). The values through which the constructed object is enriched may never be reflected in his or her "real" features—it is enough if they have a certain meaning for the receiver. However, in order for such an image to be reliable and for the candidate to be efficient in his or her actions, the candidate needs a balanced personality and oratorical skills.

In the current era of politics focused on a candidate, creating a politician's positive image becomes the fundamental element of an election campaign. European political consultants studied at the beginning of 1998 by Fritz Plasser, Christian Scheucher and Christian Senft (1999) stated unequivocally that a positive image is a very important factor influencing a candidate's chances of success. In fact, it is even more important than his or her ability to use the media or cope with particular political issues. The importance of image was appreciated in the United States a long time ago, and Polish activists are slowly beginning to realize its importance too.

Although creating a positive image is neither a simple nor an easy task, one may easily find many clues on how to achieve it. Studies conducted by social psychologists, political scientists, and academics working on communication provide a great amount of valuable data that can be very useful toward better and more targeted actions by image-creation specialists. The structure of the complete candidate image is presented in Figure 1.3.

20   A CROSS-CULTURAL THEORY OF VOTER BEHAVIOR

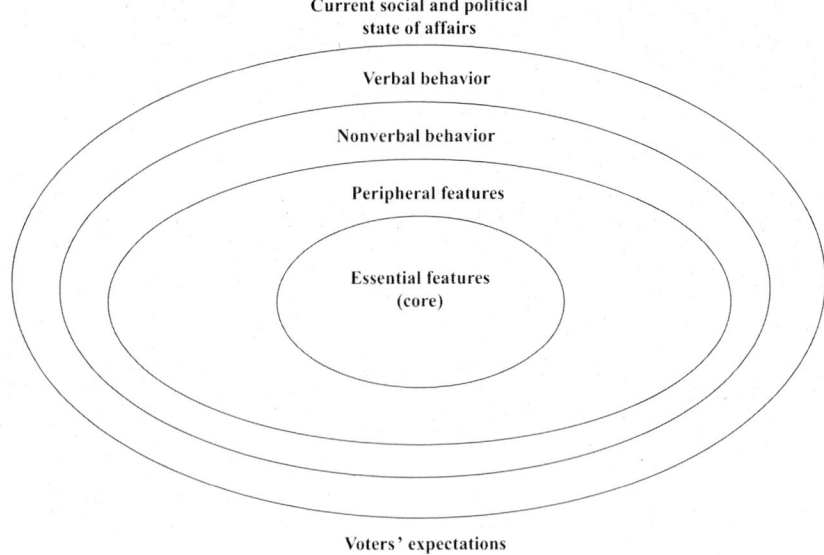

FIGURE 1.3. Candidate image structure.

The most important issue about any image is selecting those features that will lay the foundations for further actions. Such characteristics include personality features that can refer to people's beliefs connected with human nature or be a consequence of social demand in a given moment of time and particular sociopolitical situations when the campaign is conducted. They are the axis around which peripheral features are placed; they are less relevant for the voters but important for the candidate's realistic image. The model of an "ordinary Joe" clearly suggests that no need exists to always create an idea. People expect that their leaders are also "ordinary" people. Besides, not all the peripheral features have to be positive. Even the best politicians have some small sins on their conscience. It can then be said that completing the image with some peripheral features leads to the creation of a candidate's "human face."

Another stage in creating the image is "translating" the characteristics into behaviors that illustrate them or are perceived as if they did. Above all, these are nonverbal behaviors. They include both static characteristics, such as facial expressions or clothing, and dynamic characteristics, such as behavior at a wedding, rally, or some unexpected event (a car accident). Such behaviors should be completed by an appropriate "soundtrack." The candidate has to say something! He or she must present his or her own views, proposed reforms, or solutions to difficult political problems. A candidate prepared in such a way should then be presented to the voters, using all the available tools of political marketing.

One should also bear in mind that all these creation activities take place in a particular sociopolitical situation. That is why getting feedback from voters is so important. A constant monitoring of the image's perception is important for maintaining it, regardless of the political campaign.

A comprehensive description of candidate image was presented by Newman (1999a,b). In politics, an image is created through the use of visual impressions that are communicated by the candidate's physical presence, media appearances, and experiences as well as the record as a political leader, as that information is integrated in the minds of citizens. A candidate's image is affected by endorsements of highly visible people in the country who support him or her. This is no different than the successful endorsement of products by celebrities, who help ring up sales for products from beverages to long-distance telephone services. Similarly, in politics, Hollywood stars such as Barbra Streisand and Warren Beatty appeared at rallies promoting Bill Clinton during the 1992 campaign. These Hollywood stars have a strong following, and their success rubs off on a candidate when they are seen together on television.

Symbols such as a politician's hairstyle and clothing convey who that person is. For example, a Danish candidate running for office once posed naked with a big sign strategically in front of him that said "No hidden agenda." Clearly, the candidate had an impact on the image that voters had of him. In a company, the scientists and engineers in the firm's research and development department must understand the needs of the users of their products. However, customers' needs change over time (as do the attitudes of citizens bombarded by information), and it is incumbent on the company to develop a process aimed at finding ways to continue to meet consumer needs. To successfully market a product or president, a clear image must convey a single message that establishes the product's or president's major virtue. It must convey this message in a distinctive way so that it is not confused with similar messages from the competition. Also, it must deliver a message that hits the emotions as well as a person's reasoning. To be effective, an image must be consistently communicated in every message.

A president's competition is vast and varied, and their ability to shape public opinion far-reaching, thereby impeding his or her ability to communicate a clear vision to the American people. In addition to people such as Rush Limbaugh and other influential radio talk show hosts, are congressional leaders, world leaders, interest groups, and others. Because of the tendency of polls to fluctuate, thus reflecting the fluid mood of the public as a result of the torrent of information and persuasive messages coming out all the time about the president and his or her actions, it is very difficult for the president to project a clear, cohesive vision to the country when instant communication is occurring twenty-four hours a day.

Today, politics has become a big, profitable business to consultants who help manufacture politicians' images. Some say the byproduct of these consultants is cynicism of the electorate and growing armies of people involved in opposition research. The consultants have become more important because they are in a position to help a politician craft a winning image over the television that resonates well with citizens. As we move from the television era to the Internet era, the expertise necessary to be a successful consultant will have to change.

At the level of overall strategic thinking, the candidate is involved, but when it comes to creating a campaign platform, conducting polls, and setting up a promotional strategy, very few candidates get involved. The services offered by consultants include several different activities, such as direct mail, fund-raising, television and radio spots, issue analysis, and print advertising. The ability to lead in the high-tech age we live in hinges on the careful selection of the right consultants to run the candidate's campaign, both before and after entering the political office.

Results from a nationwide survey of political consultants reveal the increasingly important role they are playing in politics today. According to Newman (1999a), some survey conclusions are the following:

- 40 percent said candidates are neither very involved nor influential when it comes to setting issue priorities.
- 60 percent said their candidates were neither very involved nor influential in the day-to-day tactical operation of the electoral campaign.
- Consultants emphasize campaign activities such as fundraising, advertising strategies, and analysis of voter preferences.
- Consultants believe a winning campaign does not hinge on competence of the candidate, political organization, or the recruitment and use of volunteer workers.
- The majority of consultants do not provide services such as precinct walking, phone banking, or "get-out-the-vote" efforts (all of which are hallmarks of grassroots politicking).
- Major services consultants offer are direct mail, fund-raising, television and radio spots, issue analysis, and print advertising.
- The "permanent campaign" means consultants don't stop consulting after election day, but continue to provide advice on policymaking activities in anticipation of the next reelection campaign and follow their clients into office as formal advisors or political appointees.

This increasing power of consultants is a very serious issue concerning the general health of democracies around the world. In the past in the United States, when the political party bosses were the ones in control, a screening process was put in place to choose these people. Local officials, who were voted into office themselves, were the ones who had positions of power in a campaign.

Today, consultants are hired and fired by campaigns in the same way that a corporation might hire a consultant, based on word-of-mouth recommendation and relative success in the past. The consultants have not been exposed to the public, nor have they been screened by voters in the same way that party officials have been. So as we become a more market-driven democracy, and the power shifts from public officials to hired guns, an inherent danger to society exists that the basis on which candidates are elected will be determined by the ability, both monetarily and otherwise, to hire the right consultant. This is a serious issue, and will only be perpetuated by the rising costs of running for public office, and the need to hire consultants to manufacture images for politicians.

The media are the retailers who are given the responsibility to present the image manufactured for the president to the American people. As with product retailers, if they aren't convinced it is a good product, they will have a hard time selling it in the package it comes in.

Constructing political meanings and realities out of myriad messages coming out of a political campaign is becoming very difficult for the average citizen. It is the information that is paid for and the symbols that a politician creates that are used by voters to form attitudes and voting preferences. Political meaning is conveyed through the media and their interpretation and perceptions. At the core of candidate-manufactured images is the attempt to manipulate and control press coverage to paint the best possible television face for a candidate and at the same time mold an image consistent with the image the candidate wants to use to win over voters.

In effect, the press creates a constructed reality for the voter, based on both the substance and the images they convey. The media intensifies previously held emotional beliefs of voters by framing, highlighting, and attributing responsibility for particular events or outcomes to certain politicians. Voters then take in all of this information and attach new meaning to it based on their own perceptual filtering systems and desires. This is not dissimilar to the process that goes on for the marketing of any product or service, with the key difference being that the manufacturer has more control to convey the meaning it wants than a politician who must rely on the media to serve as the information-disseminator. Ultimately, it is critical for a politician to understand how voters perceive his or her candidacy, and to use the information that is generated from marketing research to reinforce or reposition the meaning that voters attach to a candidacy (Miller, Gronbeck, 1994).

The process of constructing a candidate's image in voters' minds is based on the same laws of constructing a reality in people's minds as those that were discovered in the information-processing approach to cognitive psychology. Therefore, one should take a closer look at this approach and apply it to political cognition.

Chapter 2

Political Cognition

The problem of getting to know the surrounding natural and social reality has been studied by philosophers since ancient times. The key question posed by ancient sages concerned our perception of the world, whether we perceive it the way it is (realism) or whether we create its subjective representation in our mind (constructivism). The modern cognitive psychology research has allowed us to analyze these issues in more detail. Although no unequivocal answer to the question about the nature of external environment cognition has been given yet, the research methodologies offer very clear and empirically proven guidelines in this area. Without a doubt, the modern achievements of cognitive psychology can be used for studying voting behaviors, perceptions of political advertising, and developing marketing strategies.

CONSTRUCTIVISM AND REALISM

Modern theories developed within cognitive psychology belong to one of the following areas: information-processing approach or ecological approach. The major issue dividing these two areas is the answer to the questions of whether during the cognitive process one creates cognitive representations of the surrounding world or whether cognition is direct and, therefore, studying cognitive representations does not make sense because they do not exist. In other words, the main object of the dispute between the information processing approach and the ecological approach is the treatment of the relationships between reality and its image appearing in a person's awareness. Does an individual actively reconstruct the image of the world, using the data provided by his or her senses and information retrieved from his or her memory? Or, thanks to perception, does the individual get a precise and real image of the surrounding world? Due to the differences in their approach to the processes of reality cognition, the first view can be defined as *cognitive constructivism,* originating from the information-processing approach, whereas the other can be classified as *cognitive realism,* originating from the ecological approach.

The process of recognizing the surrounding reality would not be complete without emotions. Each person realizes that his or her emotions influence what he or she perceives. If the emotions are positive they create a pleasant and fascinating perception in the person's mind. If they are negative, then the perception they create is threatening, unwanted, or even disgusting.

At the beginning of the 1980s, cognitive psychologists researching the problems of emotions (Lazarus, 1984; Zajonc, 1984) started the debate on whether emotions appear as a result of cognitive processes (such as recognition, categorization, thinking) that occurred previously, or whether affective judgments precede them. The answer to this question requires solving the problem of whether human cognition is based on one cognitive mechanism including both information processing and affective processes, or whether it is the result of the working of two independent systems—information processing and emotions.

The first of these two opposing views, including the affective component in the theory of information processing, can be defined as *affective-cognitive constructivism.* The other view, referring to the ecological approach, is called *affective-cognitive realism.* The criteria of assigning a given theory to one of these areas are determined by the position regarding the following two alternatives:

1. Directness versus indirectness of emotional perceptions.
2. Emotions and perception—one- versus two-mind systems.

Assuming that the creation of emotions is a perceptual process and is mediated by complex information processing methods makes this theory part of the constructivist area. Emotion is understood here as a construct that is shaped by cognitive processes. Assuming, on the other hand, that emotions are directly experienced and influence perceptual processes makes the theory part of the realistic area in which emotions precede cognitive processes. Moderate views on these two stances are represented by intermediate positions.

Emotional-Cognitive Constructivism

The epistemological stance defined as cognitive constructivism is characteristic for the information-processing approach of cognitive psychology. The constructivist view assumes that perceptual experience is not a direct reaction to an external stimulus. Cognitive perception is constructed in the mind; that is, it is created from many elements, only a few of which are provided through sensory stimuli. The other elements come from real and illusory experiences encoded in long-term memory. When a person is getting to know the world, he or she creates a cognitive representation of the surrounding reality, which is not, however, an exact copy but a certain mental construct. The constructivist approach assumes that the representation may be different every time a given situation is repeated.

It is particularly in the area of perception processes that different ways of receiving the same reality in an individual's mind are shown on the basis of perception stimuli illustrating the principles of perception organization. The stimuli that are most often used are gestalt figures, which cannot really be found in the natural environment. They create artificial situations, frequently spectacular illusions, or perception illusions, and illustrate the principles of Gestalt psychology very well, including the rule of proximity, similarity, continuity, and common fate. These principles, described in great detail by Kurt Koffka (1935) in the first half of the previous century, illustrate the cooperation of the mind with the sensory reception of stimuli quite well. It ascribes meaning to the received sensory stimulation and its meaningful organization, often by the mind adding nonexistent stimuli to this stimulation and thus creating a figure separated from the background. A classic example of such a construct is the illusory contour of the triangle, illustrating the principle of a figure's closure, and is presented in Figure 2.1.

In the figure one can see a black triangle and the contour that does not exist in reality. Perceiving the figure as a whole, we add some nonexistent elements and in our minds create an object that does not, in fact, exist. It was exactly the principles of Gestalt psychology

FIGURE 2.1. Illusory contour of the triangle.

that laid the foundation of the constructivist approach in cognitive psychology.

The results of the research on perceptions shows that the process of getting to know the surrounding reality consists in constructing certain images and events in one's mind that are the result of interpretation and inference of the received stimulation. This idea was first presented by Ulric Neisser (1967) and then discussed in detail by Jerome S. Bruner (1973).

Constructivism in cognitive processes can be illustrated by the perception of stimuli in which mind representation is completely dependent on the changing context. The best illustration of different representations of the same stimulus being created in one's mind are ambiguous figures. Looking at the same picture, one can in turn see two different figures. The example often used in psychology handbooks is the "old woman/young woman" illustration or the gestalt "duck/rabbit" figure presented in Figure 2.2.

If such stimuli are perceived, the context in which one interprets the figure as a certain one is of internal character. The cognitive structures previously remembered and stored in one's memory correspond to the events we perceived before we attribute meaning to the received stimulus. If the observer had never seen an old woman or a

Political Cognition 29

FIGURE 2.2. Ambiguous figures ("Old Woman/Young Woman" and "Duck/Rabbit").

rabbit before, he would not have recognized these figures in the ambiguous shapes.

However, the context has a broader meaning for the interpretation of the perceived objects than only mere superimposing of memory structures on the received stimuli. Contextualized internally, these memory structures also cooperate with the external situational context during object perception. John Bransford (1979) suggests that the object may have a functional character. An example is presented in Figure 2.3.

The meaningless object acquires a meaning when the two following types of contexts begin to interact:

1. External situational context showing different functions and meanings of a given object in three different situations: (a) as leaves of flower, (b) as wings of penguin, and (c) as the spout of a whale;
2. Internal context as memory structures superimposed on the received stimulus. This occurs when we know what leaves, wings, and spouts are used for and mean based on our past experiences.

The example presented here shows that the same shapeless figure may be perceived in many different ways. This perception can be interpreted as a cooperation of two different contexts and suggests a complicated process of information processing taking place in the

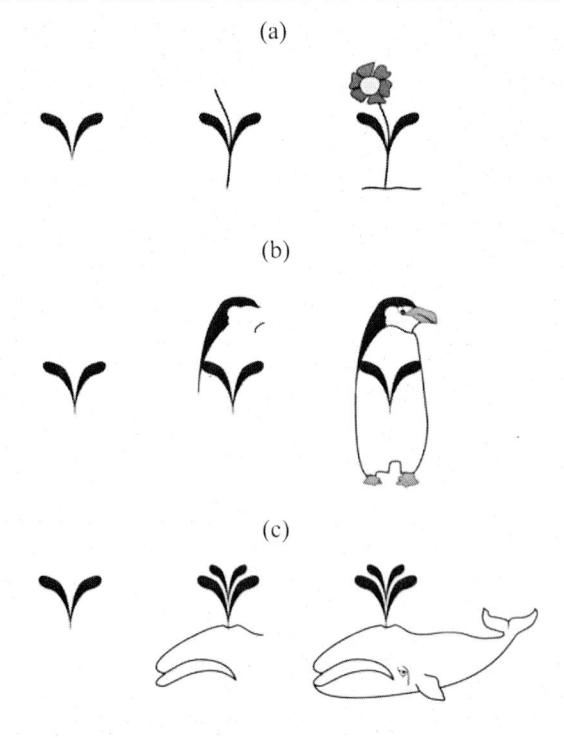

FIGURE 2.3. Meanings as a function of events.

observer's mind. It is surprising that a person, without any effort, experiences the perceived object as a concrete figure: a leaf, a wing, or a spout. The process of perceptual inference automatically and subconsciously assigns meaning to the received stimulation. The perceived object comes from the information received by the senses, which is processed according to subconsciously applied rules.

Another example of perceiving events according to the expectations connected with one's knowledge is Jerome S. Bruner's and Leo J. Postman's experiment (Bruner, 1973), in which the subjects were shown playing cards. In addition to ordinary cards, they were also presented atypical cards, including "black hearts" and "red spades." No such cards can be found in a standard deck. However, the subjects often recognized these atypical cards as if they saw a typical card: for instance they recognized a red spade as black, slightly overcolored, or

Political Cognition   31

blackish brown. Therefore, the subjects' perception of the cards illustrated the process of adapting the perceived image to the expectations created as a result of knowledge.

Another example of the influence of context on different interpretations of the same words can be shown by people understanding the meaning of different words. Let us examine the English words "the cat," presented in Figure 2.4. Although the words include identical images of two different letters, the reader is able to read the first image as the letter "H" and the other as the letter "A" without any problems. The context leading to an instant and varying interpretation of the same graphic sign is the meaning of the words "the cat" coded in one's memory.

The examples presented here show various interpretations of the same stimuli that can be subtly controlled by the context in which these stimuli appear. Obviously, such a manipulation is used in advertisements, creating a positive or a negative image of political events in voters' minds.

Controlling the way of understanding the perceived stimuli does cause different emotional reactions. Therefore, the concept of constructivism should be complemented by affections. The constructivist approach to emotions assumes that they are: (1) constructions and not biological constructs, and (2) improvisations based on a given person's interpretation of a situation (Averill, 1980). Therefore, no emotional reaction may occur without emotional processes. In other words, cognitive processes constitute emotional reactions (see also Frijda, 1988).

Richard S. Lazarus (1984; 1991a,b; Lazarus, Kanner, Folkman, 1980) develops and radicalizes the assumptions held in the cognitive-motivational-relational theory of emotion. It claims that "cognitive

THE CAT

FIGURE 2.4. The effect of context enables us to perceive the letters despite the missing features.

evaluation is the fundamental and integral characteristic of all emotional states" (Lazarus, 1982, p. 1021). Every emotion is generated and driven by a specific evaluation pattern characteristic. Learning, memory, perception, and thinking are all cognitive activities triggering certain emotional reactions (Lazarus, Kanner, Folkman, 1980). The fact that an individual's affective state is very sensitive to changes occurring in the relationships between a person and the environment and influences the way in which these changes are evaluated, makes Lazarus (1984) assume that there is one cognitive-emotional system in the human mind.

Cognitive Realism

A theoretical branch of cognitive psychology representing radical realism in cognition is the ecological approach formed by James J. Gibson (1966, 1979). It was created in opposition to the information-processing approach, which assumes that the process of getting to know the surrounding world occurs only in the human mind and what is learned is only an abstraction of the state constructed (created) by a person. In the ecological approach, the cognition of the surrounding physical and social reality occurs directly. The perceived objects and events appear to a person's mind as they are in reality, without any mediating cognitive structures.

The ecological theory has epistemological consequences. One world exists from which people extract various information depending on their past experiences, adaptability skills, culture, and social-psychological habits. Therefore, man perceives the same reality, but in its infinite variants or perspectives. Consequently, the cognition of reality comes down to its constant discoveries. It is not a process of creating reality, as the information-processing approach suggests.

The analyses conducted within the ecological approach became an inspiration for many social psychologists as well as for the debates on the relationship between affection and cognitive processes. According to Ross Buck (1984), human behavior should be considered a function of many specific systems of its organization, which can be assigned to one of the two general levels. The first one (primes) includes innate motivation and an emotional system whose main task is to adapt to the environment and preserve homeostasis within the organism. Their functioning is connected with knowledge by acquaintance. As Bertrand Russell (1980) claims, this knowledge is what we realize directly, without the mediation of an inference initiated in cognitive structures. This knowledge is collected not only as a result of cognitive characteristics of the surrounding physical and social environment, but it also includes the awareness of internal states such as feelings, desires, emotions, and motivations. The second level of behavioral organization includes the effect of the organism's relevant learning, based on experiences. This is the level at which one attributes meaning to the internal and external environment, and its functioning is based on knowledge by description, which is dependent on the previous knowledge by acquaintance.

According to Buck (1984), emotion perception should be treated as a direct process happening without the mediation of decoding rules. The object of such perceptions are emotions communicated by other people through both subtle, nonverbal expressions and "open behavior" (for instance, thumping the table as an expression of anger). The knowledge gained due to such a process is an example of knowledge by acquaintance. When the observer uses the rules of information decoding and thus begins cognitive processes including memory, interpretation, or passing judgments, then, according to Buck, emotional cognition is evident. This occurs when an analysis of an already perceived emotion reaches one's consciousness before the initiation of information processing.

The previous distinctions serve to set apart the concept of extreme emotional-cognitive realism. The most representative conception characterizing this branch is probably the theory formulated by Robert B. Zajonc (1980, 1984; Zajonc, Markus, 1982). Using Buck's terminology, one may assume that the theory attributes the dominant role in the organization of humankind's behavior to emotions. It focuses mainly on particular aspects of these emotions (emotional evaluations or judgments—*hot cognitions*), which can usually be found in preferences and which are the foundation for the distinction between the pursuit and the avoidance of something. The most fundamental thesis, put forward by Zajonc (1980), states that affections accompany cognitive processes, that they occur prior to them, and that emotions come from a parallel and partly independent system in the organism.

Cognitive psychology of emotions has also developed approaches that can be classified as moderate relativism and cognitive constructivism. The authors of these theories claim that emotions precede cognition in some situations, but a reverse relationship is also possible. Variants of the moderate approach are presented by Buck (1988) and Susan T. Fiske and Mark A. Pavelchak (1986).

SOCIAL CATEGORIZATION OF POLITICIANS

As ways of analyzing the nature of perceiving the surrounding reality, cognitive realism and constructivism are a framework that should be filled with content related to voting behaviors. One of the key elements of this content is the categorization and perception of politicians by voters. The issues of social perception and categorization have been studied by many researchers, mainly because of the important social function of this phenomenon. The quality of our social and political life depends to a large extent on how we evaluate other people, not only our colleagues at work, friends or family, but also the decision makers in the economic and political sphere. Our evaluation is important in the context of voting behaviors because it influences political choices and, as a result, has an impact on the sociopolitical development of a country. As a result, one should take a closer look at the psychological mechanisms of politicians' social categorization, which is the result of images shaped in voters' minds. The empirical structure of such a categorization in light of cognitive realism and constructivism is presented by voting behavior models in Chapter 6.

Social Image of Politicians

If we assume that people try to shape their life situations to satisfy their basic needs and realize their philosophy on life through politics, then one of the means of achieving this goal is through the democratic institution of free elections. In supporting a particular political force, an individual also indicates the direction of his or her country's development that is most in line with his or her own personal objectives. Therefore, obtaining adequate information about the sociopolitical reality is essential to achieve its optimal adaptation.

However, acquiring such knowledge of reality requires both caution when making decisions and much effort. It is no accident that the sphere of political activity has been called "the political stage" and the politicians, "actors." They perform a certain play in front of their audience-voters in order to win their support, which bestows power on them. Such a collective performance is based upon images reflecting dreams of a better standard of living, which are intended to evoke strong feelings and steer away from the rational control of reality (see also Le Bon, 2002/1895). However, to quote Francisco Goya's series of graphics, *The Sleep of Reason Produces Monsters*, spontaneity is thus eliminated, critical thinking "switched off," and an individual's original psychological acts are replaced with somebody else's feelings, thoughts, and desires (Fromm, 1965). A political performance resembles a peculiar religious rite in which masses participate. Marvin (1994) demonstrates that the institution of political elections, which are a culmination of a collective performance, is a contemporary version of the totemic ritual of rebirth, making an offering that is supposed to atone for the ruling chaos. According to Marvin, those who leave office make a sacrifice of themselves through the act of a peaceful handover of power to their successors. Those who receive power, on the other hand, commit themselves to sacrificing their own future for others and, simultaneously, become a postponed or promised sacrifice.

Thus, the term *image* is the creation of a particular type of representation for a particular purpose (e.g., voting), which, by evoking associations, provides the object with additional values (e.g., social-psychological, ethical, or personality) and thus contributes to the emotional reception of the object (Falkowski, Cwalina, 1999). The values through which the constructed object is enriched may never be reflected in his "real" features—it is enough if they have a certain meaning for the receiver.

Politicians eagerly make use of the psychological mechanism of influencing voters' cognitive processes and attitudes. Particular attention should be paid to three phenomena: creating an image of an "ideal politician" (particularly of an "ideal president"), political advertising's influence on the voters' perception of a political candidate, and the role of emotions in politics.

Prototype of an Ideal Political Leader

Every citizen wants his or her country ruled by the best, or, an almost ideal political leader. However, the following questions arise: What is this ideal? What features should he have?

According to Mark Leary (1996), five features are extremely important for a political leader to possess: (1) competency; the ability to evoke (2) sympathy, (3) morality, (4) power, and (5) the ability to embarrass others. Possession of all these attributes contributes to the leader's charisma and improves his chances for electoral success.

Competency is the key element used to select a candidate for a "political job." However, in this sphere it is more difficult to clearly state what the candidate should be about. Is a competent politician one who has been educated as a political scientist? Maybe an economist, or a lawyer? Or maybe a psychologist? Should competency relate to the ability to manage others, problem solve, negotiate, etc? Or, rather, does competency pertain to knowledge in economic rules, international relations, and legislation? It seems that "political competency" is made up of everything, in certain proportions. The goal is to make others respect you—to be professional, effective, and successful.

The ability to evoke people's sympathy seems to be one of the most fundamental elements of social relations. Respect for others, humility while in contact with others, as well as the ability to maintain one's authority are indicators of social attractiveness. Provoking sympathy, or in other words being liked, guarantees social and professional successes, and it is the foundation for one's well-being and satisfaction with life.

According to Leary (1996), a charismatic leader should also be moral and his behavior should be immaculate. Despite that we are not saints ourselves, we want our politicians to be as "saintly" as possible. Problems with morality were the reason for many spectacular political falls such as Richard Nixon's resignation from presidency after Watergate (Winter, Carlson, 1988). Nevertheless, in some cases, politicians managed to get away with scandals, such as Bill Clinton and his affair with Monica Lewinsky, which, however, has left a flaw on Clinton's image and weakened people's trust in him (Morrow, 1998). In some cases it is possible to repair one's reputation by admitting one's guilt.

A series of studies on the consequences of a politicians' public confession conducted by Bernard Weiner, Sandra Graham, Orli Peter, and Mary Zmuidinas (1991) prove that this strategy is successful only in certain cases. Confession is to a politician's benefit when it is obvious he or she has done something wrong. In other words, if evidence of his or her guilt is clear, it is better to admit to it and ask for forgiveness than to deny it. However, even in this situation it is not really possible to wholly recover the lost image. Admitting guilt also has positive consequences when it is not certain who is responsible for the wrongdoing. This strategy may also be successful if one is only accused of misconduct; it is better to anticipate the attack than to desperately defend oneself. It is better to admit something spontaneously than to be condemned. Besides, admitting one's guilt is more efficient for repairing one's image when the charges concern character and not actions. It is easier to justify one's weaknesses of character than improper behavior and the damage done because of it.

Another characteristic of an ideal leader mentioned by Leary (1996) is power. Such a politician should be calm, firm, and composed. A charismatic leader can carry through every action he or she plans. The power of politics is best visible during situations of crisis or stress, including a war, terrorist threat, or the crash of the state's finances.

Such attributes demonstrate the charismatic character of the leader and bring him or her closer to a successful election. However, Leary stresses that a leader must not only be competent, kind, moral, strong, and dominant, but he claims that the leader should also incorporate these characteristics into the repertoire of self-presented behaviors that create his or her image, which is not necessarily compatible with reality.

Another study on the characteristics of leaders was conducted by Wattenberg (1995). He analyzed the personality features of all the candidates running for the U.S. presidency between 1952 and 1988. He found that a candidate's personal attributes can be divided into the following five general categories:

1. integrity—associated with the candidate's trustworthiness and incorporates comments concerning honesty, sincerity, and any reference to corruption in government
2. reliability—a candidate being dependable, strong, decisive, aggressive, stable, or the converse of these
3. competence—refers to a candidate's past experience, ability as a statesman, comprehension of political issues, realism, and intelligence
4. charisma—a candidate's leadership abilities, dignity, humbleness, patriotism, and ability to get along and communicate with people
5. personal aspects of the candidate—appearance, age, religion, wealth, former occupation, family, and so on

The results obtained by Wattenberg demonstrate that in seven cases out of ten, the candidate who got higher ratings in public opinion polls regarding the previously mentioned personality categories won. Only three times was a less valued candidate able to win: Kennedy versus Nixon in 1960, Carter versus Ford in 1976, and Reagan versus Carter in 1980. According to the study, the best rated president, chosen two times (in 1952 and in 1956), was Dwight D. Eisenhower.

Research on Representative Samples

Another way of "discovering" what characteristics voters desire in a candidate is by simply asking them. In the poll conducted by Centrum Badania Opinii Spolecznej (The Public Opinion Research Center), before the Polish parliamentary elections in March 1997, 1,185 adult Poles were asked about the most valued characteristics of a good politician (*Portrety liderów opozycji,* 1997). The task of each respondent was to select five such characteristics from the list he or she was presented. The respondents stated that the most valued characteristics of a politician are honesty (47 percent of respondents), credibility (46 percent), intelligence (43 percent), understanding the problems of "ordinary people" (39 percent), competence (36 percent), and acting for the good of Poland (35 percent) (*Portrety liderów opozycji,* 1997).

To a large extent, these characteristics are compatible with the results obtained by Wirthlin Worldwide in a survey conducted before the 1996 U.S. presidential elections. The American respondents stated that the most important features of a good president are honesty and trustworthiness, high ethical standards and moral values, a clear vision of where to lead the country, sincerity, decisiveness, concern about "people like me," strength, and the ability to accomplish his or her plans for the country (*Election '96: Defining Mr. Right,* 1996). The results are presented in Figure 2.5.

The authors of the report sum up their results by stating that both Bill Clinton and Bob Dole, as candidates for president, must constantly develop their public images, including all the features mentioned previously as well as unselected ones. Only then can they sufficiently count on voters' supporting order to win. What is required of a candidate for president is not necessarily the possession of the desired features, but that he or she displays them in public and

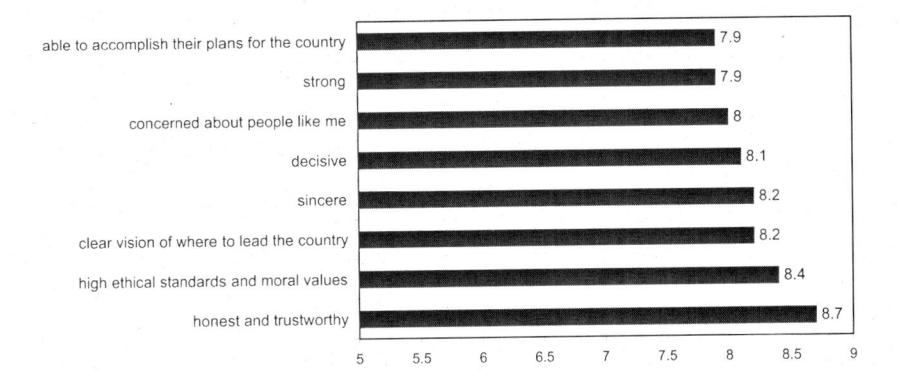

Characteristic	Rating
able to accomplish their plans for the country	7.9
strong	7.9
concerned about people like me	8
decisive	8.1
sincere	8.2
clear vision of where to lead the country	8.2
high ethical standards and moral values	8.4
honest and trustworthy	8.7

FIGURE 2.5. The characteristics of an ideal U.S. President. *Source:* Adapted from *Election '96: Defining Mr. Right* (1996).

makes an impression that he or she possesses them. To use the language of marketing, a candidate must create a proper image of himself. Such practices, however, create not a true but fictional ideal (Fromm, 1965).

The term *image* means creating a particular type of representation for a particular purpose (e.g., voting), which, by evoking associations, provides the object with additional values (e.g. social-psychological, ethical, or personality) and thus contributes to the emotional reception of the object (Falkowski, Cwalina 1999; Kaid, Holtz-Bacha, 1995). The values by which the constructed object is enriched may never be reflected in the individual's "real" features—it is enough if they have a certain meaning for the receiver.

Research on Purposive Samples

Studies on social perception demonstrate that in voters' minds, an "ideal politician" is a prototype, an example of the category of people professionally dealing with politics (Kinder, 1986; see also Cantor, Mischel, 1979; Fiske, Neuberg, 1990; Fiske, Pavelchak, 1986). Such cognitive schemes are a reference point for people when passing judgments on candidates running for a certain office or when making voting decisions.

The prototype concept is further developed by the superman/ everyman model of image formation and candidate selection proposed by John L. Sullivan, John H. Aldrich, Eugene Borgida, and Wendy Rahn (1990). The model assumes that in comparing candidates, voters make use of intuitions about human nature. Therefore:

1. They may expect that candidates for president should be supermen or superwomen who are able to rise above the limitations imposed by human nature. If none of the candidates meet these requirements, then the voters will support the one who has the smallest deficit hoping that once elected he or she will grow while in office. This way of evaluating candidates may be defined as the *superman model* of image formation and candidate selection.
2. They may accept the assumptions about human nature, yet they may choose the candidate who is most typical. For instance, Ronald Reagan's presidency (the so-called "Teflon Presidency") may have evoked a conviction on part of some voters that they should support him because he personifies "a next-door neighbor." He was not the best and most intelligent, but rather, the most typical. This model of candidate evaluation may be defined as the *everyman model* of image formation and candidate selection. The model assumes that candidates who are perceived as worse than or much better than the majority of people are rejected by voters. The first are discarded for obvious reasons, and the latter because they are too different from "everyman." Such people are usually considered overintellectualized and thus neither understood nor liked.

Sullivan and his colleagues tested the candidate selection models during the presidential elections in the United States in 1984 (Ronald Reagan versus Walter Mondale). The results they obtained demonstrate that voters want their presidents to be trustworthy, lacking egotistical tendencies, and having control over events in the country, to the maximum extent possible. In addition, most citizens placed the incumbent, Reagan, into a modified version of the everyman model. People liked him and supported him because they perceived him as being at least as good as the majority of Americans. Mondale, on the other hand, as a challenger, was measured against the superman model. If he came out well in this comparison, voters reported a positive emotional attitude toward him. However, such a situation occurred quite rarely, and Reagan won the elections. The results pointing to the superman model, though, are consistent with the hypothesis put forward by Kinder (1986): people compare candidates to their prototype concept of an ideal president.

In the studies conducted during the first and second rounds of the presidential elections in Poland in 1995 and 2000, Wojciech Cwalina and Andrzej Falkowski (2000; Cwalina, 2003b) checked the conformity of the features mentioned in answers to open-ended questions about Aleksander Kwaśniewski, Lech Wałęsa, Andrzej Olechowski, and Marian Krzaklewski, with the features of "an ideal president." The prototype of an "ideal president" was also analyzed over the subsequent presidential elections.

The studies were conducted in different parts of Poland on purposive samples differing from the demographic features of adult Poles (in 1995: N = 203; in 2000: N = 325). The task of the respondents was to write down the features that an ideal president should have and those that individual candidates were characterized by. The questions were open-ended, so the respondents were free as to the number of characteristics they could list.

All of the characteristics they wrote down were counted and categorized according to their content similarity and number of the same characteristics being mentioned. The results obtained for an ideal president and candidates participating in the presidential elections in 1995 are presented in Table 2.1.

An analysis of the features presented in the table demonstrates the importance of creating a candidate's image and evaluating it to match the prototype of an ideal president. The key features that an ideal president should be characterized by include honesty and credibility, competencies and professionalism, education, appearance and attractiveness, intelligence, efficiency, power and determination, and being open to people and the world. Aleksander Kwaśniewski's image was based on power and determination, appearance and attractiveness, intelligence and clarity, and eloquence. The dominant features of Lech Wałęsa's image included honesty and credibility, and power and determination. The results of the studies conducted during the presidential election campaign in Poland in 2000 are presented in Table 2.2.

TABLE 2.1. Comparison of features attributed to the ideal president (percentage of indications) and main candidates in presidential elections in Poland in 1995.

Feature	Ideal President	Aleksander Kwaśniewski	Lech Wałęa
Honesty, credibility	80.3	15.8	49.3
Competence, professionalism	47.3	17.2	10.8
Education	37.4	7.4	0.0
Appearance, attractiveness	33.5	25.6	0.0
Intelligence	33.0	25.1	0.0
Efficiency	31.0	9.9	6.4
Power	29.6	29.6	24.1
Openness to people and the world	26.6	11.3	5.9
Clarity, eloquence	17.2	24.1	3.5
Wisdom, reason	13.3	12.3	1.5
Activity	11.3	13.8	1.0
Calmness, self-control	11.3	9.4	0.5
Conscientiousness, reliability	9.9	0.0	1.0
Authority, charisma	7.9	2.5	10.3
Caring for others and the country	6.9	0.0	3.0
Responsibility	6.7	2.0	5.2
Seriousness	5.9	7.4	0.5
Independence, objectivity	5.4	1.0	0.0
Fairness	4.9	0.0	0.0
Being a believer	4.4	0.0	6.4
Being known abroad	3.0	0.0	15.8
Friendliness	0.5	6.9	3.0

Source: Cwalina and Falkowski (2000), p. 207.

In the year 2000, an ideal president was characterized by honesty and credibility, appearance and attractiveness, education, competencies and professionalism, intelligence, care for others and the country, power and determination, and openness to people and the world. Aleksander Kwaśniewski's image included such features as honesty and credibility, professionalism and competencies, openness to people and the world, power, and determination. His main opponent in the presidential fight, Andrzej Olechowski, was characterized by honesty and credibility, power and determination, education, and openness to people and the world. The most important features for Marian Krzaklewski's image included honesty and credibility, being a believer (Catholic), education, and care for others and the country.

With both presidential elections, one can notice the discrepancy between Poles' expectations of an "ideal candidate" and the images of particular politicians. Apart from a qualitative analysis of the features forming a politician's image, a quantitative analysis between the profiles of an ideal president and candidates was conducted, using Wilcoxon's Z-test. The results suggest that the structure of the category "ideal president" in 1995 and 2000 differed considerably from all the candidates competing for presidency in the elections. The results suggest that none of the candidates were close to achieving the image that was attributed to the ideal. From a marketing perspective, this means that the campaigns of all the candidates were unsuccessful in meeting voters' needs.

Another conclusion derived from the research is connected with the dynamics if images change. Both images of an ideal politician and president are characterized by internal changeability. This means that in time, the perception of the features of the same object undergoes significant changes (the percentage of their indications changes). The most characteristic shift relative to the changes in the image of an ideal candidate over five years (1995 to 2000) concerned appearance and attractiveness moving from fourth to second position. Also, important shifts can be observed in the following categories: care of the country (increasing from 6.9 percent in 1995 to 21.2 percent in 2000), responsibility (6.7 percent to 18.6 percent) and independence (5.4 percent to 18.2 percent). On the other hand, some features of an ideal president became less important. In 1995, 47.3 percent of the respondents stressed the role of competency whereas five years later it was only 24.2 percent. A similar situation could be observed with effi-

TABLE 2.2. Comparison of features attributed to the ideal president (percentage of indications) and main candidates in presidential elections in Poland in 2000.

Feature	Ideal President	Aleksander Kwaśniewski	Andrzej Olechowski	Marian Krzaklewski
Honesty, credibility	89.6	30.6	32.8	34.8
Appearance, attractiveness	36.7	8.9	10.9	4.8
Education	32.2	3.2	21.3	28.7
Competence, professionalism	24.2	28.2	12.6	3.9
Intelligence	23.1	8.1	10.3	2.6
Caring about others and the country	21.2	18.6	5.8	20.0
Power	19.7	21.0	29.3	10.0
Openness to people and the world	19.7	27.4	21.3	2.6
Responsibility	18.6	4.0	4.0	1.3
Independence, objectivity	18.2	11.3	7.5	0.9
Efficiency	16.3	4.8	1.2	3.5
Fairness	14.8	4.0	1.2	1.3
Clarity, eloquence	13.6	11.3	8.1	1.7
Activity	13.3	4.0	5.6	0.9
Conscientiousness, reliability	12.9	5.7	5.2	1.7
Wisdom, reason	8.7	8.1	15.5	2.6
Being a believer	7.2	0.0	1.7	29.1
Seriousness	5.3	7.3	9.2	0.9
Calmness, self-control	3.8	16.1	9.2	0.9
Being known abroad	3.0	1.6	1.2	0.0
Friendliness	2.7	16.9	12.1	2.2
Authority, charisma	1.5	4.8	12.1	0.9

ciency (decreasing from 31 percent to 16.3 percent), and intelligence (33 percent to 23.1 percent). A comparison of the importance of particular features of an ideal president is presented in Figure 2.6.

It can be stated that the results of the research suggest that the politicians running for Polish presidency between 1995 and 2000 did not meet, despite the efforts of marketing experts, the categories of an ideal politician defined by the voters. The prototype of an ideal president is a dynamic category. In time, the relevance of particular attributes changes, and so does voters' agreement in selecting particular attributes as being relevant for an ideal president.

A study comparing the features of an ideal president relative to the candidates was also conducted on the presidential elections in Romania in 1996 (Miron, Marinescu, McKinnon, 1999). As the most important characteristics of a prototype president, those surveyed mentioned professional qualities (81.6 percent of respondents); correctness (81.6 percent); dynamism, and effectiveness (68 percent); personal qualities such as calmness and self-control (58.4 percent); and a democratic and patriotic approach as well as a love for the people and the country (32.8 percent). Those surveyed by Dorina Miron and her colleagues (1999) were much more positive with regard to these qualities when rating Emil Constantinescu (200 positive evaluations, 54

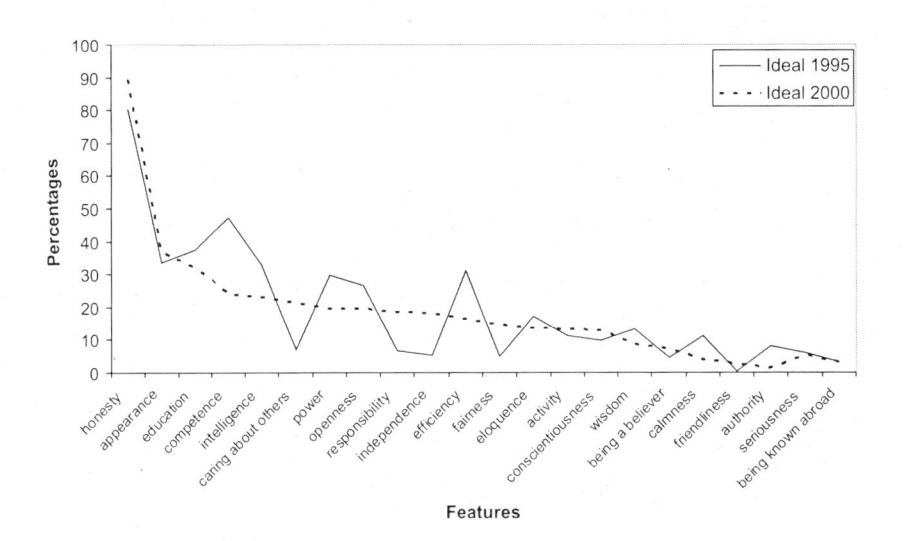

FIGURE 2.6. Image of an ideal Polish politician: 1995-2000.

negative ones, and 11 neutral) compared to his rival, Ion Iliescu (89 positive evaluations, 171 negative ones, and 17 neutral). The results of the presidential elections confirmed the Romanians' greater sympathy for Constantinescu.

The results of the studies presented here seem to bear the hypothesis that in electing candidates for public office, people vote for those who, according to their opinions, are closest to the ideal—the candidates whose image better matches the ideal attributes of a head of state. The research on social perception proves that an ideal politician is a certain prototype in voters' minds, a model of the category of people dealing professionally with politics. However, a politician's image, as well as the ideal to which it can be referred to, are not stable. They change over time, according to the sociopolitical situation in the country, as well as being a result of marketing strategies in which political advertising plays an important role. Therefore, an important challenge for image-creation specialists is their ability to "package" their candidate in order to accommodate him or her to the voters' current dream, and then monitor his or her performance.

Therefore, the first step in all political campaigns is to determine voters' expectations toward candidates and then to create an image of a politician as is desired by society. It may be an exaggeration, but we can say that what really counts is not the content, but the form, not the candidate's name and competencies, but the public mask that he or she assumes. To push this reality even further, we could venture to say that each of us is a potential political superman.

The Importance of Advertising in Forming Politicians' Images

The dynamics of change in the ideal image of a politician, and his or her image as perceived by voters is certainly modified by political advertising. Televised political advertising is a tool of political marketing that has been successfully used since the beginning of the 1950s to create an image of politicians running for various state offices (Diamond, Bates, 1992). It uses a certain image of the candidate to convey what a voter may achieve if he votes for a particular person. To create a certain image of a politician, political consultants, frequently unconsciously, rely on the principles of social perception, discovered and developed within social psychology (see e.g. Argyle, 1983; Aronson, 1992).

A detailed study on the importance of such advertising in forming a politician's image in voters' minds was presented by Lynda Lee Kaid and Mike Chanslor (1995), who theorized that perceiving and evaluating candidates for political offices is characterized by dimensionality. However, from the position of creating a candidate's image, the dimensions that are used by voters are not always favorable. If citizens "test" a given politician on his or her morality and his or her conscience is not clear, then the politician's chances of election success become smaller. If, however, he or she managed to draw attention to, for instance, his or her competencies, the candidate's chances of winning may grow. Televised political advertising often performs the function of a spotlight that focuses on the desired features of the candidate, diverting people's attention from his or her weaknesses. It thus directs voters' attention and changes the dimensions according to which the candidate is perceived and evaluated.

Kaid and Chanslor (1995) proposed a model of the influence of political advertising on changes in the perception of a candidate's image and its influence on voting behavior. The empirical research verifying this model was conducted during the presidential campaigns in the United States in 1988 and 1992, when George H. W. Bush ran first against Michael Dukakis, and then against Bill Clinton. The research from 1992 will be discussed here in detail.

In order to measure the candidate's image, Kaid and Chanslor used a twelve-scale semantic differential in which every scale had seven points. The test procedure consisted of a pretest and posttest, between which randomly chosen advertising spots of both politicians were presented. Every subject evaluated each of the candidates twice— before and after watching the spots.

In order to distinguish the dimensions according to which the candidates were perceived, the factor analysis was applied separately to each candidate and separately to each pretest and posttest. The results are presented in Table 2.3.

Analyzing the results of their tests, Kaid and Chanslor concluded that in the case of each candidate, the spots caused a change in the structure of the perception of the image by the subjects. The dimensions of Bush's images became condensed. The reconfiguration of his image consisted mainly in the elimination of the demeanor/style factor. On the other hand, the changes in perceiving Clinton were much bigger. The spots made the first two factors obtained in the pre-

TABLE 2.3. Dimensions of Bush and Clinton images before and after viewing television spots (factor analysis with orthogonal rotation).

George Bush		Bill Clinton	
Pretest	Posttest	Pretest	Posttest
F1 (56.2 percent): performance/credibility	F1 (61.2 percent): performance/credibility	F1 (43.7 percent): performance	F1 (47.9 percent): performance/credibility
F2 (12.0 percent): demeanor/style	F3 (12.1 percent): aggressiveness	F2 (13.7 percent): credibility	F2 (14.2 percent): demeanor/style
F3 (9.4 percent): aggressiveness		F3 (10.2 percent): aggressiveness	F3 (10.1 percent): aggressiveness

Note: The percentage of variations explained by a given factor is given in parentheses.

test (performance and credibility) melt into one. In addition, a new factor appeared concerning the style of Clinton's behavior.

The correlation between the results of the evaluation of the image in the posttest and the probability of voting for a given candidate was r = 0.86 ($p < 0.01$) for Bush and r = 0.73 ($p < 0.01$) for Clinton. Unfortunately, Kaid and Chanslor (1995) made no attempt to analyze the connection between the evaluation of the politicians' image and the voting intention before the spots were presented. Therefore, we cannot state whether the spots, apart from reconfiguring the image of both candidates, also influenced the changes in the support given to them.

Studies of the influence of political advertising on changes in candidates' perception were also conducted in Poland during the presidential elections in 1995, where incumbent Wałęsa fought against Kwaśniewski (Cwalina, Falkowski, 2000; Cwalina, Falkowski, Kaid, 2000; Falkowski, Cwalina, 1999). The experimental procedure was analogous to that used in Kaid and Chanslor's studies with one exception.

Namely, Kaid and Chanslor's (1995) model concerned perception and changes in perception of a candidates' image by all subjects, no matter whether they were supporters of one candidate or the other. In such an analyses, one loses the possibility of tracing the reconfiguration of a given candidate's image to people supporting him or her as well as those supporting the other candidate. Psychological knowledge about social perception also supports the division of voters into electorates; one pays attention to certain aspects of the people one likes and to other characteristics of the people one dislikes (see e.g. Argyle, 1983). It can be assumed then that every voter perceives every candidate differently, depending on whether or not he or she supports the candidate. The image of the same candidate is thus different, depending on the predisposition or the party identification of voters. The situation brings to mind experiments using *switch gestalt*, during which a person looking at the same picture may see two different things (for instance, an old or young woman, a duck or a rabbit; see Figure 2.2). Such different perceptions of a political candidate depend upon psychographic variables (attitudes, system of values) that characterize voters belonging to different voting segments.

In order to identify the dimensions according to which Aleksander Kwaśniewski and Lech Wałęsa were perceived, the exploratory factor analysis with orthogonal rotation was used. Eight such analyses were conducted, four for each candidate among his own and his opponent's supporters, before and after playing the spots. The results are presented in Tables 2.4 and 2.5. All the factor analyses conducted meet the statistical requirements of goodness of fit (χ^2 is not relevant).

A general conclusion that can be drawn on the basis of the results of factor analyses is that political advertising causes a reconfiguration, among supporters as well as opponents, of dimensions according to which presidential candidates are perceived.

In the case of Lech Wałęsa's supporters, the number of his perceptual dimensions did not change, however the spots did cause changes in their content. Before presenting the spots, Wałęsa was evaluated according to four criteria: political competence, acting according to ethical norms, power, and friendliness. After watching the spots of both candidates, two totally new dimensions emerged: keeping promises and aggressiveness. Another two dimensions were converted: political competence into social competence and power into political power. Two factors, on the other hand, fell away: acting according to ethical norms and friendliness.

The percention of Kwaśniewski's image by his opponents was also subject to considerable changes. Before the viewing of the spots, he was perceived through the perspective of five factors: acting according to ethical norms, political competence, social attractiveness, keeping promises, and aggressiveness. After the spots were presented, only one dimension did not change: aggressiveness. Acting according to ethical norms lost its element of activity and converted

TABLE 2.4. Change in Aleksander Kwaśniewski's and Lech Wałęsa's perceptual dimensions and evaluation in Wałęsa's electorate as a result of being exposed to the television spots.

LECH WAŁĘSA

Pretest—explained variance: 45.6 percent; $\chi^2 = 50.862$, df = 41, p = 0.139

Political competence	Acting according to ethical norms	Power	Friendliness
F1 (15.6 percent)	F2 (13.6 percent)	F3 (9.1 percent)	F4 (7.3 percent)
Sincere Successful Qualified Attractive Open to world	Active Honest Calm Believable Believing Christian	Strong	Friendly

Posttest—explained variance: 51.0 percent; $\chi^2 = 51.067$, df = 41, p = 0.135

Social competence	Keeping promises	Aggressiveness	Political power
F1 (25.4 percent)	F2 (12.8 percent)	F3 (9.0 percent)	F4 (3.9 percent)
Sincere Honest Friendly Attractive Active	Successful Believable	Excitable Aggressive	Open to world Strong Qualified

ALEKSANDER KWAŚNIEWSKI

Pretest—explained variance: 51.7 percent; $\chi^2 = 37.965$, df = 31, p = 0.182

Political competence	Acting according to ethical norms	Power	Friendliness	
F1 (15.9 percent)	F2 (13.2 percent)	F3 (10.3 percent)	F4 (6.6 percent)	F5 (5.6 percent)
Honest Active Believing Christian	Strong Qualified Sincere Open to world	Friendly Unsophisticated Attractive	Believable Successful	Excitable Aggressive

TABLE 2.4. *(Continued)*

Posttest—explained variance: 49.3 percent; $\chi^2 = 43.126$, df = 41, p = 0.385

Ethical norms	Professionalism of behavior	Aggressiveness	Attractiveness
F1 (14.0 percent)	F2 (13.0 percent)	F3 (12.4 percent)	F4 (9.8 percent)
Honest Believable Believing Christian Friendly	Open to world Strong Successful Active Qualified	Aggressive Excitable	Attractive

Source: Cwalina and Falkowski (2000), p. 213.

TABLE 2.5. Change in Aleksander Kwaśniewski's and Lech Wałęsa's perceptual dimensions and evaluation in Kwaśniewski's electorate as a result of being exposed to the television spots.

LECH WAŁĘSA

Pretest—explained variance: 51.0 percent; $\chi^2 = 39.336$, df = 31, p = 0.145

Ethical attractiveness	Acting according to ethical norms	Friendliness	Keeping promises	Unpredictability of actions
F1 (19.2 percent)	F2 (10.0 percent)	F3 (8.1 percent)	F4 (7.9 percent)	F5 (5.8 percent)
Calm Attractive Believing Christian Qualified	Strong Honest	Friendly	Successful Believable	Unsophisticated Active

Posttest—explained variance: 49.7 percent; $\chi^2 = 32.653$, df = 41, p = 0.821

Social competence	Ethical attractiveness	Aggressiveness	Power of acting
F1 (19.9 percent)	F2 (14.7 percent)	F3 (9.5 percent)	F4 (5.6 percent)
Open to world Honest Believable Sincere Friendly	Attractive Believing Christian Peaceful Successful Qualified	Aggressive	Active Strong

TABLE 2.5. *(Continued)*

ALEKSANDER KWAŚNIEWSKI		
Pretest—explained variance: 52.7 percent; $\chi^2 = 55.303$, df = 52, p = 0.351			
Competent political leadership	Deserving social confidence	Activity
F1 (24.3 percent)	F2 (17.8 percent)	F3 (10.6 percent)
Open to world Qualified Attractive Believable Successful Strong	Sincere Friendly Unaggressive Honest Calm	Active

Posttest—explained variance: 59.7 percent; $\chi^2=32.653$, df=41, p=0.821

Competent political leadership	Deserving social confidence	Credibility	Aggressiveness
F1 (43.3 percent)	F2 (7.8 percent)	F3 (4.9 percent)	F4 (3.7 percent)
Open to world Qualified Believable Calm Strong Successful Attractive	Friendly Sincere Honest Active	Believable	Aggressive

Source: Cwalina and Falkowski (2000), p. 214.

into more declarative ethical norms. Attractiveness lost its social aspect, and political competency converted into professionalism of behavior. The dimension of keeping promises fell apart completely, which, normally, lets a politician "breathe a sigh of relief." Neutralizing this latter factor can be perceived as Kwaśniewski's Machiavellian success while in the enemy camp. It is worthwhile to notice that the dimension of keeping promises came up after presenting the spots evaluating Wałęsa.

Among Aleksander Kwaśniewski's supporters, the influence of television spots on the perception of the candidates is also very conspicuous. The number of dimensions according to which Wałęsa was perceived decreased from five to four after the spots were viewed. The factor of ethical attractiveness was the only element that remained constant. Acting according to ethical norms, friendliness, keeping promises, and unpredictability of actions converted into social competence, aggressiveness, and power of actions.

An opposite trend could be observed in the case of Kwaśniewski's image perception. His image was developed progressing from three to four dimensions. Two dimensions remained unchanged. After presenting the spots, the independent factor of activity was eliminated, whereas two new dimensions appeared: credibility and aggressiveness.

Among Lech Wałęsa's supporters, both politicians, in a number of cases, were evaluated according to the same criteria, which made a direct comparison easier. On the other hand, Aleksander Kwaśniewski's supporters evaluated their candidate according to totally different dimensions than those applied to Wałęsa. Therefore, they had no chance to evaluate the politicians according to the same categories. Consequently, we can venture to say that Kwaśniewski's voters were constantly reassured in their preferences by their candidate, whereas Wałęsa's supporters were constantly put to the test, which may have led to a potentially high decisional uncertainty. Kwaśniewski's image was attractive for the people supporting him and, simultaneously, competitive to Wałęsa's image among the supporters of the incumbent. It seems that the objective of Kwaśniewski's advertising was met, whereas the promotional materials of his competitor proved to be less effective.

Summing up the analyses concerning the directing of perceptual dimensions, it can be said that making use of the laws of social perception, in light of which voters perceive politicians, makes citizens unaware of marketing manipulations. Political advertising shows voters what they should concentrate on. It tells them about the virtues of a given candidate, leaving out completely or blurring his or her faults. Therefore the promoted politician is perceived in consciously idealized and thus false categories. In the majority of cases, voters are not aware of this manipulation and submit to the candidates' persuasion.

THE ROLE OF EMOTION IN POLITICS

Emotions play an important role in the process of forming a politician's image. Marketing literature even makes a distinction between the issue of a candidate's socioeconomic program and his affection-modified image (Kaid, Holtz-Bacha, 1995). Models of voting behaviors also consider emotions as a separate element not only influencing voters' behaviors but also shaping the way of perceiving a candidate's agenda and receiving political information broadcast by the media. Some of these models and their empirical testing will be discussed in Chapter 6.

In 1987, Martin P. Wattenberg already stated that around one-third of voters do not know anything about particular politicians despite having strong emotions toward them. In addition, empirical researchers of voting behavior discovered that the emotional attitude toward candidates or political parties is a very good predictor of voters' decisions. Bernice Lott, Albert Lott, and Renee Saris (1993) for instance, stated that in the U.S. presidential elections in 1988 a preference for a candidate correlated significantly with the emotions toward him on the level of $r = 0.68$ for George Bush and $r = 0.60$ for Michael Dukakis. Kulwant Singh, Siew Meng Leong, Chin Tiong Tan, and Kwei Cheong Wang (1995), analyzing the attitude of voters immediately before parliamentary elections in Singapore in 1988, using the multiple regression equation obtained a voting intention prediction based on emotions toward a party and its candidates on the level of $R^2 = 0.36$ ($p < 0.001$).

In the research conducted by Wojciech Cwalina and Andrzej Falkowski in Poland in 1995 during presidential elections, the coefficient of point-biserial correlation between emotional attitude toward candidates and voting intention was $r_{pbi} = 0.85$ (p < 0.001), which points to a very strong link between affection and voting behavior. (Cwalina, 2000; Cwalina, Falkowski, 1999; Cwalina, Falkowski, Kaid, 2000; Falkowski, Cwalina, 1999).

Similar results were obtained by other researchers analyzing the relationship between people's emotional attitude toward candidates and their decision to vote for them during the elections (e.g. Abelson et al., 1982; Masterson, Biggers, 1986). Elliot Aronson, Timothy D. Wilson and Robin M. Akert (1994) metaphorically suggest that today people vote with their minds more than with their hearts.

Another group of analyses concentrates on the importance of the affective attitude toward candidates and evaluations of their views and features for citizens' voting behaviors (Holbrook et al., 2001; Rahn, Krosnick, Breuning, 1994). Two types of processes are considered here that may characterize a voter making his or her decision: derivation and rationalization. Derivation is defined as a process in which voting decisions are the consequence of an individual evaluation of information about candidates and their features. In this way, the choice is based on analyzing the available implications. ("I know what features of a candidate make me support him or her. I know what features will prevent me from supporting him or her. What prevails determines my positive or negative evaluation of him or her. Based on that, I vote.")

Rationalization assumes that choosing a candidate is based on this general evaluation. But the implications of this evaluation are hardly retrievable from memory (hardly available). In this way, the choice is based on the generalized impression that can be justified only after the event, and often occurs creatively. ("I know that I support and like the candidate. Why? I may have to think for a while. . . .")

In order to determine which decision processes, derivation or rationalization, are more characteristic for a voter, Wendy Rahn, Jon A. Krosnick, and Marijke Breuning (1994) conducted a study during the governor elections in Ohio in 1990. The research consisted of two parts: the first one a month before the elections and the other in the week preceding the elections. The task of the subjects was to define their general attitudes toward candidates and write down what they liked and disliked particular candidates for. Using multiple regression analysis, the researchers established that voters make their decisions on which candidate to support based on whether or not they liked him or her. Asked to justify their choice, they started combing their memory and often simply made up some arguments. In this way, the research supported rationalization as a dominant process for voting decisions.

However, the results of other analyses from the *National Election Study* from 1972 to 1996 proved less categorical (Holbrook et al., 2001). It turned out that wondering before making their final decision on who to support caused many voters to thoroughly analyze the available information. Consequently, the problem that still needs to be resolved is the participation of issues and emotion-filtered images. Particular models of voting behaviors precisely define the relationships between cognitive and emotional predictors of voting behaviors. (See Chapter 6.)

Chapter 3

Political Marketing

In close to 50,000 pictures of Franklin Delano Roosevelt, president of the United States from 1933-1945, at his summer home in New York, only two show him sitting in a wheel chair (see Figure 3.1). Was the president really holding back from his voters his partial paralysis (due to polio) and his inability to move on his own? If this was really the case, and this seems to be confirmed by analyses of the behavior of politicians and their staffs, one may ask about the purpose of such behavior.

FDR's actions were the result of marketing techniques used by his staff whose main goal was to create an image of the president as a physically strong person. During Roosevelt's presidential campaign, specialists responsible for his image created an image of a man who could walk freely, whereas in fact Roosevelt was confined to his wheelchair. He'd mastered the technique of self-presentation, in which he would prop one of his hands against his son's arm and the other one against a stick. Such a presentation created the impression that the president was able to walk, but it was only an illusion, projecting a false image of the president. The image of the president constructed in voters' minds was not congruent with reality. The voters had a false image of Roosevelt in their minds, created by the modified stimuli. Such a construction of a candidate for public office is called *candidate positioning,* i.e., finding in voters' minds a clear and desired place relative to the competing candidates (Newman, 1994). A candidate who can hold the best position is guaranteed voting success, just as a commercial product with the best position on the consumer market is guaranteed financial success.

Many modern researchers into political behaviors, including Bruce I. Newman (1994), Philip Kotler and Neil Kotler (1999), and Andrew

FIGURE 3.1. Franklin Delano Roosevelt (1882-1945). *Source:* Franklin D. Roosevelt Presidential Library and Museum. Online Photos. Available at: http://www.fdrlibrary.marist.edu/photos.html.

Lock and Phil Harris (1996), find analogies between voter and consumer behavior. In fact, it seems that making political voting choices has much in common with making purchasing decisions. Therefore, voters are often treated as consumers, consumers of political information (see also Cwalina, Falkowski, 2005a; Wolfsfeld, 1992). The inevitable consequence of applying methods of political marketing to voting behaviors is the "packaging" of the candidates, i.e., creating their images for the purpose of election to public office. It often leads to their being compared to particular consumer products, such as laundry detergent or toothpaste. However, as Alex Marland (2003) clearly sees and demonstrates, such comparisons are outdated and hardly appropriate in modern marketing. He stresses that politicians are not consumer products that one can own. Rather, they should be treated as relators hired for a particular period of time, similar to doctors or lawyers. One should not forget, however, that "political products" prepared in such a way are launched on the market to be sold for a profit. They are accompanied by a great amount of advertising in the press, on the radio and TV, and by presentations and "promotions" during election rallies.

Applying the methodology of commercial marketing to political behaviors during presidential and parliamentary campaigns led to the establishment of a new research discipline called political marketing. Lock and Harris (1996) define political marketing as a discipline, the study of the processes of exchanges between political entities and their environment and among themselves, with particular reference to the positioning of those entities and their communications. Government (the parliament) and the legislature exist both as exogenous regulators of these processes and as political subjects.

ECONOMIC VERSUS POLITICAL MARKETING

In order to understand the links between marketing and politics, one should also understand specific marketing concepts. Above all, marketing as a process involves creating exchange, where the two sides involved are the seller of products or services on one side, and the customer (consumer) on the other. Marketing strategies, developed on the basis of the *marketing mix,* serve to realize this exchange in such a way that the two sides are satisfied.

The similarity of a candidate to consumer products presented at the beginning of this chapter is an oversimplification, which, as Bruce I. Newman (1994) demonstrates, is a myth perpetuated by the press and is based on candidates employing commercial marketing specialists for the purpose of their political campaigns (see also Marland, 2003). Those specialists use their knowledge of advertising products to advertise candidates or political parties. However, one should remember that a candidate is rather a provider of certain services for his or her electorate. The candidate offers his or her services the way an insurance agent does: the product is the insurance policy provided by insurance companies and sold by the agent, and not the agent himself or herself. Although the marketing strategies used during political elections refer to the candidate, which may suggest an analogy to the product, the real product is *the campaign platform* (Newman, 1994). It consists of a number of elements, including (1) the general election program of the candidate based on the political and economic guidelines of the party he or she belongs to or the organization set up for the time of the elections; (2) his or her positions on the most important problems appearing during the campaign; (3) the image of the candidate; and (4) the candidate's reference to his or her political background and the groups of voters supporting him or her (e.g., labor unions, associations, nongovernmental organizations, etc.). Such a platform is flexible and evolves together with the development of the voting campaign and changes in the voting situation.

In order to understand the specificity of marketing actions in politics, one should take a closer look at the differences between economic and political marketing. A detailed analysis was conducted by Lock and Harris (1996), who point out seven major differences between the two spheres:

1. Those eligible to vote always choose their candidate or political party on the same day that the voting takes place. Consumers, on the other hand, can purchase their products at different times, depending on their needs and purchasing power. Very seldom do the majority of consumers simultaneously want to purchase a certain product. Besides, although one can talk about similarities between opinion polls and tracking measures, the latter often refer to the purchasing decisions that have already been taken, unlike poll questions referring to the future and unknown reality.

2. Whereas the consumer purchasing a product always knows its price—the value expressed in financial terms—for the voter no price is attached to his or her ability to make a voting decision. Making a voting decision may be the result of analyzing and predicting the consequences of this decision, which can be considered as possible losses and gains in the long-term perspective between elections. In this respect, a great similarity exists between post-purchase behavior and voting behavior. In both cases, one may regret making a particular decision; the product one purchased or the candidate one chose

may not meet the expectations of the customer or voter. Of course, one may also feel satisfaction after making a decision. However, it seems that such a state is much more often experienced by customers than voters. Besides, it would be odd if, before going to the polls, the voter would be informed of how much he or she needs to pay to be able to choose a party or a politician, whereas it is natural that such a price be attached to consumer products.

3. The voter realizes that the choice is collective and that he or she must accept the final voting result even if it goes against his or her voting preferences. Geoffrey Brennan and James Buchanan (1984) even claim that the relationship between how an individual voter votes and the final result of the election is hardly relevant. What is really important is the distribution of support across the whole society. In other words, this is a social rather than an individual choice. This is very different from consumer choices, in which the purchasing decision is completely independent of the attitude toward a given product that other consumers may have.

4. Winner takes all in political elections. This is the case in majority elections, including, for example, the presidential elections in Poland, mayoralty elections, and single-member districts in Senate elections. The closest equivalent to commercial marketing in this case would be gaining a monopoly on the market.

5. The political party or candidate is a complex, intangible product that the voter cannot unpack to see what is inside. Although commercial marketing includes as well products and services that the consumer cannot unpack and check while buying them, the proportion of such packages that cannot be unpacked is much greater in the political market. Besides, the consumer may change his or her mind and exchange products or services almost immediately for others when he or she does not like the product purchased; such exchanges may be quite expensive, though. If the voter decides to change his or her mind, he or she has to wait till the next election, at least a few years.

6. Introducing a new brand in the form of a political party is quite difficult and always remote in time. Many short-lived parties are created (in Poland, for instance: Center Agreement, Liberal-Democratic Congress, or Solidarity Election Action). Besides, politics has no supranational parties, although transnational groupings exist in the European Parliament, for instance. In commercial marketing, on the other hand, there are many brands that have acquired international

status, including the supermarket chain "Géant," for instance, which is present in many European countries, or the Coca-Cola company, which is represented all over the world.

7. In commercial marketing, brand leaders tend to stay in front. In political marketing, one can often witness a situation when, after winning the elections, a political party begins to lose support in public opinion polls. Such a situation is connected with the ruling party often making decisions that are not well received by various social groups (e.g., unfavorable budget decisions or tax increases).

In addition to this, Bruce I. Newman (1994) points to further differences between economic and political marketing, stressing that in business the ultimate goal is financial success, whereas in politics it is strengthening democracy through voting processes. Besides, not infrequently, elections are won by a small margin of a few percentage points, whereas gaining the leading position on the consumer market is the result of a huge advantage over the competition. Using various marketing strategies in economic practice is the result of conducting market research that promises satisfactory financial profits. In politics, on the other hand, a candidate's own philosophy often influences the scope of marketing strategies. This means that although marketing research may suggest that a politician's chances will increase if he or she concentrates on particular political or economic issues, the politician does not have to follow these suggestions if his or her own conception of political reality is incongruent with these issues.

Therefore, one can assume that the often mindless assumption that research methods developed for influencing consumer behaviors can directly be transferred to controlling voting behaviors is wrong. The differences between economic and political marketing are big enough to make one think about developing an independent concept for studying voting behaviors. However, creating such a concept is closely connected to the development and understanding of democratic processes. Therefore, it is natural that currently, when the discipline of political marketing is only in its developmental stage, the practitioners and politicians use already verified methodology from commercial marketing, making analogies between the consumer and voter. In political marketing one can find concepts drawn from studying consumer behaviors as well as market research, market segmentation, positioning, the development of marketing strategies and their implementation. At the current level of research, the models and theories of political marketing assume that the consumer and voter are roughly similar. No matter what markets they describe, be they economic or political, the models always assume that competitiveness lies at their very foundation.

MARKETING ORIENTATION IN POLITICAL CAMPAIGNS

Campaigning for office has always had a marketing orientation. Kotler and Kotler (1999) state that to be successful, candidates have to understand their markets, that is, the voters and their basic needs and aspirations, and the constituencies they represent or seek to represent. Marketing orientation means that candidates recognize the nature of the exchange process when they strive for votes. If a candidate is able to make promises that match the voters' needs and is able to fulfill some of these promises once in office, then the candidate will increase voter, as well as public, satisfaction. It is obvious, then, that it is the voter who should be the center of attention during political campaigns.

The essence of marketing strategy leading to voting success is to create, during the campaign, in a relatively short period of time, an organization able to mobilize the forces of various, often conflicting social groups in order to build a strong coalition supporting the candidate. Until recently, candidates, mainly on local levels, faced what they believed were quite homogenous and close-knit voting districts. Such homogenous understanding of the voting market allowed for a homogenous message about a candidate, concerning both his or her political program and personal qualities.

In recent years, however, one could observe, applying, among others, the tools of commercial marketing for politics, that the political voting arena has become very diverse. It consists of groups of various interests, likings, preferences, and lifestyles. More efficient and successful political campaigns need to accommodate this diversity by creating strategies for various market segments. Issue-oriented voters exist, but so do voters influenced by a candidate's personal charm. Politicians often face a difficult task: they have to build a voting coalition based on and reflecting a certain compromise among various social groups. This requires a great amount of skill on the part of a candidate in creating a cognitive map of different opinions, emotions, or interests. Then the candidate has to refer to such a map while constructing his or her information messages in order to establish the foundations of an agreement between various voter groups and the candidate.

Electoral districts and the political campaigns connected with them can be very diverse. A candidate from a small, single-issue political district can be either the champion of an issue, a rebel against it, or a reformer, seeking ways to mobilize and gain support for a brand-new idea. In order to achieve success, he or she has to identify the interest groups in society that would support new solutions and to define ways of presenting himself or herself and his or her ideas in the media. Such activities require financial means whose importance increases considerably once the voting fight becomes closer, fiercer, and more aggressive (Kotler, Kotler, 1999). Whereas in 1980 approximately $220 million was spent on political campaigns in the United States, in 1996 the figure exceeded $894 million, and campaign expenditures continue to grow.

Kotler and Kotler distinguish five factors playing key roles in organizing political campaigns and establishing a political market that they call voting market segments:

1. *Active voters,* who are in the habit of casting ballots in elections.
2. *Interest groups and nongovernmental organizations,* social activists and organized voter groups who collect funds for election campaigns (for example labor unions, business organizations, human rights groups, civil rights groups, or ecological movements).
3. *The media,* which make the candidate visible. The candidate may be foregrounded during the campaign or kept in the shadows of campaigns.
4. *Political party organizations,* which nominate a candidate, express opinions about him or her, and provide the resource base for the campaign.
5. *Donators (contributors),* who are private persons making donations for the candidate and his or her campaign.

These factors are graphically presented in Figure 3.2.

Among these five elements, it is the media that is the most important for the success of a political campaign. The media influences the ultimate image of the candidate in the direct process of communica-

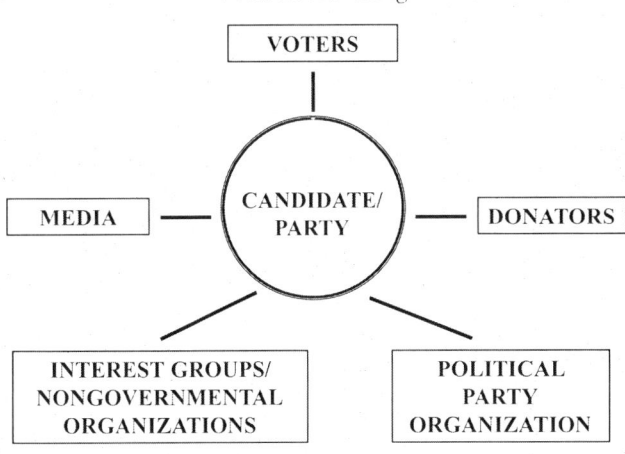

```
                    ┌─────────┐
                    │ VOTERS  │
                    └─────────┘
                         │
                    ╱────────╲
    ┌───────┐      │CANDIDATE/│      ┌──────────┐
    │ MEDIA │──────│  PARTY   │──────│ DONATORS │
    └───────┘      ╲────────╱       └──────────┘
                   ╱         ╲
    ┌──────────────────┐   ┌──────────────┐
    │ INTEREST GROUPS/ │   │  POLITICAL   │
    │  NONGOVERNMENTAL │   │    PARTY     │
    │  ORGANIZATIONS   │   │ ORGANIZATION │
    └──────────────────┘   └──────────────┘
```

FIGURE 3.2. Factors influencing the political voting market.

tion with his or her voters. The media's influence on voting preferences can be either open or hidden. The media's open influence may be demonstrated by their supporting a given political option and sponsoring and publicizing various events connected with the political campaign. The media's hidden influence is represented by the extent to which a given candidate appears in the media. Becoming known to the voters is an important factor that has an influence on voting preferences. The media may also manipulate the message, exaggerating or marginalizing a candidate's position on various social and political issues. It may also shape his personality and emotional image, highlighting positive or negative features in information programs.

THE PROCESS OF POLITICAL MARKETING ACCORDING TO PHILLIP B. NIFFENEGGER

Phillip B. Niffenegger (1988) proposed a concept of political marketing in which he tries to show the use of the mix of marketing tools in political campaigns. The author shows the evolutionary process of the development of political marketing using the examples of the actions of candidates and their staffs during the U.S. presidential elections campaigns. He stresses that in political marketing, one can notice efforts aimed at integration within the *marketing mix* (the "four Ps") to more efficiently control the voters' behaviors. Advertising is not set apart here as an independent research discipline, but is closely connected to the process of marketing research, for which the segmentation of the voting market plays an important role. Niffenegger's concept of the political marketing process is presented in Figure 3.3.

Niffenegger's concept is based on Kotler's definition of political marketing research. According to this definition, a political party participating in parliamentary elections or a candidate running for president must identify the needs, interests, and values of voters and present himself or herself in such a way so as to best fit these requirements. Even if he or she is able to identify the country's key social, economic, or political problems, without systematic research the candidate is not able to determine how these problems are perceived by various voter groups. It can be assumed that they hold different weights for particular groups. Therefore, the candidate should try to fit his or her voting strategy to different voter segments, that is, to find the best position for himself or herself in each of them. Such a procedure refers to the candidate's positioning and requires marketing research.

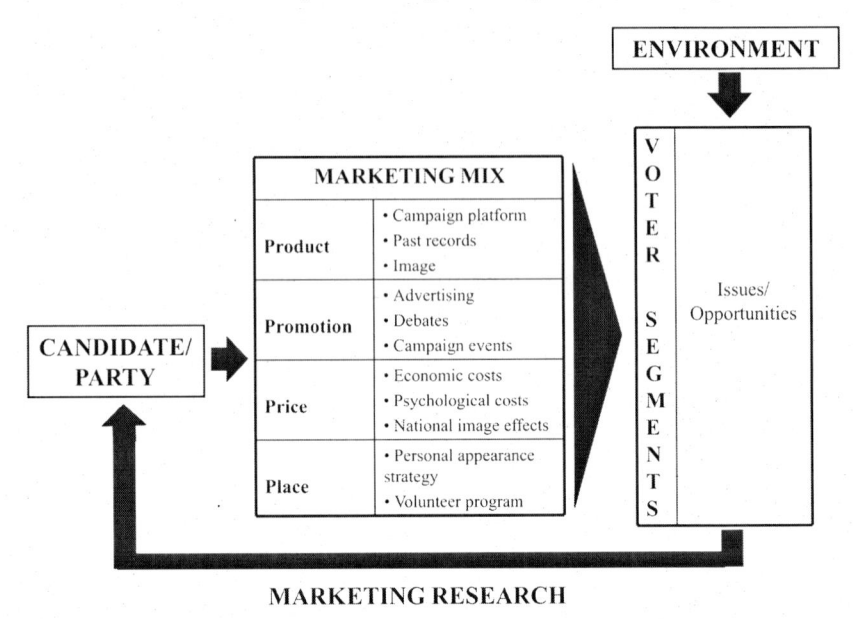

FIGURE 3.3. The process of political marketing according to P.B. Niffenegger.

This is illustrated by the arrow in Figure 3.3 connecting the four Ps marketing program with voter segments. It should be stressed that this link is mediated by marketing research whose results, given to the candidate, show him or her what marketing mix he or she should use to be most successful. In political marketing, being successful mainly means expanding one's electorate.

Marketing research, in the form of prevoting polls whose goal was to position the candidate, was first conducted by Dwight Eisenhower's staff in 1952. The purpose of the research was to define the position of Eisenhower relative to the position of his main rival, Adlai Stevenson. The research procedure was quite simple. First, the voters were presented thirty-second political spots, and then an interview was conducted to determine which problem presentation made the greatest impression on the voters. One could then predict the voters' behavior by controlling the problems presented in the spot.

Prevoting marketing polls very quickly began to be commonly used to position candidates in various voter segments. Richard Nixon's consultants used them in the presidential campaign of 1968. They first tried to determine the voters' ideas of the ideal U.S. president, and then the next step was to position, in such a context, the images of Nixon and his main opponents, Hubert Humphrey and George Wallace. Defining the differences between the image of an ideal president and his own, Nixon was able to determine which characteristics should be improved and presented in television spots in such a way as to approach as closely as possible the voters' expectations.

In 1984, Ronald Reagan's political consultants tried to define the characteristics of the image of an ideal candidate by using prevoting telephone polls. His staff also conducted polls on the major social and economic problems of the country and ways presidential candidates might solve them. When the data was entered into PIN, Political Information Network, set up for the purpose of the campaign, one could track the dynamics of the changes of voters' attitudes toward particular candidates.

In his model, Niffenegger distinguishes four fundamental marketing stimuli, using the same names that the classical commercial marketing mix uses: product, promotion, price, and place.

According to Niffenegger, *the product* offered by the candidate is a complex blend of the many benefits voters believe will result if the candidate is elected. The major voting promises are spelled out in the candidate's party platform. Then they are publicized through political advertising and press releases and during the candidate's public appearances. Whether the offer is recognized as reliable and really meeting their expectations mainly depends on voters' knowledge of the candidate and his or her achievements, the candidate's personal profile formed by his or her staff, and the evaluation of the state's economic condition connected with the previous ruling team. Ronald Reagan, for instance, in his presidential campaign in 1984, very cleverly used the arguments of his Democratic opponent Walter Mondale for increasing taxes. Reagan showed what the consequences of such a policy might be by referring to the economic crisis during Jimmy Carter's presidency. This tactic led to a decrease in the support for Mondale.

Whereas creating the product in political marketing is, as a matter of fact, the purpose of the candidate and his or her staff, the "packaging" part is almost solely the task of political consultants. An example showing how various "packaging" is created for various situations is the changing of strategy by Reagan's consultants during his presidential campaign in 1980. They were quick to spot that in his speeches the Republican candidate was perceived as a warmonger and as dangerous and uncaring. Instead of using the phrase the "defensive position," the candidate began to talk about the "peace position." The "armaments race" was replaced by the phrase "a need to restore a margin of safety." After such changes, the image of Reagan came closer to the image of an ideal president. He was perceived as a politician who would strengthen peace.

The price of the product offered by the candidate refers to the total costs that voters would bear if the candidate were elected. It includes economic costs, such as tax increases or budget cuts. Other costs listed by Niffenegger include national image effects: whether the voters will perceive the new leader as a strong one, someone who will increase people's national pride, or someone who will be a disgrace to his or her compatriots on the international stage. One should also remember psychological costs: will voters feel comfortable with the candidate's religious and ethnic background? The general marketing strategy for the price consists in minimizing the candidate's own costs and maximizing the opposition's. In his presidential campaign, John F. Kennedy recognized a potential cost in being the first Catholic president, a thought that made some non-Catholics feel uneasy. But he was able to successfully minimize this cost with television spots in which he was shown meeting Protestant audiences. During his presidential campaign in 1995, Aleksander Kwaśniewski also stressed that he would be the president of all Poles, irrespective of their religion and views.

Place (distribution) is the marketing stimulus that refers to the candidate's getting across in a personal way to his or her voters. The marketing strategy for the distribution of the campaign's message combines the personal appearance program with the work of volunteers who are used as a personalized extension of the candidate into local markets. This includes the work of activists (door to door) who by canvassing, distributing the candidate's badges, registering voters, and soliciting funds, familiarize the voters with the candidate's program and his or her image during direct contact with the electorate. The places and forms of a candidate's meeting with voters can vary—from rallies in city centers to club meetings and meetings at workplaces. Since the goal of the politician on the campaign trail is to meet as many voters as possible, he or she tries to be in as many places as possible in the shortest possible time. Gary Hart, a candidate for the Democratic presidential nomination in 1984, used a plane to move quickly from one town to another. His press conferences were staged in every airport he flew into. Listening to the evening news, one had the feeling that Hart had been in many towns at the same time. More recently, satellite technology has made it easier for candidates to stage interviews with journalists who are in remote places.

Promotion consists, to a large extent, of advertising efforts and publicity, through free media coverage of the candidate, his or her program, and campaigning. Niffenegger distinguishes four fundamental promotion strategies:

1. *Concentration strategy:* concentrating a disproportionate amount of money and promotion efforts on particular voter segments (for instance on regions or provinces).
2. *Timing strategy:* involves spending the heaviest promotion money and the highest promotion activity where it does the candidate the most good. It forces the opposition to increase their activity and thus depletes their resources.

3. *Strategy of misdirection:* avoiding a frontal assault against a stronger opponent and trying to catch the opponent off balance to make him or her commit a mistake. This may be a particularly successful strategy for underdogs.
4. *Strategy of negative campaign:* is based on direct or indirect comparative assaults against the position of the opponent and/or his or her personal characteristics.

Recognizing the reasons for his poor showings in the political debates in 1980, Ronald Reagan decided to change the strategy he had been using. During the next election, in his political spots, he focused on evoking positive emotions in his voters. His spots featured sunrises, colorful parades, landscapes, and friendly faces. These contrasted with Walter Mondale's spots, which gave rise to negative emotions by presenting visions of an atomic holocaust, starvation, and poverty.

Specific marketing programs based on the four Ps are prepared separately for different voting market segments. A particularly important role in this division is played by the segment of undecided voters, irrespective of the demographic and psychographic criteria of segmentation. It is these voters at whom the marketing mix should be directed. This was noticed by Richard Nixon's staff, which, using marketing research, was looking for ways of reaching undecided voters. This segment is considered most susceptible to marketing influence, and it is this segment at whom the greatest efforts of a political campaign should be directed. Less attention can be given to decided and loyal voters whose preferences are hard to change. Nixon's approach to the strategy of the voting market segmentation is congruent with the position of Jay G. Blumler and Denis McQuail (1968), who stated that the image of political reality can be formed only among undecided voters, whereas voters with a clearly defined political stance are very resistant to marketing efforts.

In the presidential campaign in 1980 when Jimmy Carter and Ronald Reagan competed against each other, the segment of undecided voters (amounting to nearly 20 percent of the electorate) decided the results of the election. Maintaining a strong position among current supporters is also important. During the 1984 presidential campaign, the Political Information Network showed that Reagan needed to improve his image among blue-collar workers, Catholics, and Latinos. The support of these groups for the current leaders was decreasing, which turned this segment into undecided voters, easy for the challenger to take over.

The implications of the political marketing model proposed by Niffenegger suggest that the candidate's staff should create and update advanced marketing information systems, including collecting and analyzing data from political market research, segmentation, and channels for the distributing of the promotion message to target groups. In addition, it is important to introduce regional variants to the general strategy of the campaign and use microsegmentation, as well as take into account the specificity of local voting markets. One should also consider focusing the marketing effort on some "showroom" target areas. A spectacular success in a given area may have a positive influence on the campaign in other areas. Niffenegger suggests that negative advertising be used only as a last resort, because it may produce a backlash. In a political campaign, one should also use the specific qualities and limitations of television to gain a competitive advantage (e.g., organize rallies or meetings that can make headlines).

Niffenegger's concept of political marketing, despite that it attempts to show the efficiency of using marketing strategies for political campaigns, is in fact a copy of the concepts used in commercial marketing. It seems, then, that it does not distinguish to a sufficient extent between consumer and political choices.

A MODEL OF POLITICAL MARKETING ACCORDING TO BRUCE I. NEWMAN

One of the models of political marketing that includes all of the elements of the voting campaign is represented by the concept developed by Bruce I. Newman (1994). In his model Newman (1994) introduces a clear distinction between the processes of a marketing campaign and those of a political campaign. A marketing campaign helps the candidate go through the four stages of a political campaign, including the preprimary stage of a politician finding his or her own place in politics to his or her already formed political image at the general election stage. It is natural, then, that both campaigns are closely connected. The process of a marketing campaign is the foundation of the model, because it includes all the marketing tools needed to conduct the candidate through all the levels of the political campaign. Figure 3.4 presents a schematic representation of Newman's model. The following sections describe the particular elements of this model.

Candidate Focus

Different approaches to election campaigns can be said to be connected with the gradual evolution in understanding what the object of sale actually is on the voting market. This part presents another approach developed by Bruce I. Newman (1994) and Jennifer Lees-Marshment (2001, 2003). Figure 3.5 presents a schematic illustration of the evolution of the marketing approach to election campaigns, according to Newman's theory (1994).

The evolution of the marketing concept is depicted in Figure 3.5, which shows the four stages that describe how presidential cam-

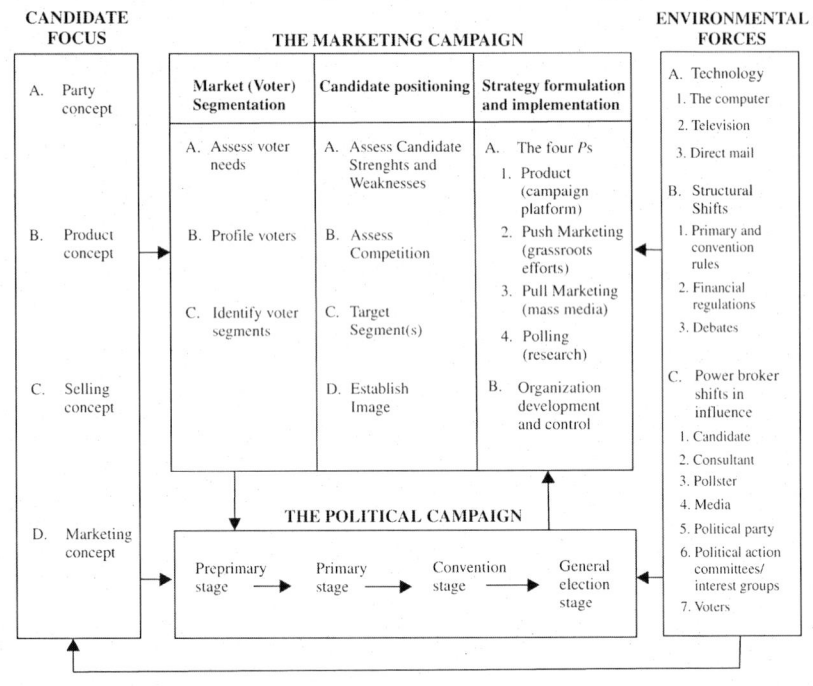

CANDIDATE FOCUS	THE MARKETING CAMPAIGN			ENVIRONMENTAL FORCES
A. Party concept	Market (Voter) Segmentation	Candidate positioning	Strategy formulation and implementation	A. Technology 1. The computer 2. Television
	A. Assess voter needs	A. Assess Candidate Strenghts and Weaknesses	A. The four Ps 1. Product (campaign platform)	3. Direct mail B. Structural Shifts
B. Product concept	B. Profile voters	B. Assess Competition	2. Push Marketing (grassroots efforts)	1. Primary and convention rules
	C. Identify voter segments	C. Target Segment(s)	3. Pull Marketing (mass media) 4. Polling (research)	2. Financial regulations 3. Debates
C. Selling concept		D. Establish Image	B. Organization development and control	C. Power broker shifts in influence 1. Candidate 2. Consultant 3. Pollster 4. Media
D. Marketing concept	THE POLITICAL CAMPAIGN			5. Political party 6. Political action committees/ interest groups 7. Voters
	Preprimary stage →	Primary stage →	Convention stage → General election stage	

FIGURE 3.4. A model of political marketing. *Source:* Newman (1994), p. 12.

Marketing concept

Selling concept

Product concept

Party concept
An internally driven organization run by the party bosses and centered on the political party

An internally driven organization run by Washington insiders and centered on the candidate

An externally driven organization run by Madison Avenue experts and centered on the candidate

An externally driven organization run by marketing experts and centered on the voter

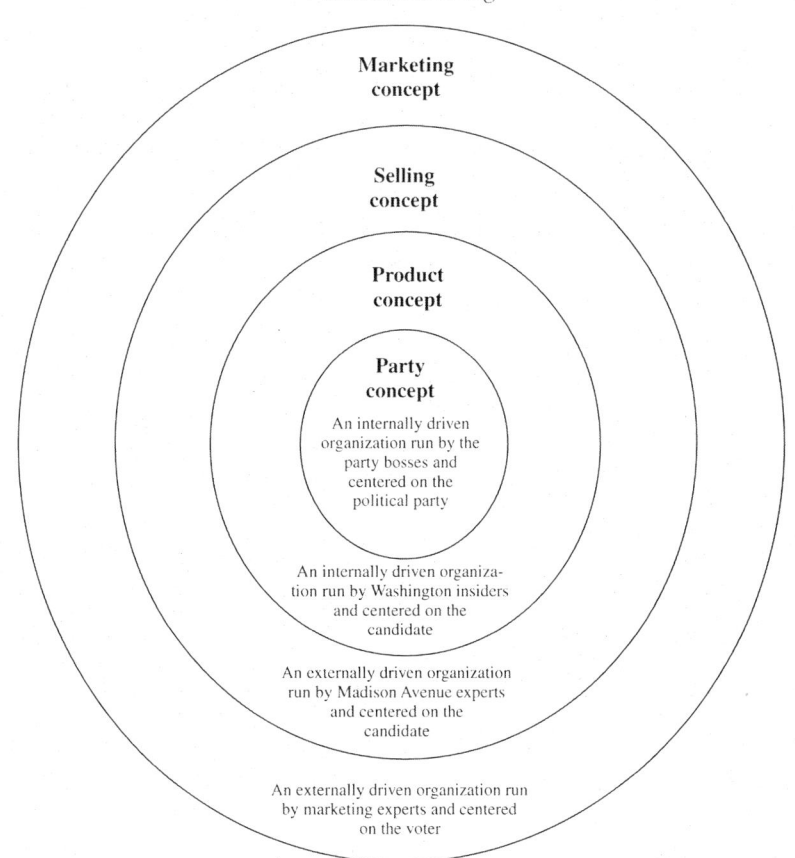

FIGURE 3.5. The evolution of the marketing concept. *Source:* Newman (1994), p. 32. *Note:* The focus of the political campaign or organization has evolved. Once centered on the political party, the political campaign became candidate-centered and then voter-centered.

paigns have gone from organizations run by party bosses to organizations run by marketing experts. The focus of the organization has also evolved from one that used to be centered on the political party to one centered on the voter.

In the *party concept* the organization has internal focus, which means that it is operated on information generated from the people within the organization and run by party bosses whose only allegiance is to the political party. Grassroots efforts to get the vote out are at the heart of the power of the political party. The candidates at that time had no choice but to rely on the party bosses within the organization to become slated as a nominee. The party concept in political elections was the leading element of voting strategies in former communist countries of Eastern Europe. Any characteristics that were not congruent with the party's political profile destroyed the candidate's electoral chances. Any departures from the party's line were treated as manifestations of disloyalty and usually led to the immediate removal of the politician from office. However, one may have the impression that the majority of Polish voting campaigns are still organized based on the party way of management. In the United States, if we look back to presidential elections up through the Eisenhower presidency, we see campaign organizations that also followed the party concept.

In time, however, attention shifted from the party to the candidate representing it. The major effort taken during political campaigns no longer focuses on the party's ideology. Although the candidate is usually put up by a particular party, it is his or her own characteristics that are important for wielding power, and these are emphasized in the electoral strategy. They include, for instance, competence or an ability to run the country's economic policy. This shift was caused by the decline in the number of people who consider themselves partisans and the increase in the number who consider themselves independents. As Holbrook (1996) notes, the percentage of the U.S. electorate identifying with a political party has declined from roughly 73 percent in the 1950s and 1960s to 61 percent by 1992. At the same time, the percentage identifying themselves as independents has increased from 22 percent in 1952 to 39 percent in 1992 (see Figure 1.1 in Chapter 1). This is consistent with Wattenberg's (1995) documentation in which he shows a broader decline in support for the parties and a concomitant increase in candidate-centered politics in presidential campaigns.

A similar picture appeared on the British political scene. Hayes and McAllister (1996) note that recent estimates suggest that not only do 24 percent of the British public leave their voting decision until the start of the election campaign (as compared to 17 percent in 1964), but swing voters—individuals who change their intended vote during the final stages of the election campaign—now constitute about one quarter of the British electorate. The data in Figure 1.2 of Chapter 1 illustrate the extent of these changes.

The proportion of voters who decided on their vote more than two years before the election campaign has declined steadily since the 1960s, and a dramatic rise in late deciders, or in individuals who decide on their vote during the election campaign has occurred. Hayes and McAllister state that most explanations attempting to account for this rise in late deciders have emphasized the importance of declining party attachments. Put simply, British voters have become less partisan. From a marketing perspective, these late deciders, called floating voters, may be considered individuals with no brand loyalty (see Chapter 1).

Marketing has developed the notion of *product concept,* which stresses the importance of manufacturing a quality product. For example, efforts went into manufacturing the Model T Ford with only one idea in mind: to built a quality automobile. Likewise, in politics, the product concept would apply to campaign organizations that have only one goal: to find the best possible candidate to represent the party. In contrast to the party concept in which allegiance is to the party, here it is directed to the candidate.

The next stage in the evolution of the marketing concept involves a *selling concept* in which the focus of the campaign organization shifts from an internally to an externally driven operation. Here the voter's reaction to the candidate's media appearances becomes critical. However, as with the product concept, the focus is still on the candidate. The best example of this concept comes from McGinniss (1969) on the Nixon presidency. McGinnis describes how great efforts were made to sell Nixon to the electorate by relying on media experts. Work went into making Nixon look as good as possible on television by using persuasive appeals in commercials to convince people to vote for him.

The *marketing concept* goes a step further by first identifying consumer needs and then developing products and services to meet those needs. The marketing concept is based on a very different philosophy than the party concept, the main difference being that the marketing concept centers on the voter as the primary focus of the campaign. The delivery of promises once the candidate begins to govern is also pivotal to the philosophy behind the marketing concept. In business, to avoid failure and ensure that consumers get what they want, companies must address their needs. This same orientation can be found in the political marketplace as well, and is used to help the candidate avoid failure and win the election. The marketing concept begins with the voter, not with the candidate. As with the business world, the marketing concept dictates what candidates do, and, as with business, candidates want to create and retain their customers. Several differences between party-driven and voter-driven campaigns have been described in detail by Newman (1994).

A slightly different approach to the evolution of marketing in politics was proposed by Lees-Marshment (2001, 2003). She set out a comprehensive theoretical framework, using comprehensive political marketing (CPM), which incorporates understanding from a wide range of areas within political science as well as from marketing literature. She states that a market-oriented party designs its behavior to provide voter satisfaction. It uses market intelligence to identify voter demands, then designs its product to suit them. It does not attempt to change what people think, but to deliver what they need and want. A market-oriented party will not simply offer voters what they want, because it needs to ensure that it can deliver the product on offer. If it fails to deliver, voters will become dissatisfied, and the party risks losing electoral support in the long term.

Marketing Campaign

At the heart of a marketing campaign is the candidates' realization that they are not in a position to appeal to all voters of every persuasion. This means that the candidate must break down the electorate into distinct voting blocs and then create a campaign platform that appeals to the candidate's following. The process of dividing the whole electorate into many different groups is called *voter segmentation*. It is obvious that the unemployed or those who may lose their jobs will be more sensitive to messages in which the candidate stresses those elements of his or her voting program that refer to fighting against unemployment and to such economic changes that will create more jobs. Entrepreneurs with high income, on the other hand, will be more sensitive to the messages presenting the candidate's position on the taxation system. It is not only demographic characteristics, including the citizens' economic status, for instance, that are important for the division of the political market, but also their needs, attitudes, interests, and preferences, all of which are part of psychographic segmentation and play an important role in the division of the market into segments.

After identifying voting segments, one needs to define the candidate's position in each of them in the multistage process of positioning. This consists of assessing the candidate's and his or her opponents' strengths and weaknesses. The key elements here include: (1) creating an image of the candidate emphasizing his or her particular personality features and (2) the candidate developing and presenting a clear position on the country's economic and social issues. Such an image and position should follow the strategy of the election fight.

In order to position the candidate in voters' minds, one should apply the political marketing mix used for the implementation of a marketing strategy. To do so one should use a strategic plan consisting of the four Ps, the previously discussed strategy commonly followed in the commercial marketplace. For a company marketing a product, the four Ps include the following components: product, promotion, price, and place. The strategy a candidate follows closely mirrors these four components.

1. *Product* is defined in terms of his or her leadership and campaign platform, particularly issues and policies he or she advocates. When the campaign's platform is being formed, two key information flow channels are created, which are also the components of the campaign's *marketing mix* through which a candidate advertises himself or herself and his or her party's platform.

2. *Push marketing*, the next P, refers to the grassroots effort necessary to build up a volunteer network to handle the day-to-day activities in running the campaign. This component is similar to place or distribution channels that are used to get the product from the manufacturer to the consumer. In politics, the distribution channel centers on transferring information as opposed to a product. The grassroots effort that is established becomes one information channel that transmits the candidate's message from his or her organization to the voter.

3. *Pull marketing*, the third P, is similar to promotion. Pull marketing becomes a second information channel for the candidate. Instead of the person-to-person channel used with a push marketing approach, this channel makes use of mass media outlets such as television, radio, newspapers, magazines, direct mail, computer, and any other form of promotion that is available.

4. *Polling* is the fourth P in the political marketplace. It represents the data analysis and research that are used to develop and test new ideas and determine how successful the ideas will be.

The foundation of marketing strategy implementation includes organizational tasks connected with assembling staff for the campaign team, defining their tasks, and monitoring their activities where soliciting funds for the campaign plays an important role.

Political Campaign

The marketing campaign is conducted simultaneously with the political campaign and serves to help the candidate get through each of the four stages—preprimary, primary, convention, and general election—successfully. Both the marketing and the political campaigns are influenced by the candidate's strategic orientation and by forces in the environment (see the previous section in this chapter titled "Marketing Orientation in Political Campaigns"). It is obvious then that both campaigns are tightly connected and interdependent, and one cannot analyze a political campaign without reference to particular elements of the marketing campaign. For example, the analysis of the market segmentation strategies of the candidates is divided into the previously mentioned stages of the political campaign.

The Preprimary Stage

One objective for a candidate in the preprimary stage is to be taken seriously by the news media. This usually means that the candidate should have won a major election for public office. In addition, the news media pay close attention to political consultants and staff being hired by the candidate. When the news media see this happening, they in turn make the formal declaration in the news that candidate X is to be taken seriously.

Before the primary season begins, candidates organize their presentation tactics in order to maintain a certain level of visibility. Investing a significant amount of time in preprimary events, the candidates raise funds and visit states that will select delegates early in the process. During this period, the candidates must be certain that they are ideologically positioned for the primary voter, who is different from the average general election voter. A much smaller percentage of citizens votes during a primary, and those who do tend to be more interested in and concerned about politics. As a result, the candidates must introduce different appeals during the primaries than during the general election.

The Primary Stage

During this stage it is critical for the candidate to try to manipulate the mass media's reporting focus. The candidate must particularly try to have some impact on the before-and-after reporting of the primary elections, especially concerning who won and who lost compared to the predictions. Interpretation of the primary results is as important as the actual outcome. The candidate who loses but does better than expected may in fact be the bigger winner than the one who wins but falls below expectations. It is therefore to the advantage of a candidate to hold his or her preelection claims to a minimum.

Primaries have major effects on candidates and their strategies because they compel candidates to raise money in order to establish credibility early in the process. Therefore, the most important aspect of the primaries is how they are analyzed in relation to their effect on public opinion and, in turn, how this information is mediated by the press. In addition, the rules of the major parties for counting primary votes make a significant difference in the development of strategy. The results of early polls and primaries are covered extensively by the press, which creates pressure on party leaders to commit themselves quickly to the front-runner. Primaries are also important because most delegates are selected during that time. Because the results represent an objective indication of whether a candidate can win the general election, the primaries also affect donations of money from interest groups and political action committees.

The primaries are to a politician what test markets are to a marketer. In a test market, a company offers a product to a carefully selected audience for a limited period of time. The audience is selected to mirror the characteristics of the whole market. Primaries serve in the same capacity for candidates, who use them to test various appeals to determine which candidate image and issues are the most attractive to voters in the various states where the primaries are held.

The Convention Stage

The convention is a meeting during which the candidates and their chief supporters try to maintain communication with as many delegates as they can. By the time of the nominating convention, most delegates are already pledged to a candidate, and a probable winner has emerged. The convention merely ratifies the result.

The main function of modern voting rallies or conventions is to create an image of the candidate or political party that can then be developed and distributed during the following months of the campaign (Holbrook, 1996). If the media get interested in such an event, then the profit may be much higher. Above all, meetings with voters offer a chance for the candidates to successfully present their message not only to their supporters but also to the numerous groups of undecided voters who attend them not out of curiosity, but because a well-known person came to their city.

James E. Campbell, Lynn L. Cherry, and Kenneth A. Wink (1992) point out two major functions of party conventions in the United States: the deliberative function and the rally function. The deliberative function serves to work out the voting platform and familiarize the voters with the candidate and his views. This function of the convention is currently disappearing. All the program and candidate-designation proposals are developed much earlier. The function of the rally is to give the campaign impetus and propel it into the lead. A convention should stir up enthusiasm for the candidate, show his or her strong and united political background, and stimulate activists and voters to work for him or her. Its consequence may be a convention "bump," i.e., the candidate's gaining direct benefits immediately after the convention is over.

Benefits from the convention can be divided into three spheres. First, the convention may help to heal internal party divisions. This is particularly important for getting the support of the candidate's internal party opponents and getting them actively involved in the candidate's campaign. Second, conventions may give an extra push to the nominee's bandwagon. The third benefit from a successful convention may be more favorable publicity for the party, which can also result in higher support in the public opinion polls (Campbell, Cherry, Wink, 1992).

Campbell, Cherry, and Wink (1992) conducted an analysis of the data from the Gallup and Harris surveys during seven U.S. presidential elections between 1964 and 1988 in order to find out what level of influence any of the three spheres previously mentioned may have had. The results confirmed the prediction that such voting events perform their "rally" function very well. After the nominating conventions, the support for the candidates usually went up. The general figure was by 6.3 percent: for the Republicans, the average increase in support was 7.9 percent and for the Democrats, 4.8 percent. The biggest increase was that of Richard Nixon in 1968 (from 46.8 percent to 60.8 percent). Only in one case during the analyzed period did the convention turn to the candidate's disadvantage. In 1972, support for the Democratic candidate George McGovern dropped from 41.3 percent to 39.3 percent. Campbell, Cherry, and Wink (1992) also found out that the effect of the convention was maintained during the campaign with only short fluctuations in the poll results. The greatest increase in the support for the candidate was always registered after the first convention of the voting campaign—8.2 percent on average. The second event led to an average increase of 4.4 percent. This is because the first convention during a given campaign appealed to a higher number of undecided voters than the second one (see also Holbrook, 1996).

The analyses presented previously prove that big election meetings have one particular function: to increase support. One could add: to attract undecided voters.

The General Election Stage

Once the convention is over, campaigning for the general election officially begins, and workers must be activated by giving them purpose. A second task is generating positive media coverage. The sheer size of the electorate and because many, if not most, voters get their information from television, means that the media have become more important in the election process. For the vast majority of citizens in America and Western Europe, campaigns do not function so much to change minds as to reinforce previous attitudes and behaviors. This approach seems to be compatible with a doctrine concerning the effects of information according to which, as Harrison (1965) presents, television can, at best, only strengthen viewers' beliefs, but cannot change currently held opinions. Blumler and McQuail (1968), who carried out more detailed research on this phenomenon during the 1964 British parliamentary elections, reiterated the opinion that so-called deep-seated attitudes remain impervious and cannot be changed by the influence of television.

Environmental Forces

Marketing and political campaigns are integrated into the environment and, therefore, are related to the distribution of forces in a particular environment (see Figure 3.4). The shift in power in politics is due to two basic forces, namely, technology and structural shifts in the political process. The three influential areas of innovation in technology include the computer, television, and direct mail. Each of these areas directly affects the way presidential candidates run their campaigns, forcing candidates to utilize the expertise of marketing specialists who guide them through the complex processes of marketing and political campaigning.

The structural shifts influence primary and convention rules, financial regulations, and debates. Complex primary and convention rules have altered the way candidates run for president. Limitations on individual contributions have forced candidates to rely not only on fund-raising experts but on direct-mail experts as well.

Advances in direct-mail technology have given candidates the ability to carefully target selected voter blocs with appropriate messages, and their campaigns are no longer solely financed by the coffers of national party headquarters but are dependent on individual contributors. These shifts have further pressured candidates to rely on the expertise of direct-mail wizards to navigate through each stage of the political campaign. The technological and structural changes have resulted in dramatic shifts in influence among the power brokers.

Therefore, it can be stated that the environment in which marketing and political campaigns take place consists of three fundamental component groups:

1. Technological elements, including mail, television, the Internet, and other means of voting communication (e.g. spots, direct mail).
2. Structural elements connected mainly with election law but also with the procedure of nominating candidates, financial regulations for the campaign, and conducting political debates.
3. Forces influencing the development of the campaign include the candidate, consultants, media, political parties, interest groups setting up political and election committees, polling specialists, and voters.

Each of these elements represents an area in which dynamic changes have taken place in the past few decades; these changes facilitate the development of marketing research and are becoming more and more important for the election process. Technological changes, for instance, have revolutionized a candidate's contacts with his or her voters (for example through e-mail, cable television, or cell phones). Structural changes in the development of political campaigns made candidates pay more attention to marketing strategies and to rely more on the opinions of the experts developing them. One should also note the growing importance of polling specialists. The results of their analyses given to the general electorate not only reflect the electorate's general mood, but they also influence the forming of public opinion. Therefore, it can be stated that polls are a controlled attempt to influence voter behavior. A detailed analysis of the environmental forces is presented by Newman (1994).

Focusing on the voter during political campaigns has resulted in a shift of focus from the nominees as leaders of political parties to the media, consultants, marketing research and polling specialists, and members of voting and political committees. Their importance in the course of a campaign is still growing and, therefore, a well-planned organization of all the activities combining these forces in the applied marketing procedures is becoming increasingly important.

Chapter 4

Traditional Models of Voter Behavior

The theoretical perspective of voter behavior research is very broad, and it includes any research discipline belonging either to social or behavioral sciences. A review of these disciplines (considered as different approaches to analyzing and understanding citizens' voter behavior) will help to place our theory on the map representing distinctive approaches to the problem. One will notice that the predictive model of voter behavior that we propose, and that is presented in Chapter 6, combines a number of detailed approaches discussed in this chapter.

SOCIOLOGICAL APPROACH

The sociological approach was briefly characterized in Chapter 1. In general, it focuses mainly on the rules of dividing voters into supporters of particular political options based on their sociodemographic characteristics. This approach is best represented by demographic segmentation of the voting market. One of the most important criteria for such segmentation is social standing.

For sociologically oriented researchers it is obvious that voters from different social classes identify themselves with particular parties or political candidates. Also, the analyses of politicians' and political party leaders' behavior point to their using marketing strategies directed at carefully selected social groups. Therefore, issues that become salient in political campaigns are those that are compatible with the interests of a given social group. Election polls investigating candidates' popularity often show the candidates' support in the context of different social groups. Therefore, it is worthwhile to more thoroughly investigate the practical application of the sociological approach for identifying classes' political representation. This is done so in this chapter using research conducted in Finland and Great Britain.

Political Representation of Social Classes before Parliamentary Elections in Finland in 1995

Pauli Forma (2000), using the data from two surveys conducted before parliamentary elections in Finland in 1995, verified the hypothesis that every Finnish social class has its own political party that represents its interests while making political decisions.

The first survey was conducted on a representative sample of the adult population of Finland (N = 1,737) toward the end of 1994 and the beginning of 1995 as part of the International Survey of Economic Attitudes (ISEA). The second survey was conducted on a sample of candidates running in Finnish parliamentary elections in 1995 (N = 529).

The main goal of Forma's analysis (2000) was to find out whether each of these social classes—farmers, workers, and employers—had a political party that represented them and cared for their interests. The starting point was the assumption that the more similar the views of a given party's candidates and their supporters, the better these interests were represented. Stands on three areas were analyzed: (1) land—agriculture should be subsidized to protect agricultural jobs and guarantee minimum prices for agricultural products; (2) labor—all important economic decisions, wages, and salaries should be set nationally in negotiations between the government, national union confederations, and employers' groups, and trade unions should be in place in all government enterprises and private business; (3) capital—the government should not get involved in disputes between unions and employers; employers should have the right to negotiate earnings with each individual worker.

The views in these three areas were compared and referenced to the supporters and candidates of the Centre Party of Finland (the former Agrarian Party) (representing farmers' interests), the Left Alliance (the former Communists), the Social Democratic Party (representing workers' interests), and the National Coalition Party (representing entrepreneurs' interests). The results of the research are presented in Figure 4.1.

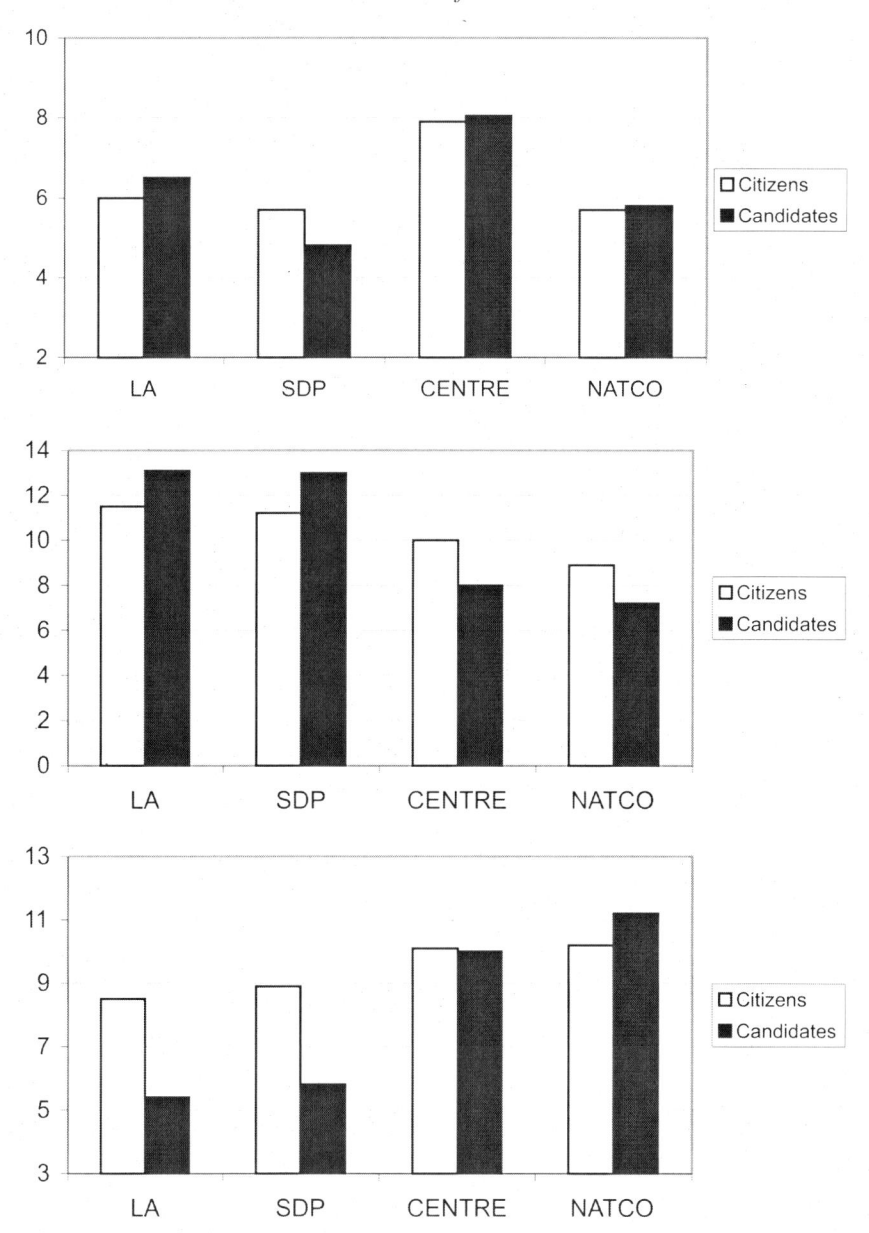

FIGURE 4.1. Opinions on the land, labor, and capital interests. *Source:* Adapted from Forma (2000).

In all the three cases it turned out that each of the social classes supported particular political groups that were considered to be the best representatives of their interests. According to Forma's analyses, the previous division between land, labor, and capital still have their consequences for the Finnish political scene and citizens' voting behavior.

Although the analyses of the political situation in Finland proves that it is possible to conduct a successful market segmentation based on social classes, it seems to be a very isolated case. In each division, based on sociodemographic features (age, gender, education, or place of living in addition to class), voters differ from one another because of the party or candidate they prefer. It is natural that in a given group more or fewer voters support a given political option, however, such minority or majority proportions may change even throughout the short period of a campaign. Election polls conducted on a regular basis show the dynamics of such changes. They are mainly caused by the media's influence used in carefully planned marketing strategies.

ACORN in the Political Marketplace: The Case of Great Britain

In 1983, in Great Britain, one could already observe that the division into social classes began to no longer matter in the segmentation of the voting market. In analyzing parliamentary elections, David Butler and Dennis Kavanagh (1984) discovered a shift of a few percentage points among working-class voters moving from supporting the Labour Party to the electorate of Conservative Party. The authors realized then that segmentation based on a single criterion (e.g., social class) is not useful, and decided to develop a division of the voting market that would simultaneously include a number of sociodemographic characteristics. Such a promising division of the voting market was the concept of ACORN (A Classification of Residential Neighbourhoods), a relatively new segmentation tool available to management.

D.A. Yorke and Sean A. Meehan (1986) examined ACORN in detail as a suitable basis for segmenting the electoral marketplace. According to them, in the 1983 general election in the United Kingdom it emerged that the link between political parties and social class was rapidly eroding: nearly 40 percent of the electorate did not vote for the party related to their social class.

The ACORN market segmentation system classifies people according to the type of area in which they live. It separates voters according to combinations of such demographic characteristics as: location of residence, age, household types, housing, and social and employment status. Yorke and Meehan (1986) distinguished eleven different neighborhood groups, three of which they tested for their voter behavior. These segments include the following:

1. *Older housing of intermediate status.* This division consists of older voters who are less mobile and live in houses close to city centers. The absence of large gardens and modern amenities is compensated for by shopping accessibility and local employment.
2. *The less well-off council estate.* This segment includes manual, semiskilled, and unskilled workers. This group tends to consist of older couples and pensioners rather than younger couples, although average incomes are increased by multiple earners and by low housing costs.
3. *Affluent suburban housing.* This is an older, high-income group inhabiting interwar suburban private housing, detached, and developed in low densities. Disposable income is spent on luxury items and invested in home improvements. Attributes of the neighborhood that particularly attract residents are quietness, privacy, and exclusiveness.

The goal of Yorke's and Meehan's analysis was to answer the following question: Are voters from these segments different because of their attitude toward political choices?

The results of their analyses (referring to the elections to the European Parliament in 1984) showed some small, statistically significant differences between voting intentions of the voters from the tested social groups. However, it should be stated that the tested individuals had a similar attitude to such questions and statements as: "When are the next European parliamentary elections?" "The outcome of the Euro election does not affect me at all," "I know little or nothing about the European Parliament, so I don't feel qualified to vote." According to Yorke and Meehan (1986), the data obtained suggest ACORN may be a suitable basis for segmenting the electoral marketplace.

The ACORN method, though it includes many demographic features in the characteristics of a given voter group, seems hardly suitable for a useful marketing division of the voting market. Psychologists and marketing specialists had long known that the key to such a segmentation that allows for a successful prediction of consumer preferences of different products brands and political parties is a personal profile of the consumer and the voter (see Chapter 1).

Personality has therefore become the foundation of the division of the market based on psychographic variables. It inspired a number of research projects on consumer and voter behavior that resulted in various proposals of psychological segmentation. Some of them will be presented in the following section, describing the social psychological approach.

SOCIAL PSYCHOLOGICAL APPROACH

The weaknesses of the sociological paradigm in explaining citizens' voter behavior led the researchers from the Institute for Social Research at The University of Michigan to concentrate on psychological processes that determine voting decisions (Campbell et al., 1960, 1967; Converse, 1964). The key element of this approach stresses the mediating function of the fixed psychological predispositions and, particularly, party identification, for creating political behavior.

Party Identification

Angus Campbell, Philip E. Converse, and their fellow researchers (1960, 1967) understood party identification as an attitude, a positive emotional approach to the objects one finds on the political stage: parties and candidates. Party identification has a filtering effect on the perception of the world of politics and provides voters with directions on how to make voting decisions (supporting their party) based on social and political events and issues. It also assumes that such identification is stable and not very sensitive to the short-term effects of political campaigns. Besides, they depend only to a small extent on the stands taken by the candidate or party in particular elections on political issues.

The supporters of models based on party identification or loyalty stress the important role of political socialization in becoming a supporter of a given party (Campbell et al., 1960; Pye, 1972; Sears, Funk, 1999). David Wood (1982) claims that every country has typical ways of raising children and typical ways in which adults fall victim to political influences. The purpose of such influences is to shape the political orientation that citizens learn in their youth and childhood. These processes, according to Wood, are only partially realized by the individual. Children taught to respect a particular political figure while they are being brought up (e.g. Józef Piłsudski in Poland, Joseph Stalin in the Soviet Union, or Charles de Gaulle in France), may transfer their liking when they grow up to his or her political successors through the halo or assimilation effect. Such a process contributes to "inheriting" party identification from parents and makes it difficult for the individual to change later in life (Däcker, Ekehammar, Sidanius, 1983).

Within the paradigm of social psychology, defined also as the paradigm of a socialized individual, one can find attempts at explaining voter behavior through such psychological variables as the system of values a voter follows (Braithwaite, 1997; Heaven et al., 1994; Rokeach, 1973), the feeling of political alienation (Reimanis, 1982), or fear (Cwalina, Falkowski, 2005a).

The social psychology approach is very often treated as a "supplement" to the sociological approach (Campbell et al., 1960) but has also been severely criticized. The first group of objections to this paradigm is methodology based. Benjamin I. Page (1977, p. 655) points to four major areas that the theories of party loyalty do not explain:

1. To what extent party loyalty is a mechanically transmitted "habit" that determines the vote
2. To what extent it is a "standing decision" based on policy preferences, which is then used as a voting cue in low information situations
3. To what extent party loyalty is itself affected (or even an artifact of) particular voting alternatives
4. To what extent apparent relationships of party and vote are spurious

The theories based on party identification are also criticized from an empirical position. Analyzing the results of many studies of voting behavior, Russell J. Dalton and Martin P. Wattenberg (1993) concluded that party bonds disappear in the majority of modern democracies. This is accompanied by people's increasing tendency to vote for a particular person, irrespective of the party he or she represents. The most dramatic example illustrating these two trends is the phenomenon of split-ticket voting. This occurs when one person supports representatives of two competing parties in parliamentary elections in two chambers of the parliament, the Sejm and Senate in Poland for instance. Therefore, one can talk about the emergence of a new, "independent" electorate: "floating voters" (Hayes, McAllister, 1996). With such phenomena becoming more and more common, one should reject or at least revise models based on party loyalty (Klingemann, Wattenberg, 1992; Wattenberg, 1995).

Voter's Personality

In light of this discussion on voter behavior one may suggest that the voter's personality is an important element influencing the political choices he or she makes. In commercial marketing, personality has become the foundation for dividing the market according to psychographic variables. The results of a series of studies on consumer behavior support psychographic segmentation, including the well-known concept of SRI International, called VALS (once an acronym for "values and lifestyles," now the system focuses on psychological traits but maintains the name) (Kahle, Beatty, Homer, 1986; SRI Consulting Business Intelligence, 2007).

A detailed proposal of psychographic segmentation of the voting market is offered by Bruce I. Newman (1999c); it stems from the model of voter behavior developed by Bruce I. Newman and Jagdish N. Sheth (1985). The authors distinguished seven cognitive domains which, according to them, determine citizen's voting behavior: issues and policies, social imagery, emotional feelings, candidate image, current events, personal events, and epistemic issues (a more detailed discussion of these domains can be found in Chapter 5). In segmenting the voting market, Newman used four cognitive domains of the behavior model referring to different values sought in a candidate by the voters. On this basis he separated voters into four groups:

1. *Rational voters.* This segment of the electorate corresponds to the social domain of "political issues," referring to the problems and directions of social and political actions. In the question-

naire developed by Newman, fields from this domain referred to the economy, foreign policy, and social issues, and were measured on binary scales: "I agree/I disagree" (e.g., "I am convinced that the candidate I voted for will decrease inflation"). It was determined that social and economic concerns are the main issues that rational voters consider when making their voting decisions.
2. *Emotional voters.* "Candidate personality" belongs to this group, which includes particular emotions that a candidate evokes among voters. Such emotions include happiness, appreciation, anxiety, pride, and disappointment. In making political choices emotional voters follow their feelings.
3. *Social voters.* This segment refers to the domain of "social imagery." The voters from this segment vote for a particular candidate associated with a particular social group, including, for instance, a national minority, a particular religion, the affluent, or the educated.
4. *Situational voters.* This segment, to which "situational contingency" corresponds, is particularly sensitive in its choices to anything that has or might have happened recently. Negative events include, among others, a higher rate of inflation or unemployment or increased corruption among civil servants. Positive events include citizens' increased access to education, lower costs of living, or fewer racial tensions. In the questionnaire, the domain of "situational contingency" is made operational by statements pointing to voters' changing their voter decisions provided certain conditions take place (e.g., "I will vote for another candidate if he or she gives people more access to education").

These segments describe voters' psychological characteristics and belong to the psychographic segmentation of the voting market. Currently, however, they are still hypothetical constructs, and we do not in fact know whether such groups really exist in political campaigns. That is why Newman designed a survey that helped to determine whether the proposed voting segmentation concept is valid. In addition to using the questionnaire referring to cognitive domains, the author asked: "To what extent does each of the candidates make it easier or harder for you to achieve your dreams?"

This question related directly to the concept of creating the president's image that Newman presented to Clinton in 1995 in the White House. He proposed a certain vision of the president, then focused around the subject "The Restoration of the American Dream." This concept, supported by detailed research, was then presented by Newman to the president's spokesman George Stephanopoulos in 1996. It became the foundation of creating Clinton's new position in voters' minds. The new position defined the way in which the president was to restore the dreams to his compatriots. Of course, "restoring dreams" is a certain metaphor made operational by cognitive domains in the model of voter behavior.

The first stage of the research compared the importance of the four domains ("political issues," "candidate personality," "social imagery" and "situational contingency") in forming voting intentions of three electorates: Bill Clinton's, and two other politicians from the Republican Party competing for nomination—Bob Dole and Colin Powell. Although the latter did not participate in the election campaign, he was included in the research because of the high popularity he enjoyed among the voters. The research was conducted when Powell was still considering running for the Republican presidential nomination in the 1996 elections. The research demonstrated that the importance of these domains was similar among all the electorates. Each domain was almost equally important for Dole's, Clinton's, and Powell's supporters. At this stage of the research, one could not determine whether the proposed voter segmentation was valid.

The decisive step in determining the validity of the psychographic model of voting market segmentation was the use of discrimination analysis. The criterion variable was the respondent's opinion regarding whether or not a particular candidate would make it possible for Americans to achieve their dreams. Obviously, in each of the electorates, most voters set their hopes on "their" politicians, despite that some respondents answered that the opponent can make these dreams come true as well.

At that point, the fundamental problem that needed to be solved was to determine which domains are important in explaining the voters' opinion on the candidate's ability to make it possible for the voters to achieve their dreams. In order to use the language of discrimination analysis, one should find out what questions differentiate from these questions significantly and what the indicator is that predicts these proportions. The results showed that a number of detailed domain items predicted the proportions of answers to the question about the dreams in each of the electorates quite well. However, they often belonged to different areas and, therefore, it was not possible to determine the types of voters in an empirical and unequivocal way by using Newman's model of psychographic segmentation.

Let us look at the results of this analysis in Clinton's electorate where three important items, predicting why this candidate may help Americans achieve their dream, come from three domains: "Clinton makes me happy" (domain: candidate personality), "Clinton will help me have more time for myself" (domain: political issues), "Clinton will contribute to the development of social equality" (domain: situational contingency). The items predicting why the candidate can make it harder for people to achieve their dreams also belong to different domains. They include: "My candidate will not stop the spread of crime" and "will not create conditions for general access to education" (both statements belong to the domain of situational contingency) and "he will not contribute to my financial stability" (the domain of political issues). Expressing an opinion on these six issues allowed respondents to predict the candidate's ability to make it possible for voters to achieve their dreams in 76.8 percent of the cases.

The concept of psychographic segmentation proposed by Newman refers to the well-known proposal of the consulting company SRI International on consumer behavior, VALS (Kahle, Beatty, Homer, 1986). Although the research on psychographic segmentation of the voting market described here did not achieve results that were as good as VALS on the consumer market, attempts continue to be made to create voter groups based on their psychological characteristics (Fiedler, Maxwell, 2000).

ECONOMIC APPROACH

The creator of the economic paradigm often called "rational choice theory" is Anthony Downs (1957). The fundamental axiom of this model is the assumption that citizens' behavior in the sphere of politics is rational. By voting, voters make a conscious, intentional choice to support the candidate or the party that in their opinion will bring them the most benefits. Rational citizens want to maximize the usefulness of their decisions. They are egotistical in their behavior and follow only their own interests. Similar to consumers, voters choose the political program on the market that satisfies them the most. As a consequence, they do not vote for a candidate but for a solution to a particular political problem, which is called *issue voting* (Nie, Verba, Petrocik, 1976).

Issue Voting

In issue voting, acquiring information about the current political situation as well as the participants of the political contest and their programs is the basis for making a voting decision. On the other hand, political parties also "specialize" in offering "the best solutions" to particular social and economic problems. This means that, according to voters, a certain political group is more efficient in solving certain issues than are other groups. Such a phenomenon was described by John R. Petrocik (1996) with reference to American parties in his theory of issue ownership. According to this theory, a party's "owning" of a certain problem is connected with a relatively stable social background and is also connected with political conflicts. The results of Petrocik's analysis suggest that American voters consider issues connected with general social welfare including the homeless, public schools, the elderly, national minorities, health care, and the environment as owned by the Democratic Party. The Republican Party is associated with better achievements in the areas of crime reduction, defense of "moral values," running foreign policy, defense, inflation, taxes, and government spending. The theory of issue ownership also has certain consequences for running a successful voting campaign. According to Petrocik, the campaign will bring the desired result if the candidate or political party manages to limit voting decisions to those issues the country faces that he or she is able to solve better than his opponent. As Stephen Ansolabehere and Shanto Iyengar (1994) have shown, the candidate should also be able to present the issues well in the media.

Campaigns that are planned in this way, however, are not free from risk. If the candidates foreground the problems that they "own," it may lead to strong polarization of the voters. The voters supporting particular candidates will join forces with them, whereas those undecided or voting from only time to time may withdraw from the elections, discouraged by the growing political conflict. Therefore, the most successful voting strategy may be to come up with an ambiguous position on political issues or focus on issues that have no reference to the program (e.g., on desirable characteristics of political leaders), confirmed by the analyses of Edward G. Carmines and J. David Gopoian (1981). More agreement always exists around general political goals than around specific ways of achieving them. However, under such circumstances, the act of choice does not express rational support for a political program, but is "washed out" and taken over by symbols and an evaluation of the candidates' personality (Petrocik, 1979).

Retrospective Voting

An important supplement to the economic theory of voting is the *retrospective voting model*. The main ideas standing behind this model were formed by V.O. Key in his posthumous book *The Responsible Electorate* (1966). Key's starting point is that "voters are not fools" (p. 7). Developing this point, he expresses his belief that voters coming to the polls remember, above all, how they were doing in the period that has passed since the last election. If the evaluation of this period and forces that were in power is positive, then they are likely to extend their support for the ruling party or candidate. If the evaluation is negative, the support will be shifted to another, more promising party or candidate.

The model of retrospective voting is also defined as *electoral reward and punishment* for those in power (Greenberg, Page, 1995). It can also be treated as one of the mechanisms of a democratic control of officeholders. Besides, as Edward S. Greenberg and Benjamin I. Page (1995) stress, it has certain consequences for politicians' behavior. If they want to remain in power, it is a strong stimulus encouraging them to care about society's welfare and solve the problems citizens face. They should also predict voters' needs and then meet them.

As far as retrospective voting is concerned, Gregory B. Markus (1988) distinguishes its two variants based on what voters concentrate on in evaluating the achievements of officeholders: *pocketbook voting* and *sociotropic voting*. Pocketbook voting occurs when citizens analyze their financial situation thinking in microeconomic categories. Sociotropic voting occurs when voters evaluate the condition of the national economy.

The question that arises, however, is whether voters follow one or the other way of "settling accounts" with those in power. The factors that are influential here include the condition of social welfare and the economy in a given country. Alexander C. Pacek and Benjamin Radcliff (1995) analyzed the patterns of pocketbook voting and sociotropic voting in seventeen democratic countries between 1960 and 1987. These countries had different social welfare states ranging from institutionalized welfare states (e.g., Denmark, Germany, Italy, or Sweden) to marginal welfare states (e.g., the United States, Spain, Canada, Australia, Great Britain, or Japan). The results of their research clearly demonstrated that in the countries with very limited social welfare systems, the voters punish or reward officeholders according to the condition of the economy. In the case of the countries with developed social welfare systems, the fortunes of those in power seem to be quite independent of the macroeconomic situation.

In addition to economic criteria (micro and macro), the object of voters' evaluation may be legislative changes introduced by the authorities or the promises of introducing laws connected with value systems including teaching religion in schools, settlement with the old communist "nomenklatura," or the right to abortion. Voting decisions may also be influenced by how authorities manage difficult and extreme situations, including, for instance, terrorist threats (Bourne, Healy, Beer, 2003) or droughts and floods (Britton, Ford, 2001).

Criticism of the Rational Voter Theory

The idea of the rational voter gained many supporters (see Lupia, McCubbins, 1997; Popkin, 1991; Struthers, Young, 1989). However, the first objection against this theory is that it does not offer a satisfactory answer to the questions concerned with how the voter is able to manage so much information about the participants of the political fight. Does he or she follow only some information? How does he or she select this information and decide which information is useful for him or her?

Also, Benjamin I. Page (1977) raises many arguments against believing uncritically in the rationality of political choices. The most important argument against economic theory is that it assumes that citizens are very well informed about the political situation. However, a deficit of information may exist, and then voters base their decisions on factors other than a given candidate's or party's program.

Cognitive Heuristics

More evidence supporting the limitations of the rationality of people's choices is provided by the widely disputed experiments conducted by Daniel Kahneman and Amos Tversky (Kahneman, Slovic, Tversky, 1982; Tversky, Kahneman, 1974) on humankind's use of heuristics while making decisions, particularly when such decisions are taken with uncertainty. Heuristics is a method or set of rules for solving problems other than by algorithm and can be called the rules of inference; such rules are useful but do not guarantee that the decision one makes is right. Bearing such rules in mind and assessing some event or information, one does not analyze them in detail. He or she focuses on some specific aspects of this information and skips others. Therefore, making a decision based on heuristics is relatively quick and requires neither much effort nor information, but can be unreliable (Chaiken, Stangor, 1987; Chaiken, Lieberman, Eagly, 1989).

The most typical cognitive shortcuts described by Tversky and Kahneman (Kahneman Slovic, Tversky, 1982; Tversky, Kahneman, 1974) are the heuristics of representativeness, anchoring, availability, and simulation. They are characterized in Table 4.1.

The statement that people relatively rarely think about events and compare available information has been considered an important argument against the existence of a fully rational voter (Carmines, Kuklinski, 1990; Ottati, Fishbein, Middlestadt, 1988). An attempt at collecting specific "political heuristics" was made by Jeffery J. Mondak (1994). By analyzing the literature on making voting decisions he distinguished seven heuristics: likeability, balance, signal-taking, "desert heuristic," availability, heuristic function of affect, and stereotypes. The characteristic of these heuristics is presented in Table 4.2.

The abundance of "cognitive shortcuts" that citizens making voting decisions use makes one realize that careful and well-thought-out decisions are rather an exception than a rule. It is not beneficial to democracy but, on the other hand, makes the job of political marketing specialists easier.

TABLE 4.1. Cognitive heuristics.

Heuristics	Characteristics	Example
Representativeness	Likelihood of an event is assessed on the basis of its similarity to the population it comes from (how representative it is for it).	Wondering who a representative of American Polonia voted for, the evaluator will tend to think he or she supported a representative of a right-wing party.
Anchoring and adjustment	Articulate information (anchors) is used while judgments on a given subject are being formed.	After receiving the news, "Another scandal in party Y," the voter's evaluation of the party and its members' achievements will be negative.
Availability	Decision maker estimates the likelihood of an event by gauging the ease with which specific examples can be brought to mind. The number of examples one can easily recall is the indicator of an event's frequency of occurrence.	The answer to the question of whether corruption in Poland is a common event is quite easy. The media's frequent references to this issue provide us with abundant examples.
Simulation	An event is more likely if the scenario of its occurrence is easily conceivable.	The answer to the question of what a terrorist attack would look like in Poland is much easier if one recalls what such attacks looked like in New York or Madrid.

Despite this, Samuel L. Popkin (1991) believes that voters are rational but that it is a *low-information rationality*. This means that if a voter does not have some information about a candidate, he or she will substitute information. For instance, when it is difficult to define a politician's views on some issues, one may infer this information by using data from his or her personal life, including, for instance, his or her education or achievements. Instead of performing a detailed analysis of particular candidates' positions on various issues, it is much

TABLE 4.2. Political heuristics.

Heuristics	Characteristics
Likeability	Enable citizens to estimate the issue positions of various political groups. The voter's own position helps in his or her evaluations of opposing political groups. The more favored force is attributed an opinion closer to his or own, and the less favored is attributed the opposite. The key role here is played by the affect for particular political groups.
Balance	Here voters draw on two known facts to infer a third. For instance, if voter V likes candidate C and has B's beliefs, he or she is likely to infer that candidate C has also the views of B.
Signal-taking	Voters draw on two known facts to infer the third; however, in this case they rely on signals from prominent political leaders in constructing their own issue evaluations. The consequence of using this heuristic is largely elite-driven public opinion.
Desert	This is based on whether or not an individual or group is perceived as "deserving." For instance, one's view regarding agricultural subsidies depends on whether he or she appreciates farmers as "deserving" such help. In a similar way one can define his or her position on, for instance, flood victims.
Availability	This political heuristic is understood in the same way as the cognitive heuristic. Topics that are widely discussed (corruption, crime) have more influence on people's perception of the scale of the phenomenon they refer to.
Heuristic function of affect	Affective reactions may serve as a foundation of voting decisions inhibiting any attempts to analyze the candidates' views or features. For example, "I don't vote because all of the politicians are thieves!"
Stereotypes	Stereotypes can also perform the function of heuristics in the evaluation of political candidates. For example, "I am not going to vote for him because he is. . . !" Stereotypes are an important element of the heuristics of representativeness.

easier to concentrate on finding the most striking differences between them. Popkin believes that for the purpose of making their decisions, voters make up stories regarding each candidate in which his or her life so far is the foundation for predicting future behavior or filling gaps with inferences. Though remote, such proceedings, from the canons of rationality suggested by Downs (1957), greatly reduce citizen's efforts while making voting decisions. As Timothy D. Wilson's and Jonathan W. Schooler's research suggests (1991), attempts to make people consider and carefully analyze the options they have may not necessarily improve the quality of their decisions.

Rationality in voting decisions is also limited by emotions. The section titled "The Role of Emotion in Politics" in Chapter 2 presents the importance of emotions in the formation of a politician's image in voters' minds and in their political decisions.

Economic Self-Interest

In addition, the issue of the voters' focusing on their own economic self-interests is not as obvious as the retrospective-voting model makes it out to be. In a number of polls and studies conducted by David O. Sears and his team (Sears, 1997; Sears, Funk, 1991; Sears, Lau, 1983) proved that a voter's economic situation does not have an important influence on their preferences, unless they are somehow made to see the connection. This link can be achieved by designing the questionnaire studying political attitudes in a certain way, by structuring questions in a particular way, or via the media or the election campaign itself.

David O. Sears and Carolyn L. Funk (1990) believe that economic self-interest does not have much influence on citizens' political attitudes. Although some exceptions exist, they usually refer to specific situations, including, for instance, heavy taxation or threats to health or life. However, even such circumstances do not have a systematic and strong effect on voter behavior. This conclusion can also be applied to pocketbook voting. This concept is slightly more likely during U.S. presidential elections when the candidates repeatedly refer to the citizens' economic situation in order to show them ways of improving it. However, during parliamentary elections both in the United States and Western Europe, voters do not analyze their economic situation to such an extent that it could influence their decisions. According to Sears (1993), the decisive role regarding their choices is played by symbolic dispositions, that is, learned affective reactions to political symbols. Instead of performing complex analyses, people follow some collective myths that are accompanied by certain symbols. They use such categories such as "the Jewish plot," "communists," or "terrorists," which allows them to immediately develop certain attitudes toward politicians and parties.

Political Programs and Views

The changes on the political stage also question the assumption that the voter differentiates between the programs of political parties present on the market and votes for the proposal that he or she considers most beneficial. Experiments conducted in the United States (Lott, Lott, Saris, 1993) and in Australia (Noller et al., 1988) prove that voters have problems with assigning particular views to the politicians who actually propagate these views. Besides, the solutions to various social and political problems proposed by the candidates are often the same in substance, which makes the voters follow extra-program factors when making their choices. The most spectacular example of the blurring of the differences between political programs of the competing parties was the parliamentary election in Great Britain in 1997. Both the Conservative and Labour Parties had similar programs referring to Margaret Thatcher's policy (McGuire, 1997). Wattenberg (1994) and Brams (1976) also confirm these findings.

Pamela Johnston Conover and Stanley Feldman (1981), after analyzing the data from the National Election Study from 1976, stated that the factor responsible for Americans' ideological self-identification is their evaluation of ideological labels of the parties (liberal versus conservative), and not their stands on issues. These labels function as socially defined political symbols and have an influence on voters' opinions on particular political issues. Stands on issues do not have a direct influence on identification. Ideological labels and, consequently, voters' own identifications, have a symbolic meaning for the society/voters (see also Sears, 1993).

The question arises in this context: "How can citizens demonstrate issue voting if their views have nothing in common with party preferences?"

MULTIDIMENSIONAL MODELS OF VOTER BEHAVIOR

Criticism of the traditional paradigms of the analysis of citizens' voter behavior has led to the development of multivariable models including the elements characteristic for all of the approaches. Much more extended models allow for a better understanding of citizens' voter behavior and are an important source of information for political marketing practitioners.

It seems that four such approaches representing a more complex approach to the problem of voter behavior are of particular theoretical and practical value. They include the sociogeographical model of British voting behavior (Johnston, Pattie, Allsopp, 1988); the model based on the theory of planned behavior (Ajzen, 1991, 1996); the marketing model of voter's choice behavior (Newman, 1999c; Newman, Sheth, 1985), and the causal-effect model of voter behavior combining theoretical and marketing theories (Falkowski, Cwalina, 2002). Since the latter two models are the foundation of the empirical cross-cultural research presented in this study, they will be discussed in detail in separate chapters (see Chapters 5 and 6).

Sociogeographical Model of British Voting Behavior

The authors of the sociogeographical model of British voting behavior (developed between 1979 and 1987) are three political geographers: Ron Johnston, Charles Pattie, and Graham Allsopp (1988). Although the original name of their model is "a revised and expanded model of British voting behaviour," due to the specificity of the variables included in it, it seems that the proposed name better renders this specificity.

While analyzing the data from parliamentary elections in Britain between 1979 and 1987 collected in the archives of the Economic and Social Research Council (ESRC) and from television polls conducted by BBC television together with Gallup, Johnston and his team put particular emphasis on two factors explaining voting decisions. The first one refers to social variables through which it is possible to characterize voters, whereas the other one relates to the spatial aspect—voters' origins throughout a country. These factors do not operate independently from each other, but enter into mutual interactions, thus shaping voting preferences of the British. The model developed and revised by these researchers is presented in Figure 4.2.

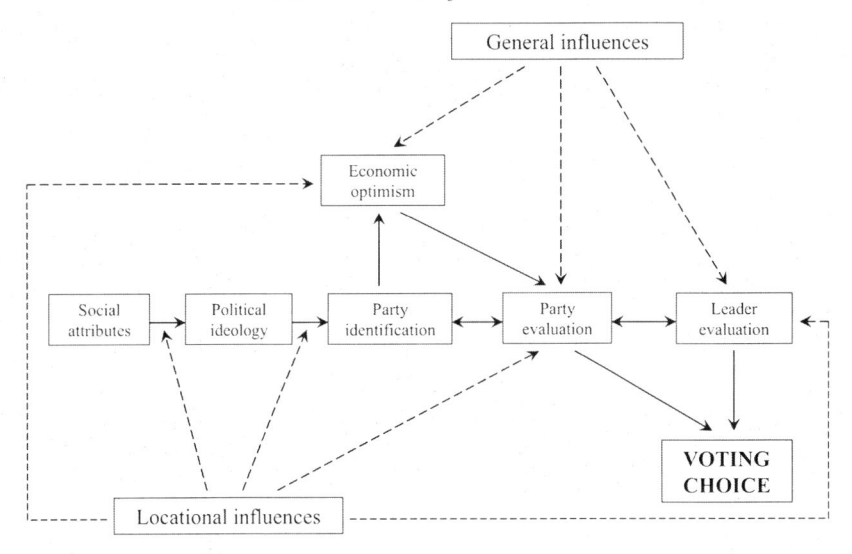

FIGURE 4.2. Sociogeographical model of British voting behavior, 1979-1987. *Source:* Adapted from Johnston, Pattie, Alsopp (1988).

Generally, the model proposed by Johnston, Pattie, and Allsopp suggests that the factors connected with locational influences modify preferences for a particular political ideology and therefore influence party identification. In addition, the regional context also influences the degree of citizens' economic optimism and their evaluation of leaders. The consequence of this complex set of influences is the reason for voting for a particular political party.

Once people enter adulthood with certain social attributes, (social class, religion, or income), they develop particular political ideologies connected with these attributes, which is part of the socialization process. These ideologies, in turn, lead to their identification with particular political parties that best represent their views. This is another manifestation of the socialization process that assumes the ideology of a given social group is followed by the acceptance of the fact that it is this particular party that is connected with the ideology one follows and, therefore, should be supported.

Such social attributes are guided by locational influences (the geographical factor). People sharing certain characteristics (ideology, party identification) may vote differently if they live in different regions of the country (see e.g. Agnew, 1996). One should not, however, assume that people of similar social attributes will follow the same political ideologies. In different regions, social class can be interpreted differently and more emphasis may be put on a particular group of socioeconomic problems. People sharing a similar ideology may also differ in their party identification when one party manages to gain a great amount of support in one area and another party in a different area. At that point, locational influences begin to interact with the political socialization process in two points of the sequence and may generate diversity both in ideological development and party identification.

Subsequently, party identification has much influence on people's party evaluation. The supporters of the British Labour Party are convinced that it offers the best political program, as opposed to the supporters of the Conservative Party. Evaluation of political parties has particular consequences for voting decisions as the voter seeks the answer to the following question: Which political party is best able to cope with what is an important political problem for me (e.g., unemployment, crime)? The evaluation process is influenced by five variables: party identification, party leader evaluation, general influences, economic optimism, and locational influences. However, it should be noted that the relationship between party identification and evaluation is bilateral. Party identification facilitates positive party evaluation, but positive party evaluation also facilitates party identification.

General influences refer to the voting context and party presentation, especially in the media. Therefore, for example, the voter may agree that law and order are important political issues and that the Conservative Party has the best policy on these issues. He or she may reach such a conclusion not because he or she has knowledge of law and order and the Conservatives' policy in these areas but because important programs broadcast by the media make the voter think so. General influences, in addition to the direct influence on party evaluation, also influence it indirectly through *economic optimism*. If the media reports on an extremely good economic situation, then the citizens are more likely to develop a positive attitude toward the ruling party.

Economic optimism is influenced both by locational influences and general influences as well as party identification. The media may suggest that the future of the country is bright, but voters from some regions may not necessarily think that this statement is true. With spatial differences in the standard of living (economic and social), one may expect similar differences in the level of economic optimism. This diversity may then account not only for party identification differences in particular regions of the country, but also for differences in political party evaluation related to the place of living.

The empirical verification of the sociogeographic model conducted by Johnston, Pattie, and Allsopp allowed its authors to draw three major conclusions regarding British voting behavior between 1979 and 1987:

1. Party identification among the British is quite long-lasting. No important changes were observed over the years during which the research was conducted except for some fluctuations in some parts of England (increased identification with Labour Party in Devon and Cornwall). Southern areas of Great Britain have more supporters of the Conservative Party than the Labour Party, whereas in northern regions the situation is reversed.
2. More satisfaction with the current government and higher economic optimism for the future lead to increased support for the Conservative Party. More dissatisfaction with the current government and economic pessimism for the future result in increased support for the Labour Party. In general, there was more optimism in northern regions of the country than in the southern ones.
3. Similarly, the north-south regional patterns (with minor fluctuations in some areas) were also valid for political party and leader evaluations.

According to Johnston, Pattie, and Allsopp (1988), the model they proposed and its empirical verification fully show how important it is to include a country's regional specificity in an analysis of voting behavior. The region where the voters live has much influence on the process of political socialization (social attributes and party identification), economic optimism, and party and leader evaluation. In consequence, they also influence voting behavior. In addition, important factors that also need to be taken into consideration include: the campaign's context and the role of the media (general influences), which influence economic optimism, party and leader evaluation, and the power of party identification.

Theory of Planned Behavior

The theory of planned behavior is a psychological proposal offered by Icek Ajzen (1991, 1996), whose purpose is to explain and predict human behavior in different life situations and with reference to different objects. It is an expanded and supplemented version of the well-known theory of reasoned action developed by Ajzen together with Martin Fishbein (Ajzen, Fishbein, 1980; Fishbein, Ajzen, 1975).

The theory is based on four fundamental assumptions (Ajzen, 1991). First, intention is an element that directly precedes a person's behavior. Second, intention is determined by the attitudes an individual assumes toward the behavior (or object of behavior), its subjective norms, and the perceived behavioral control over this behavior. Third, these intention determinants are a function of the following beliefs: behavioral, normative, and control-oriented. And fourth, these beliefs are connected with one another and depend on an individual's current experiences and his or her other characteristics. The model of planned behavior is presented in Figure 4.3.

Attitude toward behavior is understood here as a positive or negative evaluation of performing certain behaviors (e.g., supporting a candidate during the elections). Subjective norms refer to the perceived social pressure on performing or giving up certain behaviors (e.g., "What will my friends say to that?"). The perceived behavioral control refers to the perceived ease or difficulty of performing a certain behavior. It is the result of current experiences (e.g., "I am not going to vote because it will not change anything!"), anticipated impediments, and obstacles that prevent one from performing a behavior (e.g. "If it keeps raining I am not going to vote!"). According to Ajzen (1996), each of these three elements of the theory can be expressed through numbers, which allows it to be empirically verified. In order to be able to verify the model, one should also learn about someone's intentions toward a given object, for instance, a politician. Does he or she support the candidate or not, and to what extent?

The theory of planned action is the subject of very intensive research whose goal is to verify the model. It involves very different issues, including job searching, participating in lectures, going on a

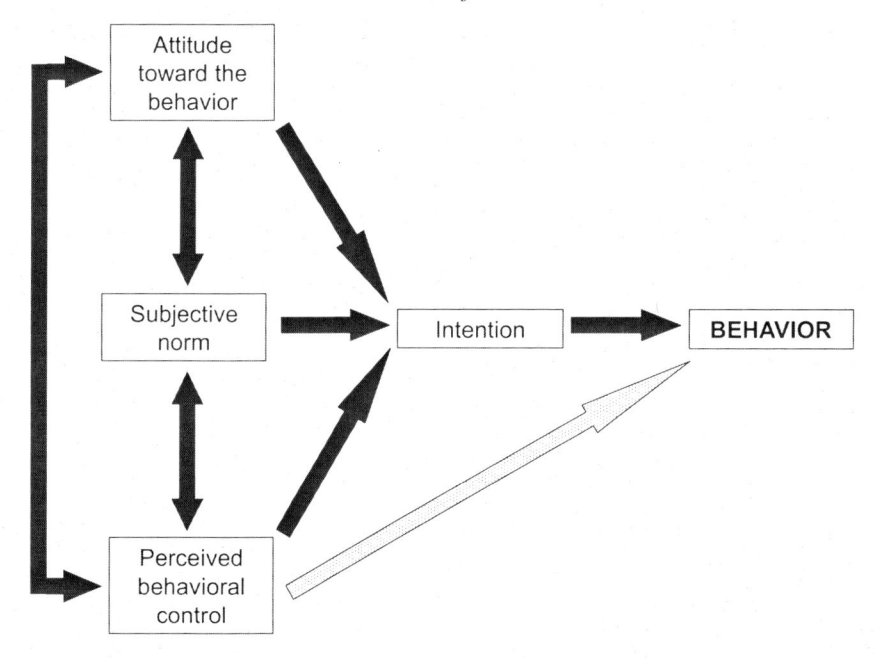

FIGURE 4.3. Theory of planned behavior. *Source:* Adapted from Ajzen (1991).

diet, or using condoms (see Ajzen, 1991). However they are all based on the same statistical procedure: regression analysis. The dependent variable here is behavioral intention, whereas the independent variables are expressed through numbers: attitudes, subjective norms, and behavioral control (see Figure 4.3).

The theory of planned action—in its current and earlier version of the theory of reasoned action—has been verified with reference to the voting behaviors of citizens in the United States (Ajzen, 1991), Singapore (Singh et al., 1995), and Spain or, in fact, in the Basque Country (Echebarria, Paez, Valencia, 1988; Echebarria, Valencia, 1994). It is worthwhile then to demonstrate an empirical verification of this theory by providing a research example.

A. Echebarria Echabe, D. Paez Rovira, and J.F. Valencia Garate (1988) conducted a survey according to the reasoned action model during the autonomous Basque Parliament election in Spain on November 30, 1986. The survey was in the form of a questionnaire; 298

people (53 percent female, and 47 percent male) participated in the survey. The average age was 31.34 years. The group consisted of students from the University of the Basque Country in San Sebastian, and, also, qualified and nonqualified workers, company directors, administration workers, the unemployed, and housewives.

Echebarria and his team tried to determine voting behaviors toward five parties running in the elections: Herri Batasuna (HB), Partido Nacionalista Vasco (PNV), Euskadiko Ezkerra (EE), Partido Socialista Obrero Español (PSOE), and Eusko Alkartasuna (EA).

Ajzen's perceived behavioral control model was replaced with past voting experience (the question inquired who the respondents had voted for in the previous elections). Two days after the election, the researchers contacted the respondents again to find out whether they participated in the election and which party they had voted for. In this way, they determined the respondents' actual voting behavior. With reference to each party, the authors conducted logistic regression to determine predictors of voting behaviors. The results for all the political groups had the same pattern. They are presented graphically on the example of HB in Figure 4.4.

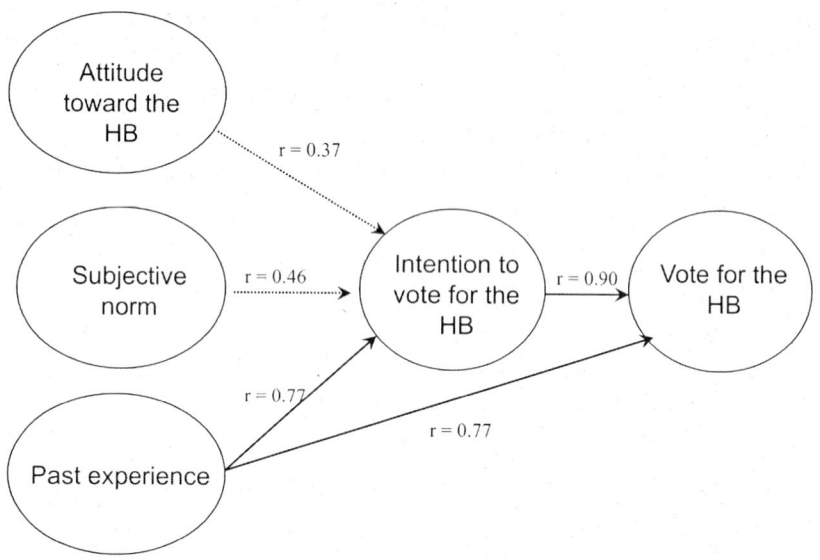

FIGURE 4.4. Theory of planned behavior. Support for Herri Batasuna in the election to Autonomous Basque Parliament in Spain in 1986. *Source:* Adapted from Echebarria, Paez, Valencia (1988).

It turned out that it was past voting experience that had the greatest influence on predicting the Basques' voting intentions. Voting intention was a very good predictor of actual voting behavior. The influence of attitudes toward a party and subjective norms turned out to be of little importance.

Models based on a combination of marketing concepts and results of modern psychological research increase the chances of predicting citizens' voting behaviors.

Chapter 5

A Model of Voter's Choice Behavior: A Newman and Sheth Approach

The most developed multidimensional model of voter behavior is the model of voter's choice behavior developed by Newman (1981, 1999c; Newman, Sheth, 1985). The basic assumption behind the model is that the same principles that operate in the commercial marketplace hold true in the political marketplace. Successful organizations, whether they are run by a corporation, political party, candidate, or interest group must have a market orientation and be constantly engaged in creating value for their customers. In other words, marketers must anticipate their customers' needs and then constantly develop innovative products and services to keep their customers satisfied. Politicians have a similar orientation and are constantly trying to create value for voters by offering them the most benefit at the smallest cost (Kotler and Kotler, 1999). A detailed analysis of marketing orientation in political campaigns is presented in Chapter 3.

Newman's model has been subject to empirical tests during elections at various levels and seems to offer a better chance to explain the foundations of voter behavior. It is also an important source of information for practitioners of political marketing. It allows them to base marketing decisions on a more solid scientific basis by providing them with knowledge as to what data might be needed to better plan a campaign and to better use funds to achieve success.

MODEL DESCRIPTION

Newman's model of voter's choice behavior assumes that voters are consumers of the services offered by politicians, similar to the consumers on the consumer market. Voters choose the best candidate from the available political options. According to this model, the following seven cognitive domains are assumed to guide voter behavior (Newman and Sheth, 1985).

Issues and Policies

Issues and policies refers to a list of salient issues and policies along four dimensions: economic policy, foreign policy, social policy, and leadership characteristics. It also represents the perceived value a candidate possesses in these salient criteria that represent the rational or functional purposes of the candidate's platform. For instance, voters interested in educating their own children will be more likely to vote for a candidate who is going to make access to education easier. Older voters who have health problems will choose a candidate who offers some ideas on how to solve problems in nursing homes/retirement communities.

The evaluation of problems and directions of political actions refers directly to the theory of the rational voter who is interested in the proposals of solving various important political and social issues offered by the candidates. This is confirmed by the research on issue and retrospective voting (see the section titled "Economic Approach" in Chapter 4).

Social Imagery

Social imagery refers to all relevant primary and secondary reference groups likely to be supportive of the candidates being studied. Candidates acquire positive or negative stereotypes based on their association with the different demographic, socioeconomic, or political/ideological segments of society. Social imagery is closely linked to creating in the voters' minds an image of the candidate that is preferred by selected social groups. Creating such imagery is an important element of forming the candidate's image; however, due to the candidate being perceived by various groups, these perceptions may be either positive or negative.

This domain also corresponds to the sociological approach to voter behavior. It stresses the importance of identifying the candidate's sociodemographic position and his or her voter background (see "Sociological Approach" in Chapter 4).

Emotional Feelings

Emotional feelings represents the emotional dimension of voting, and refers to affective feelings such as hope, responsibility, patriotism, etc. aroused by the candidate. The voter's feelings may be independent of the personality of the candidate, having been established on the basis of the issues the candidate advocates, or the voter may be aware of a candidate's personality, but may not have any feelings toward it. In his two presidential campaigns, Ronald Reagan often appeared against the background of a waving American flag, which contributed to the development of his image as a true patriot.

This dimension includes the elements of the critique of the economic approach to voter behavior, assuming that the emotions evoked by candidates are an important element influencing people's support for them (see "Economic Approach" in Chapter 4).

Candidate Image

Candidate image refers to the image of the candidate based on salient personality traits that are thought to be characteristic of the candidate.

Current Events

Current events refers to the set of issues and policies that develop during the course of a campaign, and includes the domestic and international situations that would cause the voter to switch his or her vote to another candidate. The candidate acquires utility or value because of certain issue and policy stands he or she makes that affect different situations. Current events are often unpredictable. Such an unpredictable event on the international scene was the taking of the hostages from the embassy in Iran just prior to the 1980 presidential election. The unsuccessful attempt to free the American hostages in the U.S. embassy in Tehran led to the weakening of the position of Jimmy Carter, in office then, and to the strengthening of his competitor, Ronald Reagan.

Personal Events

Personal events refers to situations in the personal life of the candidate that would cause the voter to switch his or her vote to another candidate. The candidate acquires utility or value because of certain personal or family events that precede the voter's decision. Such events include, for example, involvement in an economic scandal publicized by the media or collaboration with secret security forces in the 1940s and 1950s in the United States and under communism in Poland.

This dimension is linked, on one hand, with forming the candidate's image and, on the other hand, with planning and conducting a negative campaign whose goal is to publicize unfavorable information about political competitors.

Epistemic Issues

Epistemic issues refers to reasons that would justify the perceived satisfaction of curiosity, knowledge, and exploratory needs offered by the candidate as a change of pace.

In the 1976 presidential election, Carter was very successful at tapping the curiosity of voters who saw him as a "fresh face" on the political scene. The emergence of such a new face on the political stage may threaten the well-known candidates. Such a situation occurred during the U.S. presidential elections in 1992 when, besides Bill Clinton and George H. W. Bush, the multibillionaire Ross Perot, not connected with any of the "old" parties, joined the race. For many voters, he embodied a candidate whose position on many domestic and international issues was considerably different from the positions of the other candidates that the public was well familiar with. It led to Perot becoming a clearly distinguishable brand in politics (Newman, 1994).

An equally unpredictable but successful political entry was that of the well-known actor and former bodybuilder, Arnold Schwarzenegger. After a fierce campaign to remove incumbent governor Gray Davis, the Austrian-born candidate was chosen governor of California in the 2003 recall election (Fineman, Breslau, 2003). These cognitive domains are presented in Figure 5.1.

The model consisting of seven domains was first proposed by Bruce I. Newman and Jagdish N. Sheth (1985), and was then slightly

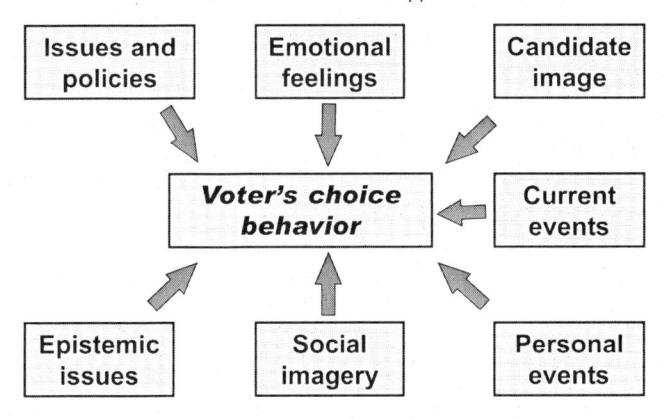

```
     ┌──────────┐    ┌──────────┐    ┌──────────┐
     │Issues and│    │Emotional │    │Candidate │
     │ policies │    │ feelings │    │  image   │
     └────┬─────┘    └────┬─────┘    └────┬─────┘
          ↘               ↓               ↙
              ┌──────────────────┐    ┌──────────┐
              │  Voter's choice  │ ←  │ Current  │
              │     behavior     │    │  events  │
              └──────────────────┘    └──────────┘
          ↗               ↑               ↖
     ┌──────────┐    ┌──────────┐    ┌──────────┐
     │Epistemic │    │  Social  │    │ Personal │
     │  issues  │    │ imagery  │    │  events  │
     └──────────┘    └──────────┘    └──────────┘
```

FIGURE 5.1. Newman and Sheth's model of primary voter behavior. *Source:* Newman and Sheth (1985), p. 179.

changed by Newman (1999c) and limited to five domains (political issues, social imagery, candidate personality, situational contingency, and epistemic value).

The model of voter's choice behavior has been verified empirically several times. The first such test was Newman and Sheth's research (1985) conducted during the primaries of the Republican Party in Illinois in 1980.

PRIMARY ELECTION IN ILLINOIS (U.S.) IN 1980: REAGAN VERSUS ANDERSON

The 1980 Illinois primary for the Republican and Democratic presidential nominations in the Champaign-Urbana area was used as the experimental setting on a sample of 839 registered voters. The respondents answered the survey questions relating to the seven cognitive domains and gave their own demographic data. In order to test the predictive and explanatory power of the model, a discriminant analysis was carried out for the Republican Party. The criterion variable in the discriminant analysis was based on a respondent's stated intention to vote for either John Anderson or Ronald Reagan. The results of the discriminant analysis are presented in Table 5.1.

Data on Table 5.2 show that the issues, policies, and social imagery components were the most significant discriminating variables and dominated the model. Reagan voters had higher means than Anderson voters on both of these components. This implies that Reagan voters placed more importance on issues and social imageries associated with the candidate. This in turn fits in with Reagan's campaign, which appealed to many voter segments. Voters also would have been much more familiar with Reagan's platform, since he had run in a previous national election.

TABLE 5.1. Classification results based on political involvement variables.

Candidate	Total voters used in study	Number correctly classified	Percentage correctly classified	Number misclassified	Percentage misclassified
Anderson	102	53	52.0	49	48.0
Reagan	77	64	83.1	13	16.9

Note: Correctly classified: 65.4 percent.

Source: Newman and Sheth (1985), p. 185.

TABLE 5.2. Two-group discriminant analysis using average scores from each of the seven components in the model.

	Coefficients	Means	
	Anderson/Reagan	Anderson	Reagan
Issues and policies	.46	.41	.62
Social imagery	.77	.35	.73
Emotional feelings	.04	.69	.68
Candidate image	−.14	.86	.86
Current events	−.7	.05	.05
Personal events	.11	.61	.68
Epistemic issues	−.9	.32	.29

Source: Newman and Sheth (1985), p. 183.

Newman and Sheth tested their model by predicting the respondents' voting behavior based on discriminant analysis and then validating model prediction with the actual voting behavior of the respondents. Data in Table 5.3 show that, in general, the prediction rate was very accurate and received 90.5 percent correct classification. In the case of Reagan's electorate, the indicator was 92.2 percent, whereas for Anderson's it was 89.2 percent.

The authors also conducted a comparative analysis of their seven cognitive domains model with models using demographic variables, political involvement variables, or a combination of both types of variables. To test a model using demographic variables, a second discriminant analysis was carried out. In this case, the dependent variable was the respondent's stated intention. The predictor variables covered a series of demographic questions that included degree of education, occupation, age, and socioeconomic status. The classification results of the discriminant analysis are presented in Table 5.4. When the model using demographic variables was validated, it predicted 70.4 percent of the respondents correctly.

Another widely used set of explanatory variables included party affiliation and general political involvement. In order to test for the influence of political involvement on voting behavior, a third discriminant analysis was carried out. The criterion variable was the respondent's stated intention, and predictor variables included a series of questions that tapped various aspects of party affiliation and political involvement. Table 5.1 presents the classification results of discriminant analysis for these predictors. When the model based on political involvement variables was validated, the prediction rate dropped to 65.4 percent.

TABLE 5.3. Classification results based on average scores from each of the seven components in the model.

Candidate	Total voters used in study	Number correctly classified	Percentage correctly classified	Number misclassified	Percentage misclassified
Anderson	102	91	89.2	11	10.8
Reagan	77	71	92.2	6	7.8

Note: Correctly classified: 90.5 percent.

Source: Newman and Sheth (1985), p.184.

A particularly interesting result was the combining of the demographic and political involvement variables into one discriminant analysis (see Table 5.5). This analysis yielded a prediction rate of 73.7 percent, slightly higher than the 70.4 percent prediction rate found in the analysis using only demographic variables.

It is obvious that the seven cognitive domain model is more effective than a model using demographic or political involvement variables. Certainly it is much closer to the concept of dividing the voter market based on psychographic segmentation. The results derived from this model allow the candidate to know what to communicate in his or her messages.

U.S. PRESIDENTIAL ELECTION IN 1996: CLINTON VERSUS DOLE

The study carried out by Newman (1999c) was designed to serve as the basis for segmenting the voters vis-à-vis their perception of what

TABLE 5.4. Classification results based on demographic variables.

Candidate	Total voters used in Study	Number correctly classified	Percentage correctly classified	Number misclassified	Percentage misclassified
Anderson	102	70	68.6	32	31.4
Reagan	77	56	72.7	21	27.3

Note: Correctly classified: 70.4 percent.

Source: Newman and Sheth (1985), p.184.

TABLE 5.5. Classification results based on demographic and political involvement variables.

Candidate	Total voters used in study	Number correctly classified	Percentage correctly classified	Number misclassified	Percentage misclassified
Anderson	102	72	70.6	30	29.4
Reagan	77	60	77.9	17	22.1

Note: Correctly classified: 73.7 percent.

Source: Newman and Sheth (1985), p.186.

the American Dream meant to them and the specific beliefs related to it. The study sought to determine meanings attached to the American Dream, the extent to which voter choice is based on the ability of a candidate to make it easier or harder to achieve the American Dream, and the ability of Clinton, Bob Dole, and Colin Powell to appeal to the following four main voter segments: rational, emotional, social, and situational voters. What is characteristic for this approach is that one cognitive domain corresponds to each of these segments, which differ from one another due to voters' psychological characteristics. In this way, Newman combined his model of voters' choice behavior with psychographic segmentation. The question arises, then, whether Clinton's, Dole's, and Powell's voters belonged to different psychographic segments during the presidential elections in 1996.

A total of 400 respondents were surveyed in person in several malls in the greater metropolitan Chicago area. Only those respondents who indicated that they planned to vote in the 1996 presidential election were invited to fill out the questionnaire. The crucial part of the questionnaire covered the statements for each of the four segments of voters and specific issues related to the American Dream.

The principal statistical technique used to carry out the data analyses and test the voter model behavior related to psychographic segmentation was discriminant analysis. Pair discriminant analyses were carried out between respondents who indicated that each candidate would make it either easier or harder to achieve their American Dream. In this analysis, the criterion variable was the following question: "To what extent do you think each of the following political leaders would make it easier or harder for you to achieve your American Dream?" The predictor variables were the items referring to particular voter groups. The results of the discriminant analysis for each of the candidates are presented in Tables 5.6, 5.7, and 5.8.

Respondents who believed that Clinton would make it easier for them to achieve their American Dream indicated that they would switch to another candidate who would create more equal opportunity. They also indicated that they felt happy as they attempted to achieve their American Dream and that they believed the dream would lead to more personal time for themselves.

Respondents who believed Clinton would make it harder for them to achieve their American Dream indicated that they would switch to another candidate who would reduce crime rates and make education

TABLE 5.6. Discriminant analysis results for Clinton supporters. Three most important variables listed for each segment.

A. Segment 1: President Clinton will make achieving the American Dream easier
 1. I would switch to another candidate who would create more equal opportunity (discriminant coefficient = 0.68)
 2. I feel happy in my attempt to reach my dream (discriminant coefficient = 0.52)
 3. My American dream will lead to more personal time for myself (discriminant coefficient = 0.38)

B. Segment 2: President Clinton will make achieving the American Dream harder
 1. I would switch to another candidate who would reduce crime rates (discriminant coefficient = −0.52)
 2. I would switch to another candidate who would make education more accessible (discriminant coefficient = −0.39)
 3. My American Dream can offer me financial stability (discriminant coefficient = −0.39)

	Predicted		
Actual	Easier	Harder	Number of participants
Easier	75	19	94
Harder	18	48	66

Note: Correctly classified: 76.8 percent.

Source: Newman (1999c), p. 274.

more accessible. They also said that they thought their American Dream would offer them financial stability.

Other predicted variables were found among Dole's supporters, and they are presented in Table 5.7. The results of the discriminant analysis for Dole supporters suggest that those who believed Dole would make it easier for them to achieve their American Dream were afraid of failing and, at the same time, felt increased confidence as they attempted to achieve the dream. They also said they were willing to switch to a candidate who would reduce the crime rate. Respondents who believed that Dole would make it harder for them to achieve their American Dream believed that the dream would offer them more freedom to take risks in life and work and, at the same time, to feel proud or good about themselves as they attempted to achieve the dream.

TABLE 5.7. Discriminant analysis results for Dole supporters. Three most important variables listed for each segment.

A. Segment 1: Dole will make achieving the American Dream easier
  1. I am fearful of failing in my attempt to reach my American Dream (discriminant coefficient = −0.52)
  2. I feel increased confidence in my attempt to reach my American Dream (discriminant coefficient = −0.41)
  3. I would switch to another candidate who would reduce crime rates (discriminant coefficient = −0.37)
B. Segment 2: Dole will make achieving the American Dream harder
  1. My American Dream can offer me more freedom to take risks in my life and work (discriminant coefficient = 0.51)
  2. I feel proud/good about myself in my attempt to reach my dream (discriminant coefficient = 0.49)
  3. Foreign-born people are least likely to achieve the American Dream (discriminant coefficient = 0.39)

Actual	Predicted Easier	Predicted Harder	Number of participants
Easier	54	12	66
Harder	8	78	86

Note: Correctly classified: 86.8 percent.

Source: Newman (1999c), p. 275.

Predicted variables for Powell supporters can be found in Table 5.8. As Newman emphasizes, the discriminant analysis performed for Powell revealed a broader base of reasons explaining why respondents thought he would make their American Dream both easier and harder. That means that Powell as a candidate appealed to voters on more levels. Respondents who believed Powell would make it easier for them to achieve their American dream indicated that they believed he would make the dream possible for high school educated people and that it would be difficult to realize the dream because of the increased cost of living. They said that they would switch to another candidate if he would increase levels of self employment. Respondents who believed Powell would make it harder for them to achieve their American Dream thought that it would be difficult to realize the dream because they have no control over achieving it, and that Powell would make the dream possible for foreign-born people. These re-

TABLE 5.8. Discriminant analysis results for Powell supporters. Three most important variables listed for each segment.

A. Segment 1: Powell will make achieving the American Dream easier
   1. I would switch to another candidate who would increase the level of self-employment (discriminant coefficient = –0.48)
   2. High school–educated people are most likely to achieve the American Dream (discriminant coefficient = –0.42)
   3. My American Dream can be difficult to achieve due to the increasing cost of living (discriminant coefficient = –0.32)
B. Segment 2: Powell will make achieving the American Dream harder
   1. My American Dream can be difficult to realize because I have no control over achieving it (discriminant coefficient = 0.58)
   2. I would switch to another candidate who would increase job security (discriminant coefficient = 0.40)
   3. Foreign-born people are most likely to achieve the American Dream (discriminant coefficient = 0.38)

	Predicted		
Actual	Easier	Harder	Number of participants
Easier	92	17	109
Harder	8	27	35

Note: Correctly classified: 82.6 percent.

Source: Newman (1999c), p. 276.

spondents indicated a willingness to switch to another candidate who would increase their job security.

The key question that arises about the psychographic context of the model of voter's choice behavior is, can one classify a given candidate's voters into a particular psychographic segment on the basis of the results of discriminant analyses that were applied? Are, for instance, Clinton's voters rational, emotional, social, or situational? In answering this question, one should look at the cognitive domains to which the most powerful discriminating variables belonged in the classification analysis for each candidate.

The most important variables in discriminant analysis results for Clinton supporters, presented in Table 5.6, belong to the three cognitive domains referring to rational voters, emotional voters, and situational voters. The variables for discriminant analysis results for Dole refer to exactly the same psychographic voter segments. But variables in discriminant analysis results for Powell supporters include all the psychographic segments defined by the model of voter behavior, that is situational voters, social voters, rational voters, and emotional voters.

One should check, therefore, whether or not "pure" psychographic types exist when discussing a given candidate's supporters. This is not unusual, because no "pure" personality types exist in personality psychology either, and the classification is made either by comparing a person to the prototype, as is the case in Eysenck's psychological theory (1990), or by configuring the profiles of a number of personality traits, as is the case in the concept of the "Big Five" (McCrae, Costa, 1996). Therefore, psychographic segmentation of the model of voter's choice behavior should be made more specific in one of the following ways: (1) A given candidate's supporters can be located on a multidimensional cognitive map, on which are previously selected "pure" psychographic segments. In this way, one can specify in what way the voters combine features of different psychographic segments. Such an approach to positioning candidates on the cognitive map of preferences is presented by, among others, Johnson (1971) and Fiedler and Maxwell (2000) presenting voter space in the United States in 1968 and 2000, correspondingly. (2) A concept can also be developed based on profiles of many personality features, in which a specific configuration of a given candidate's voter features will be their psychographic segment.

U.S. PRESIDENTIAL ELECTION IN 2000: BUSH VERSUS GORE

In research on voter behavior during the U.S. presidential elections in 2000, Newman (2002) applied the model of voter's choice behavior to predict preferences not only for the candidates (George W. Bush and Al Gore), but also for political parties (Republican and Democrat). The study was carried out with the participation of 151 students, faculty, and staff of DePaul University in Chicago. Approximately two-thirds of voters in both the Republican and Democratic parties were loyal to their party.

The questionnaire included statements that were operationalized along the lines of each of the following five components in the predictive model of voter behavior: political issues, social imagery, candidate personality, situational contingency, and epistemic value. As in previous research, the principal statistical technique used to carry out the data analysis was discriminant analysis. In this analysis, the criterion variable was the respondent's preferred candidate and party identification. The predictor variables were questions generated for each of the components in the theory.

Let us first look at the discriminant analysis carried out between voters who identified themselves as either Republicans or Democrats. The most important values to voters who identified themselves as Republicans were, in order of importance:

1. Gun control
2. Desire for change in the administration
3. Low inflation
4. Support of patriotic candidates by the party

A review of these issues suggests that the Republican Party was successful in positioning itself as a party that would respond to two key issues: gun control and low inflation. On the other hand, the strong desire for change in the administration is not surprising, as these are voters who had seen Democrats in the White House for the past eight years. The importance of the fourth issue is the result of Bush's campaign in 2000, in which the theme of patriotism was a key component.

The four most important values to voters who identified themselves as Democrats were, in order of importance:

1. Support of the poor
2. The issue of women's equality in the job market
3. Support of blue-collar workers
4. Support of the unions

These four issues suggest that the Democrats were able to successfully target their campaign to the stronghold of their party, namely unions, blue-collar workers, and the poor. They also appealed to women voters with a promise to fight for their equality in the workforce. Naturally, these values were expressed by the questionnaire statements corresponding to them. The results of the discriminant analysis are presented in Table 5.9.

For Republicans, the statements explaining voter preferences belong mainly to the cognitive domain of political issues and situational contingency. For Democrats, on the other hand, their statements belong just to social imagery. It can be said, therefore, that the research has shown that during the 2000 presidential campaign in the United States one could differentiate better the voters of the Republican and Democratic Party than during the 1996 presidential campaign (see section titled "U.S. Presidential Election in 1996: Clinton versus Dole" in this chapter). The discriminant model predicted the respondents' voter behavior with an exceptional level of accuracy, 98.9 percent, an indication that the predictive model of voter behavior worked very well at the party level.

A look should also be taken at the discriminant analysis carried out between voters who identified themselves as either Bush or Gore supporters. The four most important values to voters who identified themselves as Bush supporters were, in order of importance:

1. Desire for a change in the administration
2. Support by middle-aged adults
3. Support by white-collar workers
4. Support by executives

It is quite understandable, then, that after eight years of Clinton's presidency, voters were mainly seeking a change in administration. But a key base of support for Bush came because of the perception that he was aligned in people's minds with the traditional base of Republican voters, namely white-collar workers and executives. Sup-

TABLE 5.9. Discriminant analysis results for party supporters.

Actual	Predicted Republicans	Predicted Democrats	Subjects
Republicans	33	1	34
Democrats	0	59	59

Note: Correctly classified: 98.9 percent.

Source: Newman (2002), p. 167.

port from middle-aged adults came as a result of the issues that Bush advocated in his platform, especially his promise to offer a tax cut to the American people.

The four important values to Gore supporters were:

1. Support of the poor
2. Promise to reduce unemployment
3. Promise to initiate a broad-based health care program
4. Plan affordable housing for young families

The support generated by Gore was connected to issues that he strongly advocated: health care, housing, and unemployment. Along with these issues was the strong link that Gore made between his programs and the poor. The results of the discriminant analysis are presented in Table 5.10.

For Bush supporters as well as for Gore supporters, the statements explaining voter preferences belong to different cognitive domains, such as political issues, social imagery, and situational contingency. At the candidate level, voters could not be differentiated according to the model of voter behavior during the 2000 presidential campaign, although they could during the 1996 election (see "U.S. Presidential Election in 1996: Clinton verus Dole" in this chapter). The discriminant model predicted the results with 97.8 percent accuracy, indicating that it worked equally well at the party as at the candidate level.

The predictive model of voter behavior isn't able to clearly differentiate voters according to cognitive domains and the psychographic segments related to them. However, it is invaluable in reporting the specific appeals that have proven to be most effective for both the

TABLE 5.10. Discriminant analysis results for candidate supporters.

	Predicted		
Actual	**Republicans**	**Democrats**	**Subjects**
Republicans	40	0	40
Democrats	2	50	52

Note: Correctly classified: 97.8 percent.

Source: Newman (2002), p. 169.

candidates and parties in their attempt to win over voters in a presidential campaign.

As democracies continue to evolve around the world, the model of voter behavior has already become a useful tool to examine the comparative role and influence that both the candidate and party play in winning over voters. Let us look at its application in the parliamentary elections in Slovenia and the presidential elections in Poland.

PARLIAMENTARY ELECTION IN SLOVENIA IN 2000

Verčič and Verdnik (2002) tested the predictive model of voter behavior in Slovenia, that is, in a different cultural and political setting than the United States, and also in a different electoral setting: in a proportional instead of a majority system of voting. The model in their study was operationalized at both the candidate and party levels. The study sought to identify those questions that were unique to both candidates, and the political parties that influenced the behavior of the voters in this election. Although Newman's (2002) research in the United States indicated that this model of voter behavior works equally well on the candidate and party levels, this was not possible to test in Slovenia. As Verèiè and Verdnik pointed out, among potential voters, candidates had low visibility, so it was not feasible to measure data separately for candidates and parties. Because voters were able to identify only parties, the model was tested on the party level.

Let's look first at the Slovenian electoral system, since this country belongs to the so-called evolving democracies, in comparison to a well-established democracy such as the United States. The electoral system is essentially proportional, that is, each party gets a number of deputies equal to the share of votes they received at the polls. However, it also has elements of a majority system. Voters vote for individual candidates within each of the eighty-eight electoral districts. The electoral districts are integrated into eight electoral units. Because the candidate lists are comprised of those candidates who received the highest share of votes in the electoral units, candidates within the same party also compete against one another. A detailed description of the Slovenian electoral system is found in Verčič and Verdnik (2002).

The study was carried out about two weeks before the parliamentary elections in the Vrhnika electoral district. This district was selected based on the similarity of its electoral results to previous parliamentary elections in 1996. Based on preelection polls by several research institutions, the three political parties predicted to win the most votes were selected for study. They were the LDS (Liberal Democrats of Slovenia), the ZLSD (United List of Social Democrats), and the SDS (Social Democrats of Slovenia).

Respondents were interviewed via telephone. Interviewing started two weeks before elections and was completed in four days. The day after the elections, a postelection contact was made with the respondents of the study to obtain information on the previous day's electoral decision of the respondents. The study was carried out on samples of 200 voters per each selected political party. The questionnaire included statements that were operationalized along the lines of the five components of the model of voter behavior (see "U.S. Presidential Election in 2000: Bush versus Gore" in this chapter, and Newman, 1999c). A total of 230 questions were included in the survey.

The principal technique used in the data analysis was discriminant analysis. In the analysis, the criterion variable was the respondent's preferred political party. The predictor variables were questions generated for each of the components in the theory using a series of paired T-tests between the following respondent groups: LDS versus ZLSD, LDS versus SDS, and ZLSD versus SDS. The results of the analysis of each of the three groups are discussed in the following sections.

LDS versus ZLSD

The four most important values to voters who identified themselves as LDS supporters were, in order of importance:

1. Orientation toward the future
2. Support for the poorest
3. Higher salaries
4. Quality education

A review of the top four issues shows why the LDS was capable of being a party of a relative majority in the parliament throughout the first decade of democracy in Slovenia, and why it was the pivotal player in nearly all the governments in that period. The main reason is that voters perceived it as being capable of bringing about a good future. At the same time, it was perceived as being compassionate, considerate of government and public service employees, and as investing in the educational system. It is no wonder that with such a profile, the party won these elections.

The four most important values to voters who identified themselves as ZLSD supporters were, in order of importance:

1. Women's rights
2. Situational contingency—switch if taxes rose
3. Situational contingency—switch if party's leaders were caught drinking while driving
4. Situational contingency—switch if party's leaders evaded taxes

These four values show a high level of situational contingency involved in voter behavior in Slovenia. This can partly be explained by a lack of profound political choices European emerging democracies face, which forces all political parties that compete for the central stage to support the same policies: liberalization and privatization (domestic policies), and EU and NATO membership (foreign policies).

The values described were expressed by the questionnaire statements corresponding to them. The discriminant model predicted respondents' voter behavior with a 90.4 percent level of accuracy, as shown in Table 5.11.

TABLE 5.11. Discriminant analysis results for party supporters, LDS versus ZLSD.

Actual	Predicted LDS	Predicted ZLSD	Subjects
LDS	59	8	40
ZLSD	3	44	52

Note: Correctly classified: 90.4 percent.

Source: Verčič and Verdnik (2002), p. 129. Reprinted with permission from The Haworth Press, Inc.

LDS versus SDS

A similar discriminant analysis was conducted for the pair LDS and SDS. The four most important values to voters who identified themselves as LDS supporters were, in order of importance:

1. Situational contingency—switch if inflation rose significantly
2. Situational contingency—switch if party's leaders were involved in an economic/business scandal
3. Vote for my party because of the personalities who endorse it
4. The party will lower the crime rate

An examination of these data shows that in the choice between LDS and SDS, LDS supporters chose it over SDS because of its leaders on the national level. This result also confirms that voters in the selected electoral district were voting based on national party preferences and not for their local candidates. It looks as if these voters were satisfied with the way LDS was running the economy, and would switch if inflation significantly rose. (People learned how difficult it is to live with inflation above 1,000 percent.)

The four most important values to voters who identified themselves as SDS supporters were, in order of importance:

1. Blue-collar workers' support
2. Focus on domestic, not international issues
3. A change in the administration
4. Farmers' support

These values confirm the positioning of SDS as the main opposition to LDS. Its supporters are from a lower social segment and nonurban areas, demanding more radical changes in the evolution of a new Slovenia. The discriminant model predicted respondents' voter behavior with an 85.4 percent level of accuracy. The data are presented in Table 5.12.

ZLSD versus SDS

The results of the discriminant analysis of the last pair, ZLSD and SDS, are as follows. The four most important values to voters who identified themselves as ZLSD supporters were, in order of importance:

1. Belief that the party will offer job security
2. Belief in the sincerity of the party
3. Situational contingency—switch if economic results aggravated
4. Vote for the party because of the personalities who endorse it

Of all the parties in Slovenia, ZLSD is generally perceived as representing continuity and moderation in its support for social, economic, and political transformations. To many people, the status quo equals security. This would change only if the economy became worse. Also, this result confirms that voters in the selected electoral district were voting based on national party preferences and not for their local candidates.

The four most important values to voters who identified themselves as SDS supporters were, in order of importance:

1. Belief that the party will raise salaries
2. Foreign-born voters will most likely vote for this party
3. Situational contingency—switch if party's leaders were not healthy enough to follow through with their mandate
4. Situational contingency—switch if inflation rose significantly

Foreign-born voters in this context means descendents of people forced to leave Slovenia when the communists were in power. The support of descendents of the Slovenian political diaspora for the SDS was communicated well and noticed by potential voters. It is interesting to note what voters expected from these two social democratic parties (which ZLSD and SDS are, at least in name), in labor-related terms. ZLSD supporters expected job security, which confirms that ZLSD is more a middle-class social democratic party, whereas SDS supporters wanted higher salaries, SDS being more a blue-collar so-

TABLE 5.12. Discriminant analysis results for party supporters, LDS versus SDS.

Actual	Predicted LDS	Predicted SDS	Subjects
LDS	56	11	67
SDS	12	79	91

Note: Correctly classified: 85.4 percent.

Source: Verčič and Verdnik (2002), p. 131. Reprinted with permission from The Haworth Press, Inc.

cial democratic party. Table 5.13 presents the results of the discriminant model.

The Verčič and Verdnik research shows that the primary model of voter behavior proved itself in Slovenia. Their study found low visibility of individual local candidates in parliamentary elections in Slovenia. Although this may be partly explained by a proportional electoral system, it also demonstrates low effort on the part of individual politicians—first as candidates, but maybe even later, if elected, as officials. From a marketing perspective, it is important that further adoption of political marketing models and methods in evolving democracies may well be linked to the question of individual responsibility of politicians.

The 2000 parliamentary elections viewed through the model used here show that voters selected LDS for its orientation toward the future, ZLSD for its stability, and SDS for change. This makes the top three choices of the Slovenian electorate a balanced selection, which proves that democracy has gained ground in Slovenia during the past decade. The balance between stability and change with a view to the future is an indication that democracy in Slovenia is transforming itself from evolving into evolved.

PRESIDENTIAL ELECTION IN POLAND IN 2000: KWAŚNIEWSKI VERSUS OLECHOWSKI

A deeper analysis of Newman's primary model of voter's choice behavior was presented by Cwalina (2003a), on the basis of the presidential election in Poland in 2000. A number of sociological, demographic and worldview variables were incorporated into Newman's

TABLE 5.13. Discriminant analysis results for party supporters, SDS versus ZSLD.

Actual	Predicted SDS	Predicted ZSLD	Subjects
SDS	81	10	91
ZSLD	7	40	47

Note: Correctly classified: 87.7 percent.

Source: Verčič and Verdnik (2002), p. 133. Reprinted with permission from The Haworth Press, Inc.

original model of seven domains (see Table 5.2). It seems worthwhile to present systematically the results of the testing of the original models of voter behavior in light of testing the discriminating power of the other variables; this is what Newman did in his research on the primary election in Illinois (U.S.) in 1980 (see "Primary Election in Illinois [U.S.] in 1980: Reagan versus Anderson" in this chapter). In different combinations, these variables create the models of voter behaviors described in the following sections.

Sociodemographic Model

The sociodemographic model assumes that voter behaviors are formed within social groups to which an individual belongs. For the purposes of the planned analysis, the sociodemographic model was defined by the following characteristics of the respondents:

- Gender
- Age
- Education
- Place of residence
- Average monthly income
- Occupation (blue collar/white collar worker)

Political Involvement Model

The political involvement model includes elements of the social psychological approach for the purpose of conducting a voter behavior analysis (see "Social Psychological Approach" in Chapter 4). It stresses the mediating role of permanent psychological predispositions and, particularly, partisan and ideological orientation for the forming of political decisions.

The model was defined by the following variables for the purpose of the planned analysis:

- Interest in the 2000 presidential elections
- Belief that a person's voice is important for the result of the election
- Ideological orientation

- Partisan orientation (The levels of this variable were determined by voters' identification with AWS [Solidarity Election Action] and SLD [Democratic Left Alliance], relative to the support offered by particular political groups to A. Kwaśniewski and A. Olechowski.)
- Importance attributed by the media to the election campaign

Sociodemographic Model and Political Involvement Model

This model assumes the citizens' voter behaviors can be successfully predicted on the basis of the variables included in the two basic models: sociodemographic and political involvement. The other models include various combinations of Newman's seven domain model, resulting in the following three proposals discussed in the following sections.

Sociodemographic Model and Newman's Model

This model assumes that citizens' voter behaviors are the result of a combination of factors included in the sociodemographic and Newman's seven domain models.

Political Involvement Model and Newman's Model

This model assumes that voting preferences are the result of political involvement and the seven-domain Newman model.

Sociodemographic, Political Involvement, and Newman's Models

This model treats voter behaviors as a result of a combined influence of the set of variables included in all the models of candidate preference forming presented here.

The research was conducted in eastern and central Poland, in Lublin and Łódź provinces in November 2000, a month after the presidential election. The study was carried out using (nonrepresentative) samples from 238 voters. Because 52.94 percent of the respondents out of the whole study preferred the incumbent president, Aleksander Kwaśniewski (the actual election result was 53.90 percent), and 34.45 percent supported Andrzej Olechowski (the actual election result was 17.30 percent), all subsequent analyses were only limited to the supporters of these two presidential candidates during the election in 2000.

The respondents filled out a nine-part questionnaire on an individual basis. Part 1 referred to the political preferences of the respondents. They were asked to mark which of the twelve candidates running for the Polish presidency in the 2000 election they voted for. In addition, they defined their ideological orientation on a three-point scale: left-wing, center, or right-wing. Parts 2 through 7 included questions referring to the seven cognitive domains defined in Newman and Sheth's model.

Part 8 of the questionnaire was concerned with the voters' perception of the media. In the contemporary world dominated by the media, one cannot afford not to include this powerful tool of influencing people into models of voter behaviors. The media variable used in the current analysis is of particular importance. It does not specify the direct influence of the media on voter behaviors. However, it defines the way of perceiving media influence on such behaviors. Sample statements concerning the influence of the media and election polls on elections included: "I used information from the media in order to choose my candidate." "Polls are very useful during elections." "I am of the opinion that voting spots serve democracy well." The media is understood here as a cognitive representation of the mass media formed in the voters' minds and influencing their political behaviors. The media is treated as an additional cognitive domain that influences voter behavior. Because the media variable in the presented model of discriminant analysis did not play an important role in predicting voter behaviors according to these models, the issue of the media will not be discussed in this chapter. However, the media was found to be of particular importance in cause-and-effect models of voter behaviors (see Chapter 6). Part 9, the final part, included an index with such items as gender, age, education, occupation, place of residence, and average income of the respondents.

As in the case of Newman and Verčič's research, the principal statistical technique used to carry out the data analysis was discriminant analysis. Therefore, in each of the studied models, predictors best discriminating Aleksander Kwaśniewski's and Andrzej Olechowski's voter decisions were sought.

We will begin the presentation of the testing of voter behavior models with Newman's original model, for which the results of discriminant analysis are presented in Table 5.14. The data in Table 5.14 shows that social imagery, candidate image, issues and policies, and personal events were the most significant discriminating variables of the model. What is interesting is that the means of these components are comparable for both candidates. This implies that both candidates in their campaigns placed similar importance on these domains. The correctness of voter behavior prediction based on the conducted discriminant analysis is presented in Table 5.15.

The data in the table shows that, in general, the prediction rate was fairly accurate and achieved 75.73 percent correct classification. This indicator, however, turned out to be much higher for Kwaśniewski's electorate (81.54 percent) compared to Olechowski's (67.07 percent).

One should also take a look at the results of discriminant analysis for the other models. Table 5.16 presents prediction results for the sociodemographic model, in which only education and occupation were the significant discriminating variables of the model. The prediction results are less accurate here compared to Newman's model. However, one should realize that considerable differences exist among such prediction processes for particular candidates. The voter behavior predictors selected in discriminant analysis turned out to be much better for Kwaśniewski's electorate (86.29 percent) compared to the very poor prediction rate for Olechowski's electorate (35.80 percent).

The next model that was tested was the political involvement model, in which the significant discriminating variables were party

TABLE 5.14. Two-group discriminant analysis using average scores from each of the seven components in the model.

	Coefficients	Means	
	Kwaśniewski/ Olechowski	Kwaśniewski	Olechowski
Social imagery	.86	9.83	8.05
Candidate image	−.62	12.68	13.91
Issues and policies	.54	3.95	3.46
Personal events	−.33	5.99	6.62

TABLE 5.15. Classification results based on average scores from each of the seven components in the model.

Candidate	Number of voters	Percentage correctly classified	Number correctly classified	Number misclassified
Kwaśniewski	124	81.45	101	23
Olechowski	82	67.07	55	27

Note: Correctly classified: 75.73 percent.

TABLE 5.16. Classification results based on the sociodemographic model.

Candidate	Number of voters	Percentage correctly classified	Number correctly classified	Number misclassified
Kwaśniewski	124	86.29	107	17
Olechowski	81	35.80	29	52

Note: Correctly classified: 66.34 percent.

identification (identification with the left-wing SLD and the right-wing AWS) and ideological orientation. The results of voter behavior predictions are presented in Table 5.17. The prediction results of this model are analogous to the results obtained from Newman's model. This time the predictors of voter behavior turned out to work better for Olechowski's electorate (86.59 percent) than for Kwaśniewski's (69.84 percent).

The combined models of voter behavior are presented in Table 5.18. The combination of the sociodemographic and political involvement models resulted in the prediction rate presented in the table.

Important voter behavior predictors in this combined model included the following elements: identification with the left-wing party, education, and occupation. It is worthwhile to notice that the combination of these two models resulted in the highest prediction rate so far. One can assume, therefore, that other combinations of voter behavior models will result in an even higher prediction rate for voter behaviors. Because Newman's model turned out to be a very good pre-

TABLE 5.17. Classification results based on the political involvement model.

Candidate	Number of voters	Percentage correctly classified	Number correctly classified	Number misclassified
Kwaśniewski	126	69.84	88	38
Olechowski	82	86.59	71	11

Note: Correctly classified: 76.44 percent.

TABLE 5.18. Classification results based on the sociodemographic model and the political involvement model.

Candidate	Number of voters	Percentage correctly classified	Number correctly classified	Number misclassified
Kwaśniewski	124	75.81	94	30
Olechowski	81	80.25	65	16

Note: Correctly classified: 77.56 percent.

dictor in the United States and Slovenia (discussed previously in this chapter), the subsequent combinations already included this seven-domain model. The results of discriminant analysis of this model combined with the sociodemographic approach are presented in Table 5.19. Although, many significant predictors, including social imagery, education, candidate image, issues and policies, personal events, age, and occupation, explained voter behavior, prediction rates for correct classifications were not very high (76.14 percent) compared to the previous models.

Combining Newman's model with the political involvement model brought about a much better effect. The results of discriminant analysis for this combination are presented in Table 5.20. In this analysis many significant predictors explained voter behavior. They included such variables as identification with the left-wing SLD or the right-wing AWS, social imagery, candidate image, issues and policies, personal events and ideological orientation. However, the prediction rate of correct classification was much higher and amounted to 84.95 per-

TABLE 5.19. Classification results based on the sociodemographic model and the Newman model.

Candidate	Number of voters	Percentage correctly classified	Number correctly classified	Number misclassified
Kwaśniewski	119	82.35	98	21
Olechowski	78	66.67	52	26

Note: Correctly classified: 76.14 percent.

TABLE 5.20. Classification results based on the political involvement model and the Newman model.

Candidate	Number of voters	Percentage correctly classified	Number correctly classified	Number misclassified
Kwaśniewski	124	81.45	101	23
Olechowski	82	90.24	74	8

Note: Correctly classified: 84.95 percent.

cent. It can be assumed, therefore, that the combination of all these models will yield the best results.

Table 5.21 presents the results of discriminant analysis with the combined variables of all of the analyzed models. In fact, the results based on voter behavior predictions combining the three models, sociodemographic, political involvement, and Newman's, turned out to be the best of all the tested models. Significant discriminating variables included: social imagery, identification with the left-wing SLD, education, candidate image, occupation, personal events, and issues and policies. The predicted percentage of correct classifications based on these predictor variables was 88.24 percent.

Discriminant analyses of a number of models of voter behavior during the Polish presidential elections also show the dynamics of testing various combinations of these models in order to arrive at the best prediction results for correct classifications through predictor variables. This method might constitute a certain methodology of re-

TABLE 5.21. Classification results based on the sociodemographic, political involvement, and Newman models.

Candidate	Number of voters	Percentage correctly classified	Number correctly classified	Number misclassified
Kwaśniewski	123	88.62	109	14
Olechowski	81	87.65	71	10

Note: Correctly classified: 88.24 percent.

search into voter behavior with discriminant analysis. According to this methodology, Newman's model becomes a much more powerful predictive tool if combined with other approaches to voter behavior, including the sociodemographic approach as well as the political involvement approach.

COMPARATIVE ANALYSIS OF PREDICTIVE MODEL OF VOTER'S CHOICE BEHAVIOR AND TRADITIONAL MODELS

The research described here using discriminant analysis and based on predictive voter behavior model in the United States, Slovenia, and Poland should also be presented from the perspective of the theoretical research into voter behavior discussed in Chapter 4 as traditional models. Wide research paradigms exist based on various theoretical principles in the area of political marketing that concerns the controlling of voter behavior. Therefore, the empirical methodology of the predictive model of voter behavior must include *implicitly* a number of principles included in the traditional models. Understanding the paradigm context of this methodology will increase many political consultants' knowledge and skills of planning research on the determinants of voter behavior. The predictive voter behavior model will then be compared with the sociological approach, social-psychological approach, economic approach, and multidimensional approach.

Predictive Model of Voter Behavior and Sociological Approach

The sociological approach to voter behavior stresses the importance of dividing voters according to demographic characteristics, which include education, occupation, age, and socioeconomic status, and of defining their social class. Despite that in this approach socioeconomic status often defines party affiliation, which is closely connected with political involvement, this variable (following the traditional models presented in Chapter 4) will be included in the social psychological interpretation of predictive model behavior according to discriminant analysis.

A review of classification results of discriminant analysis should be based on demographic variables. The results of the research into voter behavior in the United States in 1980 show that the model based on demographic data is a worse voter behavior predictor than Newman's seven-domain model. The results of discriminant analysis in the United States and Poland presented in Table 5.3 should be included in the sociological approach. The results clearly show that the sociological approach in the interpretation of discriminant analysis is less accurate than Newman's model. This confirms the conclusions from Great Britain and the United States, namely that the division into social classes is no longer important for the segmentation of the voting market. However, it may be surmised that the model of discriminant analysis according to the sociological approach could have been a better predictor during the parliamentary elections in Finland in 1995. It was such a variable as the division into social classes that proved important for voters supporting a given political party (see "Sociological Approach in Chapter 4). In the Polish research, the sociological approach is operationalized by the sociodemographic model of discriminant analysis presented in Table 5.16. The analysis of the data allows one to state that the sociological approach in Poland, as in the United States, is a poor voter behavior predictor (compare Tables 5.3 and 5.16).

Predictive Model of Voter Behavior and Social-Psychological Approach

In the social-psychological approach, the key variables are psychological variables; however, this approach also includes some elements of the sociological approach. Therefore, the foundation of this approach is party identification closed to political involvement (see "Social Psychological Approach" in Chapter 4). Taking a look at the significance of this variable in the presented research will be worthwhile.

The model of discriminant analysis testing the value of this variable only in voter behavior prediction is presented in Table 5.17 (the Polish research). Although the results of discriminant analysis according to this model turned out to be better in Poland than in the United States, in both cases they are less accurate than the complete presentation of the social-psychological approach. In the case of the United States, the results obtained with this model are even worse than the results from the sociological approach including only demographic variables (compare Tables 5.3 and 5.4). This result points to the low importance of the political involvement variable for voter behavior prediction. The decreasing importance of this variable observed here on the basis of the results of discriminant analysis is very well illustrated by the charts in Figures 1.1 and 1.2 in Chapter 1. They present a systematic decrease in the number of voters identifying themselves with one or another party and an increase in the number of independent voters in the United States and Great Britain.

However, a complete presentation of the social-psychological approach in discriminant analyses should also include sociological and psychological variables closely related to the psychological segmentation of the voting market. According to the analysis of this approach presented in Chapter 4.2, Newman's predictive model of voter behavior may be a proposal of such segmentation. Some cognitive domains related to various values sought by voters in the candidates correspond very closely to particular psychographic segments (see "Social Psychological Approach" in Chapter 4).

We should therefore first look at the comparison of the social-psychological approach expressed by a narrow degree through discriminant analysis and combining demographic variables with political involvement. For the United States, this analysis is presented in Table 5.5 and for Poland in Table 5.18. The results in both countries show better prediction rates than the results achieved through the sociological approach. An even better prediction rate should be expected if the social-psychological approach were expressed through a wider range of discriminant analysis combining, in addition to demographic variables and political involvement, the variables of Newman's model expressed by cognitive domains. Such an analysis is presented in Table 5.21; it is taken from the Polish research and it constitutes the best prediction of voter behavior.

Therefore, replacing the sociological paradigm in marketing research, due to its poor efficiency in predicting voter behavior (see Chapter 4), has a very good empirical application for discriminant analyses.

Predictive Model of Voter Behavior and Economic Approach

The fundamental assumption of the economic paradigm is that citizens' behavior in the sphere of politics is rational. A person votes for specific solutions to political problems *(issue voting)* (see "Economic Approach" in Chapter 4). Therefore, the economic paradigm in Newman's model is in fact limited to this cognitive domain that refers to issues and policies.

The importance of this domain for voter behavior prediction should be verified. In the American research from 1980, this domain in discriminant analysis methodology seems to be of highest importance (see Table 5.2), whereas in the Polish research it is in the third place (see Table 5.14). However, the dynamics of changes in voter behavior prediction on the Polish market presented in detail and combining a number of various variables (see "Presidential Election in Poland in 2000: Kwaśniewski versus Olechowski" in this chapter) shows that one cannot talk about a "pure" economic approach. In other words, a "rational" voter does not exist. In light of the results of the research conducted according to the methodology of discriminant analysis, the critique of the rational voter presented in Chapter 4 is fully justified.

Predictive Model of Voter Behavior and Multidimensional Models

As it was stated in Chapter 4, the critique of the traditional paradigms of voter behavior analyses led to the development of multivariable models combining elements of all the approaches. A particularly interesting example of such a multivariable approach is Ajzen's theory of planned behavior (1991).

In comparative analysis of the predictive model of voter behavior, the predictors of voter behavior according to the theory of planned behavior can constitute all the variables used in all the models of discriminant analyses. According to this theory, the variables would define the attitude toward a candidate, in addition to such specific variables as subjective norms and perceived behavioral control (see Figure 4.3 in Chapter 4). The empirical testing of the theory of planned behavior on the basis of the logistic regression analysis by Echebarria, Paez, and Valencia (1988) during the elections to the autonomous Basque Parliament of the Basque Country in Spain in 1986 is very similar to discriminant analysis. A predictive model of voter behavior based on discriminant analysis would be a variant of the multidimensional approach.

The following conclusions can be reached on the basis of the comparative analysis of the predictive model of voter behavior and traditional models. In the first place, the predictive model demonstrates in an empirical way a need to combine elements that are characteristic for the sociological, social-psychological, and economic paradigms. Second, it allows one to look simultaneously at the separate paradigms of voter behavior presented in literature. And, finally, the predictive model of voter behavior well established within these traditional approaches offers solid theoretical foundations for research. However, these approaches are quite divergent, and further work on theoretical justification of the empirical methodology of discriminant analysis in voter behavior would require the establishment of a uniform theory going beyond traditional paradigms.

Chapter 6

Predictive Models of Voter Behavior: A Reinterpretation of Newman's Approach

The model of voter behavior presented in Chapter 5 operationalized by the empirical method of discriminant analysis shows the influence of the seven cognitive domains on voter behavior. The model can also be presented as a simple regression analysis, in which a number of independent variables not related to one another influence the dependent variable. Cognitive domains in Newman's original model are then treated as variables independent from one another.

However, the question arises whether the domains are, in fact, distinct and separate. For example, it is well documented in psychological literature that cognitive and emotional elements should be treated not as separate, but as interactive vectors (e.g., Cwalina, Falkowski, 2000; Falkowski, Cwalina, 1999; Cwalina, Falkowski, Kaid, 2000, 2005; Singh et al., 1995). Therefore, a question can be posed regarding possible causal relationships among the set of variables previously treated as distinct and independent. Replacing the traditional discriminant models with structural ones that could specify the interrelations among different cognitive domains can provide the answers to such questions (for more information on structural equation analysis, see Loehlin, 1987). In addition, the proposed structural models of voter behavior fit a particular way of experiencing social reality either through cognitive constructivism or cognitive realism very well.

Asking which element acts on another element is a problem of causal relationship among elements previously assumed to be distinct and independent variables. This concerns, in particular, the proper placement in this causal chain of a voter's emotional attitudes toward candidates. Therefore, one should define precisely the importance of emotions for voter behavior.

EMOTIONAL FEELINGS AS A PREDICTOR OF VOTER BEHAVIOR

An introduction to the problem of the importance of emotions in politics was presented in Chapter 2. This chapter seeks to present the procedure of defining empirically the relationship between emotions and voter behavior.

The precise relationship between emotion toward a candidate and intention to vote for him or her was also empirically verified during the Polish presidential election in 1995, when Lech Wałęsa (the incumbent) and Aleksander Kwaśniewski (the challenger) were the two main competitors (Cwalina, Falkowski, 1999; Cwalina, Falkowski, Kaid, 2000; Falkowski, Cwalina, 1999). In order to verify whether general emotional attitude toward a candidate is a good predictor of voting intentions, a discriminant analysis was conducted. Table 6.1 shows the results obtained, including the percentages of the participants correctly classified as Wałęsa's and Kwaśniewski's electorates, based on the feeling thermometer. The support for the candidate pre-

TABLE 6.1. Number and percentage of the subjects attributed to particular electorates based on the general emotional attitude toward the candidates. Results of discriminant analysis.

Observed intention from general feeling thermometer to vote on	Predicted intention from general feeling thermometer to vote on					
	Kwaśniewski		Wałęsa		Overall	
	n	%	n	%	N	%
Kwaśniewski	91	94.8	5	5.2	96	100
Wałęsa	5	6.1	77	93.9	82	100
No declaration	6	24.0	19	76.0	25	100

Source: Falkowski and Cwalina, (1999), p. 290.

dicted on this basis was very good: 94 percent of the participants were attributed correctly (94.8 percent for Kwaśniewski's electorate and 93.9 percent for Wałęsa's electorate). In addition, the coefficient of the point-biserial correlation between the emotional attitude toward the candidates and the voting intention was very high ($r_{pbi} = 0.845$, $p < 0.001$).

The results pointing to the power of the relationship between emotions and decisions led to the already mentioned suggestion by Aronson, Wilson, and Akert (1994) that people vote with their hearts rather than with their minds (see section titled "The Role of Emotions in Politics" in Chapter 2). Naturally, the question arises of how voters' emotions are formed. Obviously, their affective attitude is influenced by the media, whose main goal is to develop a candidate's image. Emotional attitude can then be the consequence of such an image or can modify this image. These mutual relations between these two key psychological elements influencing political behavior are under strong influence of the media and have been thoroughly tested according to the sequential model of advertising influence on voting behavior by Falkowski and Cwalina (1999) and Cwalina, Falkowski, and Kaid (2000, 2005) (see section titled "Sequential Model of the Influence of Political Advertisements" in this chapter). The reinterpretation of Newman and Sheth's voter's choice behavior model needs, besides an attempt to determine causal relations between particular domains, to be completed by another factor—the media. Therefore, it is important to better characterize the importance of the media that will be introduced to the structural models of voter behavior (see "Structural Equation Models of Voter Behavior: A Constructivist Approach" in this chapter).

MEDIA IN ELECTION

A common view exists that the media is the "fourth estate," and the supporters of this view stress the importance of mass media as an element in the political fight and as a way of influencing society. John B. Thompson (1994), trying to define the mutual relations between social development and mass communication, suggests that the media plays an important role in the mechanisms of power. The close relations between the world of politics and the media is made even closer by the specific characteristics of mass communication discussed by Denis McQuail (1969), which point to its very powerful character. In this context, the power of the media (discussed by Thompson, 1994) using symbolic forms while transferring information in order to influence events becomes a temptation for those who want to use it to achieve particular ideological, economic, or political benefits.

No matter how the mass media is organized, how it functions and what information it provides citizens with, it is a part of the political system. Therefore, all the strategies of political actions, both before and between the elections, include using the mass media for distributing particular messages and influencing the society. It is because of this (Denton, Woodward, 1990) that most common qualities of political life include its concentration on immediate issues and short-term horizons. Politicians prepare and deliver their addresses hoping for immediate benefits. Trying to step into the incessant rhythm of public debates, they must find a suitable moment, one that fits the requirements of the mass media and the public's expectations.

In the 1960s an important shift occurred in the way political communication was carried out. Television became its main channel. This change meant, above all, that political parties lost control of the content that their supporters received. The viewers had access to information about various political groups, including their strengths and weaknesses. This led to the emergence of a bigger and bigger segment of politically neutral citizens. The era of television also led to an increase of the viewing public whose support politicians were seeking. This communication channel reached groups that those seeking power had not previously been interested in. Their growing importance made their voices more and more needed.

The multiplicity of channels providing information led—according to Blumler and Kavanagh (1999)—to politicians beginning to treat the new system of the media as a hydra with many heads always hungry for food. Such a situation leads politicians who want to gain support to hire professional assistants for contacts with the media. Their main task is to provide the media with information about politicians and their actions (or prevent such information from spreading) and criticize political opponents. Such contacts with the media have consequences for the organization of government or party structures. The role of the party leader or premier grows and his or her task is to centralize and coordinate communication with citizens. This is no longer limited to television; other ways of presenting politicians are used more and more often: the Internet, billboards, press articles under a politician's name, or events that attract the attention of journalists and society. Intensive contacts with the society make politicians flatter citizens. Therefore, populist slogans become more and more widespread.

Finding mutual relations between the mass media and political institutions and society became a starting point for Ralph Negrine (1994) to propose his own model of political communication, presented in Figure 6.1.

According to Negrine, the key elements of the political communication process include: media content, the influence of political institutions and other political/social actors on the context of the messages, specific audience and interaction processes between sources of information, and the media diffusing information. The content of media messages is the result of the work of media practitioners (owners of media corporations, editors, journalists, reporters, etc.) and political actors or events covered by the media. Sometimes it is the poli-

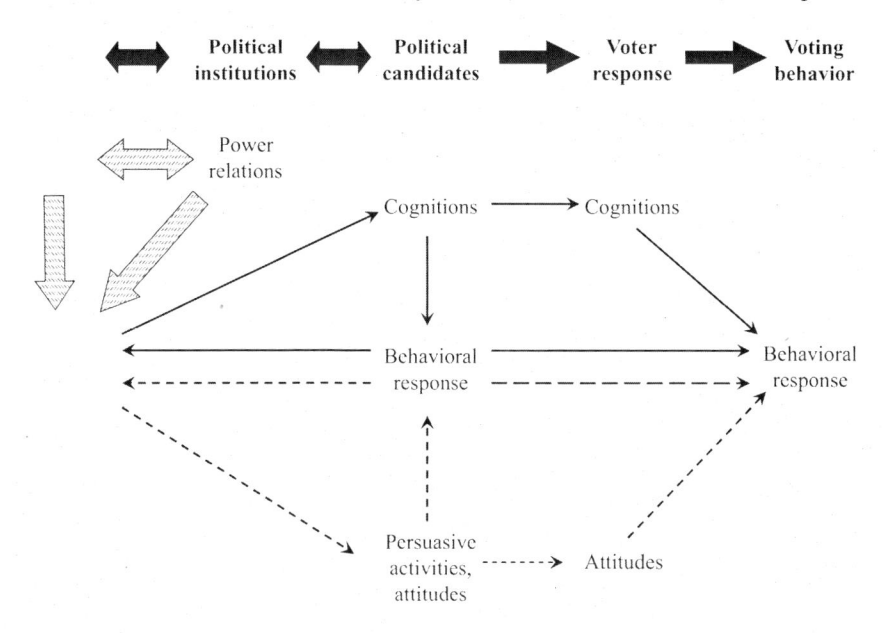

FIGURE 6.1. Model of political communication. *Source:* Adapted from Negrine (1994).

ticians who have the most influence on such reports by creating some events, but most often the final message and the opinions expressed through it are connected with the people related to the media.

Negrine stresses that groups that influence the content of political communication have different levels of power in this area. In their interactions with the media, political actors, including parties, certain politicians, the government, etc., try to achieve their own goals, and sometimes they manage to do so by dominating the content of the message. On the other hand, society at large does not have such influence. Society does not play an active role in creating messages, and the feedback from the messages is also very limited. In fact, the influence of the recipients of media messages can only be indirect. This happens when certain ideas of the audience are included by the specialists designing the message to make it fit the audience. The specialists often make use of various social studies on reading or viewing figures, dominant problems (e.g., pedophilia), or society's opinions about certain issues (e.g., the presence of Polish and American troops in Iraq). In this way, the creators of media messages are also indirectly the agents of citizens' influence on the content of political communication.

The third important component of the model proposed by Negrine (1994) is recognizing that no one uniform public political communication exists, but rather a collection of different segments of viewers. Each of them has their own preferences related to newspapers or television channels from which they gain knowledge of the surrounding world.

The fourth characteristic of political communication is that the process of creating news requires some level of interaction or strategic negotiations between the sources of information and the media that diffuse it. For instance, such relations can be based on the promise that the informer will remain anonymous. On the other hand, media representatives may have the exclusive right to report some events. Such relations are then based on feedback. What finally reaches the audience is the result of such agreements or negotiations.

Negrine's model also focuses on the cognitive processes formed by media messages and the behavioral reactions resulting from them. They shape voters' beliefs about the importance of the media for political elections and strengthen voters' feelings that they participate in the decision-making process. It is such an understanding of the media (according to Newman's model) that allows it to be classified as a cognitive domain. The media's operationalization in structural models of voter behavior will be presented in the section titled "Structural Equation Models of Voter Behavior: A Constructivist Approach" in this chapter.

One attempt at a precise specification of the media's influence is Falkowski and Cwalina's sequential model of the influence of advertising on voting behavior (1999), developed further by Cwalina, Falkowski, and Kaid (2000, 2005). Because this model is based on cause-and-effect relations, as is the reconstruction of Newman's model, it is worthwhile to analyze this research concept more thoroughly.

SEQUENTIAL MODEL OF THE INFLUENCE OF POLITICAL ADVERTISEMENTS

Existing studies conducted in many countries confirm the hypothesis that political advertisements influence voters' changing image of a candidate and lead to a reconfiguration of the structure of features that make up his or her image (Falkowski, Cwalina, 1999; Cwalina, Falkowski, Kaid, 2000, 2005; Holtz-Bacha, Kaid, 1995; Kaid, Chanslor, 1995; Sullivan et al., 1990; Mazzoleni, Roper, 1995).

Most frequently a candidate's image is operationalized by semantic differential or other adjective scales (Kaid, 1995; Noller et al., 1988; Osgood, Suci, Tannenbaum, 1957). Some scientists use the measurements relating to a candidate's personality features (Douglas, 1972; Winter, 1995) as well as the analysis of his or her interpersonal communication behaviors (Harrison et al., 1991).

Despite different operationalizations of the notion of image, most scientists try to reduce the number of variables in their models (e.g., the number of adjective scales of the differential or the number of personality features used to describe the candidate) using the methodology of factor analysis. Such studies were conducted by Lynda Lee Kaid and her colleagues (Kaid, Gerstlé, Sanders, 1986; Kaid, Holtz-Bacha, 1995; Kaid, Nimmo, Sanders, 1986). In order to measure image, Kaid and Chanslor (1995) used a twelve-scale semantic differential, where each of the scales consisted of seven points. In both cases the research procedure consisted of a pretest and posttest, between which political advertisements were presented. Factor analysis was used to determine changes in candidate images at the two points in time, before and after viewing the ads, with the result that the researchers showed a compacting of Bush's image and a more substantial reconfiguration of Clinton's image. The results obtained by Kaid and Chanslor may turn out useful for people preparing an election campaign, because they allow some extent of control when creating an image of a candidate.

The hypothetical dynamic process of the impact of advertising on voting behavior is presented in Figure 6.2. The arrows indicate the causal relationship between the components. The model assumes that in order to recognize whether the television spots change voters' decisions, it is necessary to find a link between the following four components: (1) cognitive/affective elements (image), (2) general feelings toward the candidate, (3) intention for whom to vote, and (4) decision for whom to vote.

A causal link between these components, which can be presented as a sequential model of the influence of advertising on voting behaviors, is assumed. In most of the studies on the influence of a candidate's image presented in advertisements, cognitive and emotional elements were analyzed separately (Atkin, Heald, 1976; Kaid, Holtz-Bacha, 1995; Lott, Lott, Saris, 1993). On the other hand, the key element of the sequential model is that these elements are mutually connected and should not be analyzed separately. This model was adapted for each electorate separately; therefore, a given candidate's

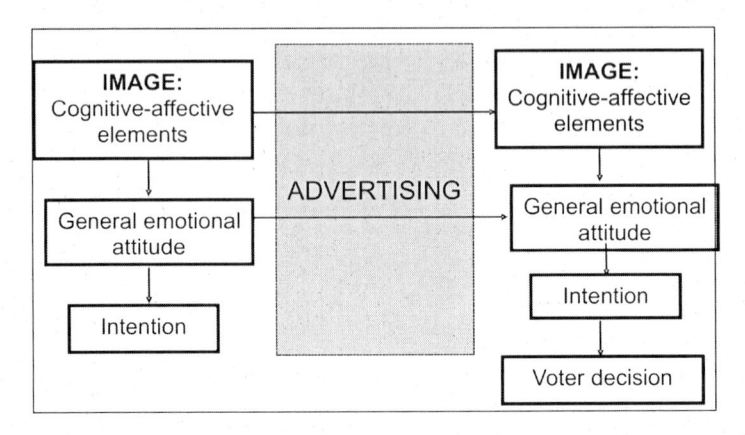

FIGURE 6.2. Sequential model of the influence of television spots on voting behavior. *Source:* Falkowski and Cwalina (1999), p. 228.

voters had to be selected very carefully. The division of voters into electorates is supported by the psychological knowledge from the sphere of social perception (see e.g. Argyle, 1983; Fiske, Taylor, 1991; Nisbett, Ross, 1980). It can then be assumed that each electorate perceives their candidate differently, depending upon whether or not they support him or her. This situation resembles the experiments with *switch gestalt* in which, looking at the same pictures, a person may see two different things (e.g., an old or a young woman, a rabbit or a duck, see Figure 2.2 in Chapter 2). Such a different perception of a political candidate depends upon psychographic variables (attitudes, systems of values) that characterize voters belonging to other electorates (see "Social Psychological Approach" in Chapter 4).

The results of the empirical testing of the sequential model of advertising's influence on voting behavior during the parliamentary elections in Germany in 1994 and the presidential elections in France in 1995, in Poland in 1995 and 2000, and in the United States in 2000 demonstrated that political advertising can influence voting decisions in three ways (Cwalina, Falkowski, Kaid, 2000, 2005). First, advertisements could strengthen the already existing voting preferences. Supporters of a given candidate confirm their support for their candidate, whereas opponents confirm their place in the opposition. In other words, the polarization of voting preferences increases. This can also be connected with a certain reconfiguration of the candidate's image in the minds of his or her electorate.

Second, advertisements could weaken the already existing voting preferences and, in extreme cases, may even cause a change. This influence leads to an increase in uncertainty among voters about whom to support. It is usually accompanied by a reconfiguration of the candidate's image.

Third, advertisements could neither weaken nor strengthen political preferences, but they could lead to the reconfiguration of the candidate's image in voters' minds. This type of influence can be called a cognitive influence because, as a result of it, the argumentation of a previously formed decision does change, but the direction and certainty with which it was made do not change.

Finally, no situation was found where advertising had no influence at all on voters. If the media and advertisements placed there always have an influence on voters, then it is fully justifiable to complete Newman and Sheth's model with a media component.

STRUCTURAL EQUATION MODELS OF VOTER BEHAVIOR: A CONSTRUCTIVIST APPROACH

This section presents an analysis of the research results according to the cause-and-effect model of voter behavior based on a constructivist approach in which cognitive domains influence emotional feelings. From a further perspective, one may think about a realistic approach, which points to the relevance of effects in forming the cognitive domains (see "Constructivism and Realism" in Chapter 2). This realistic approach in cause-and-effect models of voter behavior will be presented later in this chapter.

The distinction between the constructive and realistic approach demonstrates that political marketing strategy should follow the assumed and empirically tested epistemic background of voter behavior: Do voters recognize the political reality on an affective basis, or is affect a consequence of political cognition and the image that politicians have little in common with the real world? Thus, taking into account the simple sequence, *cognition* → *affect* or *affect* → *cognition*, we are using either a constructivist or realistic approach to perceive the social environment.

The division into constructivist and realistic paradigms in the research on voter behavior may better demonstrate the differences between traditional and evolving democracies. Some analyses of changes in voter behavior under the influence of political advertising in constructivist and realistic paradigms are presented by Cwalina and Falkowski (2003) in comparative research on Poland, France, and Germany. It would require developing a sequential model of the influence of political advertisements in the methodology of structural equation.

While proposing a reconstruction of Newman and Sheth's model of voter's choice behavior using structural equation methodology, it is necessary to consider the theoretical consequences of various causal dependencies between the variables mentioned in this model, with particular emphasis on the relationship between the emotional domain and the other six cognitive domains. We will start from a simple constructive structural model presented in Figure 6.3, which intuitively describes the dynamic process of voter behavior, and can be treated as the first hypothesis to be empirically tested. The results of the research presented in this chapter have already been published

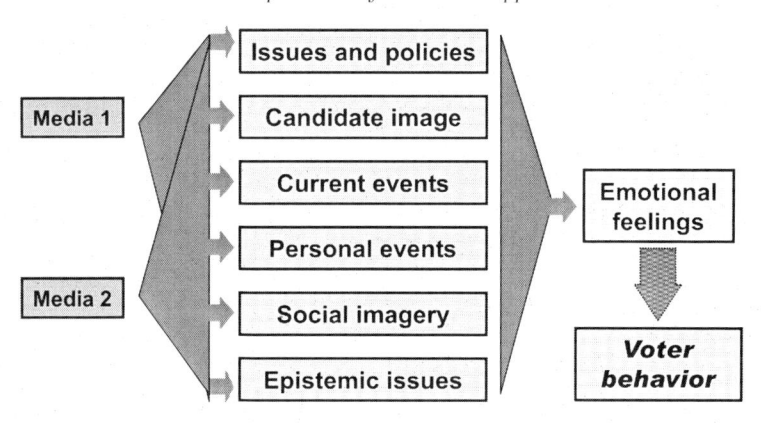

FIGURE 6.3. Structural equation model of voter behavior I. *Source:* Falkowski and Cwalina (2002), p. 144.

and presented in conferences by Falkowski and Cwalina (2002), Cwalina, Falkowski, Newman, and Verčič (2004), and Cwalina and Falkowski (2005b).

Figure 6.3 shows that it is intuitively obvious that the six cognitive domains concerning the candidate are shaped by the media. That is, the media are the cause, and each of the cognitive domains is the effect. The group of paths connecting the elements in question represents this assumption.

The next group of paths in this complex causal relationship connects the cognitive domains with emotional feelings. In Newman and Sheth's model, this element stands for a separate domain as one of the independent elements that influences a voter's choice. However, based on the results of the research on the relationship between emotions and voting intentions presented previously, it can be assumed that emotional feelings are a good predictor of voting intentions, i.e., the voter will choose the candidate who is "warmer," and evokes more positive emotions.

It is easy to see that different combinations of the structural model presented in Figure 6.4 can be presumed. It is quite reasonable to assume that the media also influence the voter's emotional feelings. Therefore, besides the paths from media to cognitive domains we can add an additional path that directly connects the media with emo-

158   A CROSS-CULTURAL THEORY OF VOTER BEHAVIOR

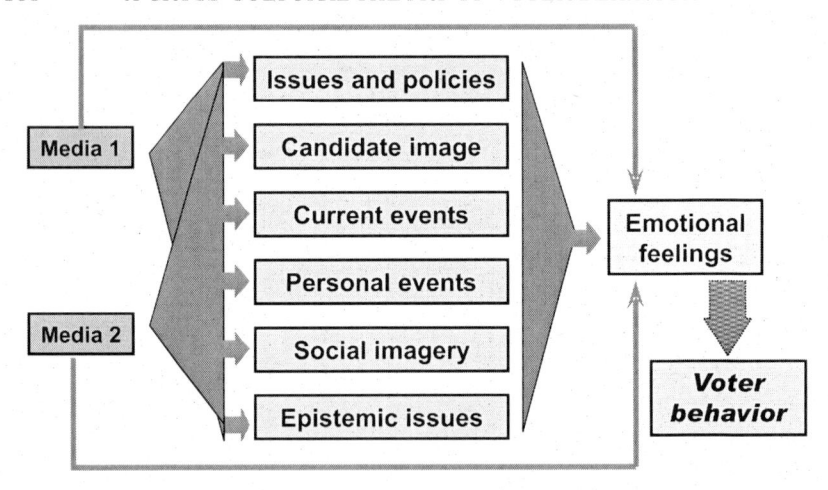

FIGURE 6.4. Structural equation model of voter behavior II. *Source:* Falkowski and Cwalina (2002), p. 145.

tional feelings. This second hypothesis is presented in Figure 6.4. It may also be assumed that a mutual interaction exists between the media and cognitive domains. That is, media influence the cognitive domains and cognitive domains influence the media.

The assumptions concerning the role of the media in forming voting preferences or even the political scene are corroborated by various studies (e.g. Ansolabehere, Iyengar, Simon, 1995; Chaffee, Zhao, Leshner, 1994). Many of them concentrate particularly on agenda-setting effects (McCombs, 1981; McCombs, Shaw, 1972). These analyses demonstrate that the subjects on which voters' discussions, as well as the attentions of political marketers, concentrate are selected by certain TV channels according to their information policy (Newman, 1994; Perloff, Kinsey, 1992). On the other hand, social and political events have a feedback influence on the contents of the media's message. Besides, this message is often based (sometimes unconsciously) on preferences and political beliefs of the creators of information programs or owners of a given channel. Voters also add their own interpretations of the information they receive, depending on their knowledge or ideology, which can be identified with particular domains of the model.

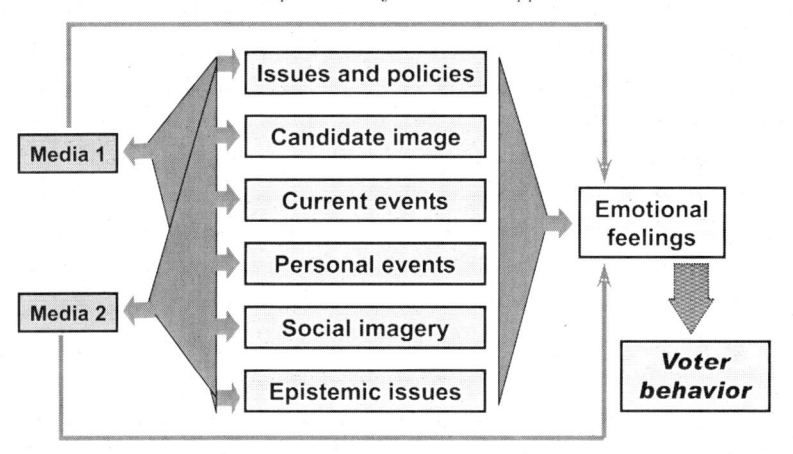

FIGURE 6.5. Structural equation model of voter behavior III. *Source:* Falkowski and Cwalina (2002), p. 146.

Figure 6.5 presents this third hypothesis of mutual relations between the media, cognitive domains, emotional feelings, and voter behavior. The empirical research was conducted in Poland, Slovenia, and the United States in 2000 during the presidential (Poland and United States) and parliamentary (Slovenia) elections.

During the presidential elections in Poland, the main candidates running for office were Aleksander Kwaśniewski, the incumbent, supported by leftist parties, and Andrzej Olechowski, the challenger, not connected with any political party, representing center-liberal options.

The 2000 U.S. presidential election pitted against each other candidates who had very different challenges. Al Gore, the vice president in the Clinton administration for the previous eight years, was working to separate himself from President Clinton in an effort to create his own identity. His opponent was a candidate of the Republican Party, Governor of Texas, George W. Bush.

In the parliamentary elections in Slovenia, based on pre-election polls by several research institutions, three political parties predicted to win the most votes were selected for the study. They were the LDS (Liberal Democrats of Slovenia), the ZLSD (United List of Social Democrats), and the SDS (Social Democrats of Slovenia).

Research Method

The same questionnaire was used for voters in each country. The only differences between particular versions of the questionnaire consisted in including political and social questions specific for particular countries (e.g., membership in the EU, cooperation with communist secret services, or caring about U.S. interests abroad).

The questionnaires used in Slovenia and the United States included the same set of questions about the supported candidate and the supported political party. This is particularly important in the case of research conducted in Slovenia during the parliamentary elections, where voters in different voting districts could vote for different representatives of the same party. Therefore, the research includes part of the questionnaire concerning the support and evaluation of the main political parties.

All the questionnaires consist of nine sections. The theoretical foundations of the questionnaire are included in Newman's original model of voter behavior (see Chapter 5).

Section 1: *Background questions* is concerned with political preferences. The subjects marked the candidate or party they were voting for during the elections. In addition, they defined their own political affiliation, their interest in politics, and the political options they supported (from left wing to right wing). The question about the candidate or party the subjects voted for was a question directing answers to other parts of the questionnaire. That is, in answering certain items, the subject always referred them to the given candidate and only to him.

Section 2: *Issues and policies* specifies the respondent-supporter views of the candidate's standing on the economy (nine items), foreign affairs (four items), and domestic social issues (seven items). The subjects had to mark whether their candidate supported a given issue or not.

Section 3: *Social imagery* included questions on what support, according to the respondent, his or her candidate or party received from various social groups (workers, farmers, entrepreneurs, religious believers, women, men, etc.). In the Polish version of the questionnaire, nineteen such groups were mentioned, in the Slovenian, ten, and in the American, fifteen. The respondent marked "yes" or "no" depending on whether his or her candidate would get support from representatives of a given group. The more groups the respondent marked, the wider social support the candidate or party enjoyed.

Section 4: *Candidate/party image and emotional feelings* is related to the image of and emotion toward the candidate (in the Slovenian sample, toward the party). This section consists of fourteen identical scales of semantic differential, among others: qualified/not qualified, honest/dishonest, trustworthy/untrustworthy (see Cwalina and Falkowski 1999; Kaid 1995), and a standard thermometer of feelings (from 0 to 100). In addition, the subjects were asked to mark whether the candidate they supported had the enumerated personal traits ("yes" or "no"). The Polish questionnaire included sixteen such traits, the American version, twelve, and the Slovenian, nine.

Section 5: *Current events* was concerned with the respondent's attitude to possible events that could change his or her voting decision. The Polish questionnaire included a list of ten such events, the American version, eight, and the Slovenian, five. The subject marked "yes" or "no" for every event, indicating whether he or she might transfer his or her vote to another candidate.

Section 6: *Personal/party events* included ten possible pieces of information from the candidate's personal life that could change the respondent's voting decision. The Polish and Slovenian questionnaire included a list of ten such events, whereas the American version had nine. The subject marked "yes" or "no" for every event, indicating whether or not he or she might transfer his or her vote to another candidate if such an event occurred.

Section 7: *Epistemic issues* refers to reasons that would justify the perceived satisfaction of curiosity, knowledge, and exploratory needs offered by the candidate/party. The Polish questionnaire included a list of twelve such reasons, whereas the American and Slovenian questionnaires had ten reasons each. The subject marked "yes" or "no" for every reason, indicating whether it was the basis of his or her choice.

Section 8 of the questionnaire referred to the media. The respondents expressed their own opinions on several five-point Likert scales (from 1—"strongly agree" to 5—"strongly disagree") on the influence of the media and polls on voting decisions and democratic processes. The Polish and the Slovenian versions consisted of seven items each, and the American poll had nine.

Finally, Section 9 covered such demographical information as gender, age, education, occupation, family status, income, and place of residence.

Structural Equation Models in the Polish Presidential Election of 2000

Empirical research was conducted all over Poland in November 2000, a month after the Polish presidential election. Respondents were chosen randomly, taking into account demographic features. Out of 240 respondents, men were 45 percent of the sample, women, 54.17 percent.[1] As far as age is concerned, the 45 percent of the sample consisted of respondents between 18 and 29 years of age, 29.17 percent of the sample were between 30 and 44 years old, and 25 percent of the sample were above the age of 44. The percentage of respondents with a primary and vocational education was 12.92, 57.91 percent with a secondary education, and 27.92 percent with a higher education. The majority of the respondents, 52.92 percent, came from big cities, whereas 31.67 percent came from small towns, and 14.58 percent from rural areas.

During the first and the last balloting, twelve candidates participated in the Polish presidential election. On the basis of the respondents' marked voting records, the research sample was divided into twelve electorates. Only two candidates were seriously considered in the election process: Aleksander Kwaśniewski, the incumbent, and Andrzej Olechowski, the challenger. In the research sample, Kwaśniewski received 52.9 percent of the votes while Olechowski got 34.5 percent. The official results of the Polish presidential election show that Kwaśniewski obtained 54.5 percent, and Olechowski received 17.4 percent.

Therefore, in our analysis, we have taken into account only the two dominant candidates, as only their sample research electorates are sufficiently large to enable us to perform statistical analysis. In the end, data received from 208 respondents were analyzed, 126 of whom were supporters of Kwaśniewski and 82 supporters of Olechowski.

---

[1] Percents do not add up to 100 percent because not every respondent completed the section on demographic characteristics.

Emotional Feelings As a Predictor of Voter Behavior

Unfortunately, the data obtained do not allow us to determine directly the connection between emotional feelings measured by the feeling thermometer and the respondent's voting behavior, because the respondents mentioned the candidate they were voting for and then, in the following parts of the questionnaire, they described their beliefs concerning only this particular candidate. Therefore, it is impossible to compare emotional feelings of the same respondent toward different candidates. However, based on the results of previous research on the power of this relationship, it is possible to conduct some indirect analyses on the collected data (see Table 6.1).

Among Kwaśniewski's electorate, the average temperature of feelings toward him was $M_K = 69.77$ ($\sigma_K = 14.64$), whereas among Olechowski's electorate it was $M_O = 68.49$ ($\sigma_O = 17.71$). It can be assumed that for the whole population, the average is $\mu = 50$, since the distribution of the temperature of feelings is a normal distribution and has no known standard deviation (Cwalina and Falkowski, 1999). Therefore, if the temperatures toward Kwaśniewski and Olechowski are considerably higher than the average for the population, then it is legitimate to say that voters voted for the "warmer" candidate.

In order to verify this hypothesis, a test was conducted for the average in the population with the unknown standard deviation based on students' t-distribution (Blalock, 1960). Both in Kwaśniewski's and Olechowski's case, the average temperature of their supporters differed considerably from the average in the population: $t = 15.03$, $df = 124$, $p < .001$; and $t = 9.28$, $df = 79$, $p < .001$, respectively. The average of feelings toward these two candidates did not differ considerably from one another ($t = 0.56$, $df = 203$, $p = .58$). Therefore, it can be assumed that the respondents actually voted for the candidate toward whom they had more positive emotional attitudes.

Media

In order to simplify the structure of data with reference to the importance of the media in forming voting preferences, we conducted a principal component analysis on the items from the media section in the questionnaires separately for Kwaśniewski's and Olechowski's electorates. We obtained two different factors for each of them (see Table 6.2).

Among Kwaśniewski's electorate, a two-factor solution was obtained, which accounts for 58.07 percent of the total variance. The first factor, called "Media 1," refers to the media and polls in elections and explains 40.97 percent of the variance, whereas the second factor, defined as "Media 2," may be defined as money and media in democracy (17.09 percent). Among Olechowski's electorate, two factors

TABLE 6.2. Results of the principal component analysis for the media.

Aleksander Kwaśniewski		Andrzej Olechowski	
Media 1 *Media and polls in elections*	40.97 percent	**Media 1** *Polls and money in elections*	27.39 percent
I used information from the media to make my choice in this election.	0.82	I used information from the polls to make my choice in this election.	0.79
The media serves a useful role in elections.	0.56	Polls serve a useful role in elections.	0.76
I used information from the polls to make my choice in this election.	0.80	Money has influence on the media.	0.54
Polls serve a useful role in elections.	0.69		
Media 2 *Money & media in democracy*	17.09 percent	**Media 2** *Media in elections & democracy*	15.72 percent
I think that polling strengthens democracy.	0.55	I used information from the media to make my choice in this election.	0.49
I think that advertising strengthens democracy.	0.71	The media serves a useful role in elections.	0.64
Money has influence on the media.	0.74	I think that polling strengthens democracy.	0.48
		I think that advertising strengthens democracy.	0.67
Total variance accounted for	58.07 percent		43.11 percent

Source: Falkowski and Cwalina (2002), p. 149.

were also distinguished which accounted for 43.11 percent of the total variance. Media 1 for Olechowski is 27.39 percent, and Media 2 is 15.72 percent.

The previously mentioned factor solutions were used in testing individual structural equation models, depending on a given candidate's electorate. The results of factor analysis on the items from the media section in the questionnaires are presented separately for Kwaśniewski's and Olechowski's electorates.

In order to verify the structural models, a methodology based on the analysis of structural equations was used, defined also as path analysis (see Loehlin, 1987). This is a statistical method making it possible to verify hypotheses concerning the structure of causal dependencies in a defined set of variables.

Figure 6.6 presents the empirical structural equation model I for Aleksander Kwaśniewski. The arrows represent relevant statistical relations between particular elements of the model. A relevant statistically standardized parameter of the path was marked above each arrow. The bold arrows represent a "complete" causal sequence, that is, one starting from media and finishing with voter behavior. The arrow connecting emotional feelings with voter behavior represents a hypothetical established connection between these domains.

The structural solution presented in Figure 6.6 does not meet the statistical requirements of a good fit ($\chi^2 = 258.91$, $p < .001$). Therefore, we have to reject model I for Kwaśniewski as it doesn't fit

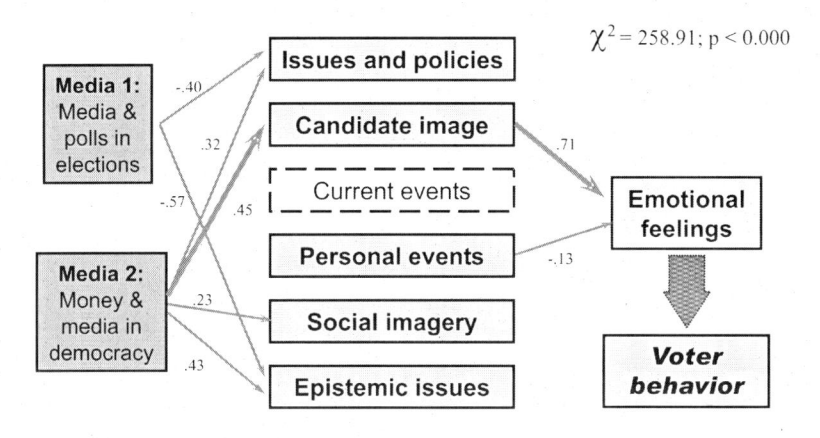

FIGURE 6.6. Empirical structural equation model of voter behavior I: Aleksander Kwaśniewski. *Source:* Falkowski and Cwalina (2002), p. 150.

the empirical data. However, some paths are significant. The cognitive domains that "warm up" the voters' feelings toward Kwaśniewski are: positive candidate image and lack of important personal events. The media significantly influence four domains: issues and policies, social imagery, candidate image, and personal events. Besides, only one "complete" causal sequence (bold arrows) is shown on the figure. The more the respondents recognize the importance of money and media in democracy, the more positive Kwaśniewski's image seems to them. This, as a result, leads to an increase in emotional attitudes toward him and finally influences their voting behavior.

A somewhat different picture emerges when we look at this same structural model concerning Olechowski's electorate (see Figure 6.7). This model also does not fit the empirical data ($\chi^2 = 123.25$, $p < .001$). Nevertheless, it is worth noticing that the path structure differs from that of Kwaśniewski's model. It seems that the media impact is lower than in model I for Kwaśniewski, as only three cognitive domains—social imagery, candidate image, and epistemic issues—are significantly influenced by this factor. Emotional feelings toward Olechowski depend on three domains: issues and policies, social imagery and candidate image. However, in the case of the two first domains, it is a negative relation (negative parameters of the path).

Two "complete" causal sequences were distinguished: Media 2 (media in elections and democracy) → candidate image → emotional feelings, and Media 2 → social imagery → emotional feelings. It is

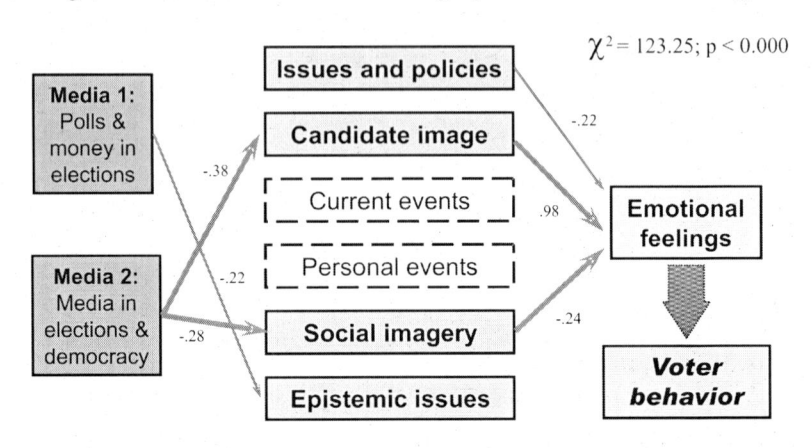

FIGURE 6.7. Empirical structural equation model of voter behavior I: Andrzej Olechowski. *Source:* Falkowski and Cwalina (2002), p. 151.

interesting to observe that if the respondents believe the media play a large role, it influences in a negative way both Olechowski's image and the perceived social support for him.

In the hypothetical structural model presented in Figure 6.4, two paths were added that directly connect the media with the thermometer feeling. The fit of the model to empirical data is better than in the previous Kwaśniewski model; however, it is still very poor ($\chi^2 =$ 173.22, $p < .001$). The path structure is presented in Figure 6.8.

The media influence most of the cognitive domains, but only personal events impact emotional attitudes. The hypothetical, direct connections between the perception of the media's role and emotions toward Kwaśniewski turned out to be statistically irrelevant; however, adding them to the initial model II changed the structure of the paths in the empirical model II. No "complete" causal sequence occurred.

The path structure for Olechowski also didn't change with reference to model I at all, except that the χ^2 is lower than in the first model ($\chi^2 = 115.52$, $p < .001$), but still its goodness-of-fit is very weak. The empirical model II for Olechowski is presented in Figure 6.9. The significant paths are similar to those obtained in the case of the empirical model I for Olechowski. Also, the "complete" causal sequences are connected with the same domains as in the previous case.

The better fit of model II to the empirical data of Kwaśniewski's and Olechowski's electorates show that the media's influence on emotional feelings toward the candidates does make sense. It is use-

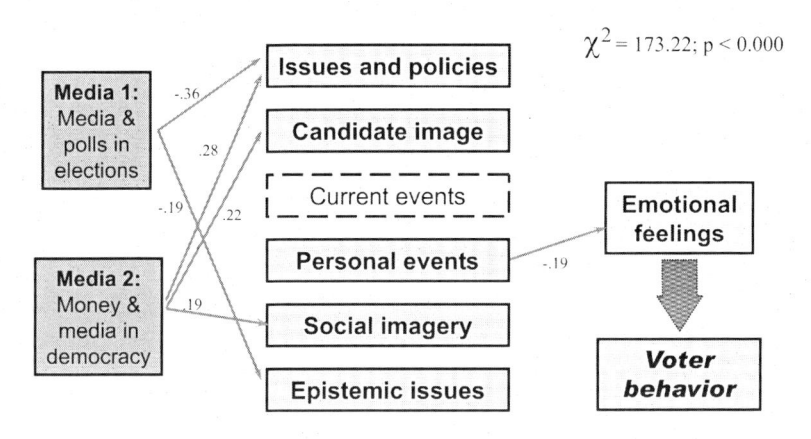

FIGURE 6.8. Empirical structural equation model of voter behavior II: Aleksander Kwaśniewski. *Source:* Falkowski, Cwalina (2002), p. 152.

ful to remember that "media" is understood here as the voters' beliefs that the media exert an influence on elections.

The final, third model assumes the mutual relationship between the media and the six cognitive domains, and all six domains plus the media directly influence the thermometer. This hypothetical model is presented in Figure 6.5. The results of fitting model III to the empirical data of Kwaśniewski's electorate are presented in Figure 6.10.

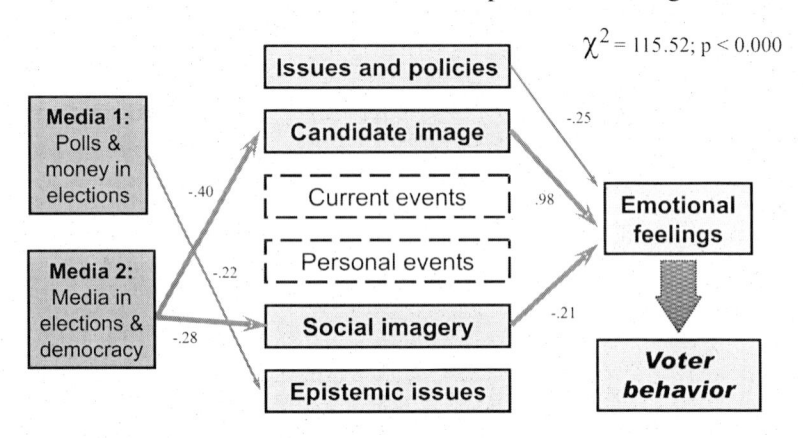

FIGURE 6.9. Empirical structural equation model of voter behavior II: Andrzej Olechowski. *Source:* Falkowski and Cwalina (2002), p. 153.

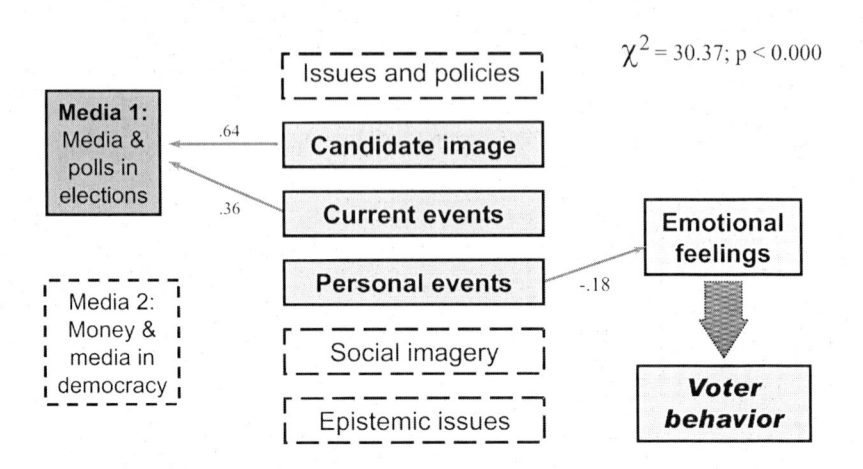

FIGURE 6.10. Empirical structural equation model of voting behavior III: Aleksander Kwaśniewski. *Source:* Falkowski and Cwalina (2002), p. 153.

The goodness-of-fit model parameter ($\chi^2 = 30.37$, $p < .001$) allows us to treat this model as an adequate approximation of the empirical data. The model structure shows that only three paths are significant: candidate image, current events influence media, and personal events exert a negative impact on emotional feelings. No "complete" causal sequence was found in Figure 6.10.

The empirical model III structure describing Olechowski's electorate is much more complex (see Figure 6.11). The χ^2 coefficient ($\chi^2 = 19.10$, $p < .005$) is the lowest of all, and even though it is not fully satisfactory, it allows us to treat this model as an adequate fit for the empirical data.

We see that the media influence some of the cognitive domains as much as the cognitive domains influence the media. Media 1, polls and money in elections, influence emotional attitudes toward Olechowski. As in the case of model III for Kwaśniewski, no "complete" causal sequence was found.

Structural Equation Models in the Slovenian Parliamentary Election of 2000

The study was carried out approximately two weeks before the parliamentary elections (October 15, 2000) in the electoral district of Vrhnika, a suburban area near Ljubljana, the capital of Slovenia. This

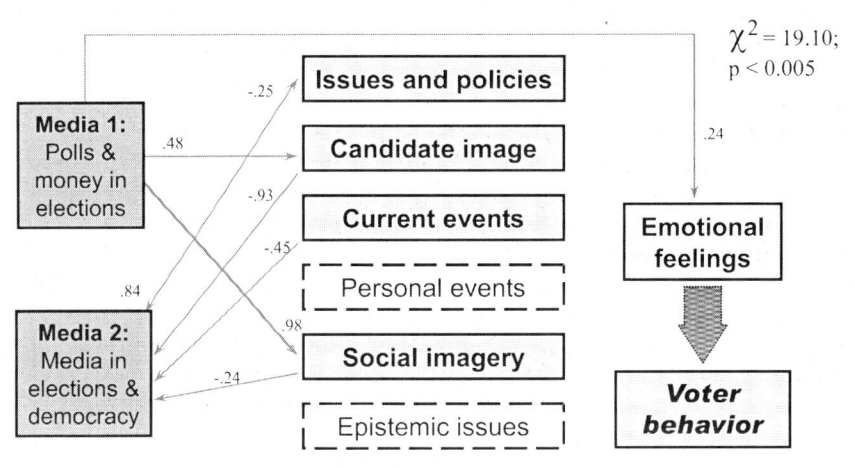

FIGURE 6.11. Empirical structural equation model of voter behavior III: Andrzej Olechowski. *Source:* Falkowski and Cwalina (2002), p. 154.

district was selected based on the similarity of its electoral result (on the party level) to previous (1996) parliamentary elections.

Respondents were interviewed via telephone. Interviewing started two weeks before the elections and was completed in four days. The computer-assisted telephone interviewing (CATI) was used to obtain respondents' intentions regarding voting. The day after the elections, a postelection contact was made with the respondents of the study to obtain information on the electoral decision of the respondents of the previous day.

The study was carried out on samples of 200 voters per each selected major Slovenian political party (LDS, ZLSD, and SDS). Random sampling was based on households and the respondents within them, and 4,564 contacts and 617 interviews were made in accordance with the sampling procedures before the elections.

The day after the elections, 87.5 percent of the original sample (N = 519) were interviewed to obtain data on the actual voting decision. The average age of the researched subjects was 48.4 years (σ = 16.5). The sample consisted of 59 percent women and 41 percent men. The percentage of the subjects with either a secondary or lower education was 21 percent, 68 percent were attending or graduated from a college, and 11 percent had a graduate degree.

In the Slovenian preelection purposive research sample in Vrhnika, the LDS received 33.5 percent of the votes; the ZLSD, 31.9 percent; and the SDS, 31.4 percent. In the postelection research sample, the LDS was supported by 33.2 percent of respondents, the ZLSD by 22.5 percent, and the SDS by 18.0 percent. The official results for Vrhinka were: LDS, 35.47 percent; ZLSD, 12.39 percent; and SDS, 22.13 percent; and for Slovenia as a whole: LDS received 36.26 of the votes; ZLSD, 12.08 percent; and SDS, 15.81 percent. Because the number of SDS supporters was so small, they were excluded from further analyses. These analyses are based on post-election reports about voting behavior.

As in the Polish case, in the Slovenian research, the principal component analysis of items from the media section in the questionnaires was also done separately for LDS and ZLSD. Two factors were obtained for each of the parties, Media 1 and Media 2.

The two-factor solution for the LDS electorate accounts for 52.12 percent of the total variance: Media 1, election polls, explaining the 33.91 percent variance, and Media 2, media and money in election, explaining the 18.21 percent variance. For the ZLSD electorate, a two-factor solution accounted for 50.77 percent of the total variance. Media 1 refers to the "polls and information in election" and explains the 32.22 percent total variance. Media 2 refers to the "money and media in election" and explains the 18.55 percent total variance.

Similar to the analysis of the Polish sample, the structural solutions for model I and model II for LDS and ZLSD were much worse than in the case of model III. The respective good fit indices are presented in Table 6.3.

Because of the best fit of model III (it differs significantly from the fit of the other models), only the results of the path analysis for this model will be discussed in detail.

For LDS, the results of the fit of structural equation model III for empirical data can be assumed to be satisfactory ($\chi^2 = 4.77$, p = .573). Two domains, the party image and the epistemic issue, have a direct and positive influence upon voters' emotional attitude toward LDS, and current events have a negative influence. Figure 6.12 illustrates the party's voting situation.

The more positive a party image, the more reasons that exist for choosing it, and the more positive an attitude toward it. The more negative the direction of domestic and international events' development, the less positive the attitudes become toward LDS. It is important to

TABLE 6.3. Structural equation models' goodness-of-fit for LDS and ZLSD.

	LDS	ZLSD
Structural equation model I	$\chi^2 = 25.66$; df = 18; p = 0.108	$\chi^2 = 55.44$; df = 18; p < 0.000 [b]
Structural equation model II	$\chi^2 = 25.35$; df = 16; p = 0.064 [c]	$\chi^2 = 53.52$; df = 16; p < 0.000 [c]
Structural equation model III	$\chi^2 = 4.77$; df = 6; p = 0.573 [c]	$\chi^2 = 23.07$; df = 17; p = 0.147 [b, c]

[a] – significant difference between model I and II

[b] – significant difference between model I and III

[c] – significant difference between model II and III.

Level of significance p < 0.001; in the case of LDS[c] – p < 0.05.

Source: Cwalina et al. (2004), p. 22.

172   A CROSS-CULTURAL THEORY OF VOTER BEHAVIOR

$\chi^2 = 4.77; p = 0.57$

[Diagram: Structural equation model with boxes for "Issues and policies", "Party image", "Current events", "Party events", "Social imagery", "Epistemic issues" (dashed: "Media 1: Polls in election", "Media 2: Media & money in election") with paths .23, -.30, .24 leading to "Emotional feelings" → "Voter behavior"]

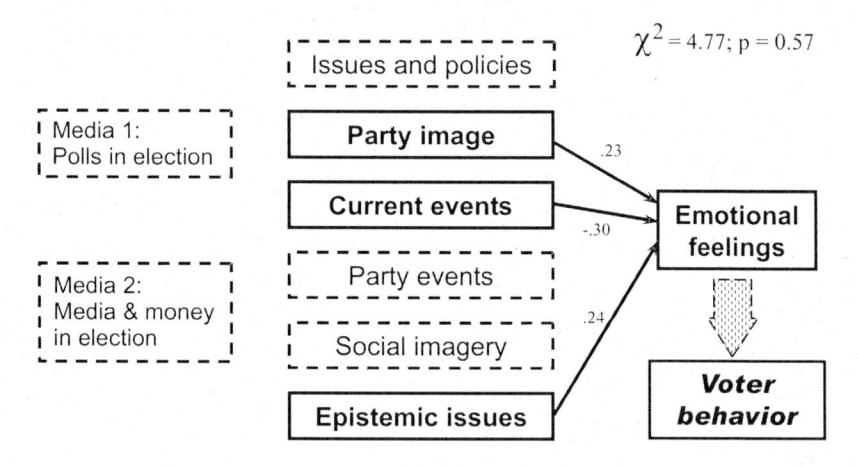

FIGURE 6.12. Empirical structural equation model of voter behavior III: LDS. *Source:* Cwalina et al. (2004), p. 22.

notice that the convictions regarding the function of the media in elections do not have any influence on the voters' decision making. From the marketing point of view, the support seems relatively independent of various situational factors that may occur during election campaigns (e.g., relations in the media, position in polls).

For ZLSD, the results of the fit of structural equation model III to the empirical data can be assumed to be satisfactory ($\chi^2 = 23.07$, p = .147; see Table 6.2). The results of the analysis are presented graphically in Figure 6.13.

In the case of ZLSD, the model is quite complex. The attitudes toward this party are positively influenced by issues and policies, party image, social imagery and epistemic issues, and current events have a negative impact on the evaluation of the party. If voters perceive that the political platform of the party might provide a chance for a better economic and social future of Slovenia, their support for ZLSD is higher. Furthermore, as previously stated, the more positive the party image, the more reasons that exist for choosing it, and the higher the social support for the party, the more positive the feelings toward it. Conversely, the more negative the direction of domestic and international events, the less positive the attitudes toward ZLSD.

Unlike the supporters of LDS, however, voters of ZLSD perceive the connections between the function of the media in elections and

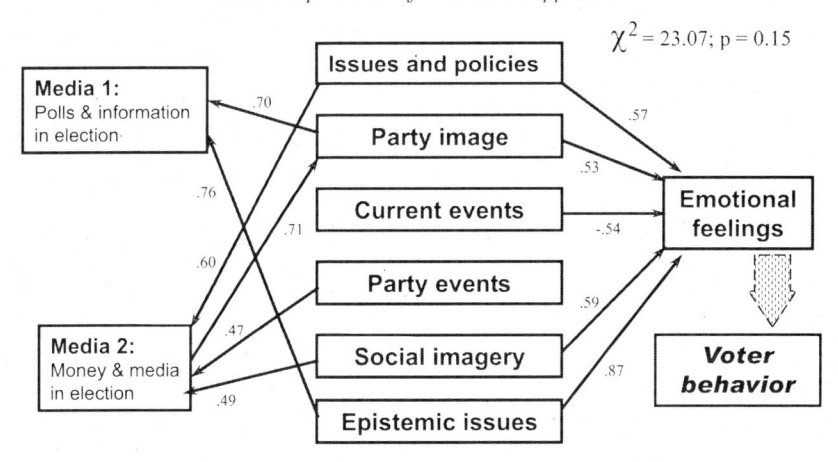

FIGURE 6.13. Empirical structural equation model of voter behavior III: ZLSD. *Source:* Cwalina et al. (2004), p. 23.

some cognitive domains referring to a particular politician. The voters' beliefs of the low relevance of "money and media in the election" connect it with the increase of the positive perception of party image. On the other hand, the relevance of money and media is negatively influenced by the political platform, social support increase, and negative personal events, which can be revealed about the candidate. The low relevance attributed to "polls and information in the election" are influenced by the number of reasons for supporting ZLSD and a positive party image.

From the marketing point of view, ZLSD supporters are more susceptible to different campaign influences. Their voting behavior depends on various factors: party image, political platform, motivation, perception of social support, and current events. Some of them are connected with the role of the media in elections and democracy. This complex pattern of connections seems to afford more possibilities for influence by marketing consultants.

Structural Equation Models in the U.S. Presidential Election of 2000

The study was carried out in Chicago, Illinois, approximately two weeks before the U.S. presidential election of 2000. The study was carried out on 151 students, faculty, and staff of DePaul University. The sample included a slightly younger, better-educated sample of voters than one would find in the population as a whole. Approximately two-thirds of the voters in both the Republican and Democratic parties were loyal to their party. Whereas close to 45 percent of the voters were very interested in the results of the election, only 2 percent were concerned about the outcome. This last statistic indicates that this was an election that was not very exciting for voters. Respondents were asked to fill out a survey before they voted, and to indicate their intention on the questionnaire.

Women constituted 68.5 percent of the sample, and men 31.5 percent. Thirty-nine percent of the subjects were between 18 and 30 years of age, 22 percent between 31 and 45, and 39 percent over 45. Fourteen percent of the subjects had either a secondary or lower education, 60 percent were attending or had graduated from a college, and 26 percent had a graduate degree.

In the U.S. research sample, Gore received 53.2 percent of the votes, while Bush received 43.5 percent. The official results of the U.S. presidential election show that Bush obtained 271 electoral votes and 47.89 percent of the popular vote, whereas Gore received 266 electoral votes and 48.40 percent of the popular vote.

The principal component analysis used for media section items for George W. Bush and Al Gore separately gave two-factor solutions. For the Bush electorate, the factors account for 43.74 percent of the total variance. Media 1 refers to "media and polls' informativeness," and explains 30.22 percent of the variance. Media 2, called "money and polls' influence," accounts for 13.52 percent of the variance. Two factors in the Gore electorate accounted for 48.7 percent of the total variance. The first one, Media 1, refers to "media in election and democracy" (33.64 percent variance), while the second one, Media 2, refers to "polls and money in election" (15.06 percent variance).

As in the case of the analyses on the Polish and Slovenian samples, the structural solutions for model I and model II for Bush and Gore do not meet the statistical requirements of a good fit and were much worse than in the case of model III. The respective good fit indices are presented in Table 6.4.

Because of the best fit of Model III (it differs significantly from the fit of the other models), only the results of the path analysis for this model will be discussed in detail.

Figure 6.14 presents the structural equation model III for George W. Bush, whose fit to empirical data is excellent ($\chi^2 = 7.12$, p = .52). What is characteristic here is a lack of dependence on emotional feelings both on cognitive domains and the media, and the occurrence of only three relevant causal dependencies between the domains and the

TABLE 6.4. Structural equation models' goodness-of-fit for George W. Bush and Al Gore.

	George W. Bush	Al Gore
Structural equation model I	$\chi^2 = 36.95$; df=18; p < 0.01 [b]	$\chi^2 = 55.99$; df = 18; p < 0.000 [b]
Structural equation model II	$\chi^2 = 34.51$; df = 16; p < 0.005 [c]	$\chi^2 = 51.05$; df = 16; p < 0.000 [c]
Structural equation model III	$\chi^2 = 7.12$; df=8; p = 0.52 [b, c]	$\chi^2 = 7.73$; df = 6; p = 0.26 [b, c]

[a] – significant difference between model I and II

[b] – significant difference between model I and III

[c] – significant difference between model II and III.

Level of significance p < 0.001

Source: Cwalina et al. (2004), p. 24.

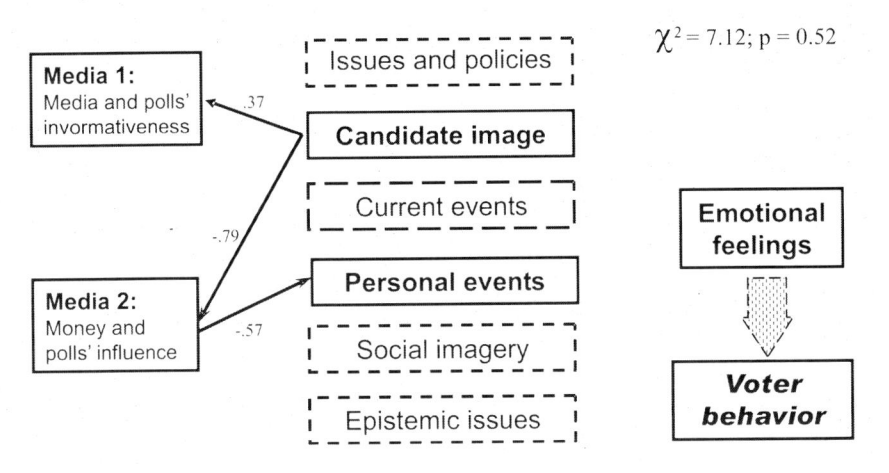

FIGURE 6.14. Empirical structural equation model of voter behavior III: George W. Bush. Source: Cwalina et al. (2004), p. 25.

media. Candidate image and personal events are directly connected with the media; however, changes in these domains, which are the result of their mutual interaction, do not translate into voting behavior. The more positive Bush's image, the greater the belief of his voters in the media's and the polls' informative function during the elections, and the smaller the relevance given to the influence of the media and the polls on their result. It suggests that on the one hand, the supporters of this candidate would like information about his strengths disseminated; on the other hand, however, they are very cautious about the quality and power of information presented by the media. Also, the smaller the relevance of the published poll results, the greater the relevance of unfavorable information about the candidate that may appear.

A similarly small number of causal dependencies occurred only in Poland with Kwaśniewski (see Figure 6.10). It suggests that Bush's electorate is stable and determined to support their candidate. As far as voter behavior is concerned, the supporters of this candidate are not sensitive to any situational factors, such as the relevance and the mutual influence of the media and cognitive domains.

The structural model III for Al Gore, presented in Figure 6.15, is more complex compared to the model for his opponent. The fit of this model to empirical data is very good ($\chi^2 = 7.73$, p = .26; see Table 6.4). No emotional feelings toward Gore directly influence issues and

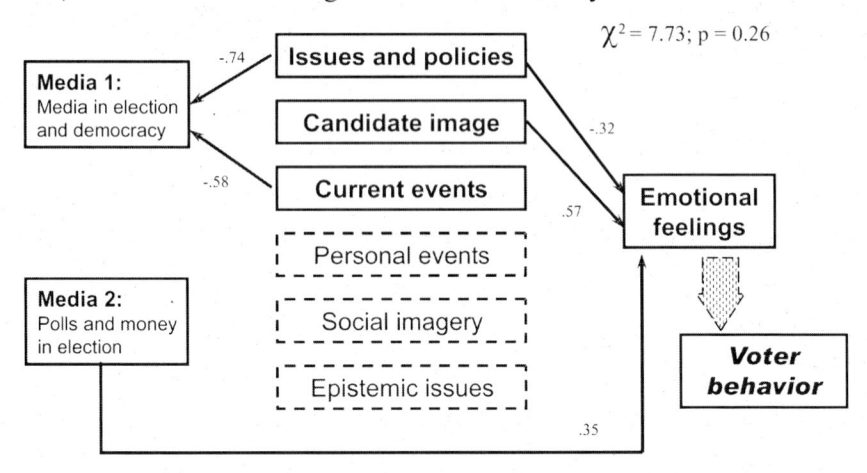

FIGURE 6.15. Empirical structural equation model of voter behavior III: Al Gore. *Source:* Cwalina et al. (2004), p. 26.

policies, candidate image, and Media 2: polls and money in the election. The more negative (more liberal) the candidate's attitude toward political issues, the more positive evaluation is given to him. In addition, emotions toward him become more favorable when Gore's image is more positive and the perceived influence of polls and money in the election is smaller. From a marketing point of view, therefore, it is possible to influence the behavior of Gore's voting electorate—unlike in the case of Bush's supporters. By presenting a more positive and coherent or a more negative image of Gore and presenting his campaign platform, it is possible to reinforce his voters in the decisions they have taken or to discourage them from supporting him.

The idea of "media in an election and democracy" depends on the issues and policies and current events cognitive domains. The more liberal the attitude toward political and economic issues and the higher the possibility of unfavorable political events happening, ones that could be a hindrance to Vice President Al Gore, the smaller the relevance Democratic voters give to the function of the media in elections and democracy. This suggests that they are ready to use the defense mechanism of denial, defending their views and their candidate.

STRUCTURAL EQUATION MODELS OF VOTER BEHAVIOR: A REALISTIC APPROACH

According to the realistic approach, the cognitive domains are formed in voters' minds on the basis of affect toward the candidate. Thus, Figure 6.16 presents the first hypothetical model assuming causal relationship between affect and cognitive domains. The structure of causal relationships is intuitively obvious here: the media influences emotional feelings which, in turn, form voter's cognitive domains, directly influencing voter choice. The assumption for this model, namely, that emotions influence the cognitive domains, is based on Zajonc's (1980) cognitive theory of affect and the results of Wattenberg's (1994) research on political behavior (see Chapter 2).

Different combinations of the structural model can also be assumed, as it is quite reasonable to presume that emotional feelings exert a direct influence not only on cognitive domains, but also on the media. Figure 6.17 presents this hypothesis. It may also be assumed that a mutual interaction exists between the media and emotional feelings. That is, the media influences the affect and the affect influences the media, as presented in Figure 6.18.

This model assumes that broadcast messages not only evoke the affect but are also perceived in the context of a voter's emotional feelings. It is well known in psychological literature that evoked emotions cause a different perception of events. Voters add their own interpretations of the information they receive, depending on their emotional state (Newirt, 2003).

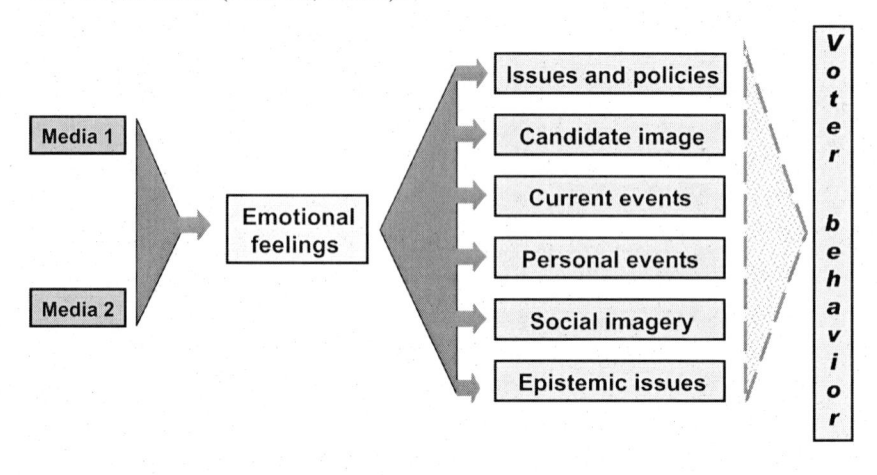

FIGURE 6.16. Structural model of voter behavior I.

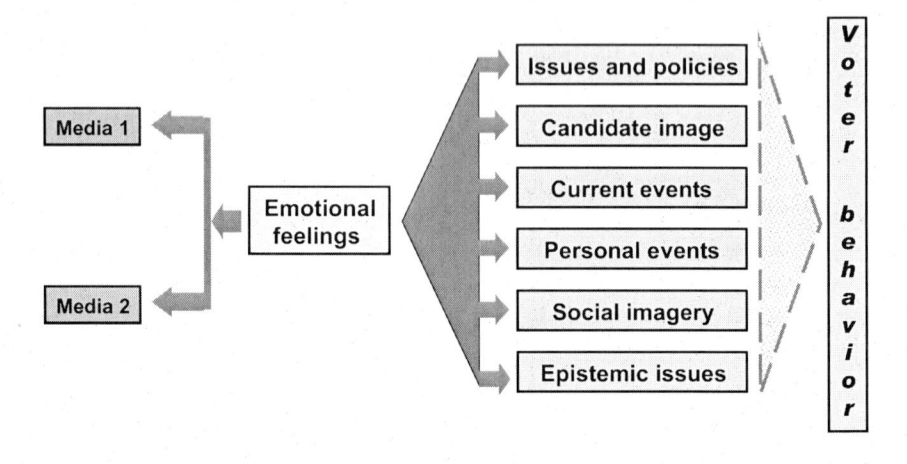

FIGURE 6.17. Structural model of voter behavior II.

A Reinterpretation of Newman's Approach 179

Each one of the three presented models can be further differentiated depending on the causal connections between the media and cognitive domains. Thus, it can be assumed that Media 1 and Media 2 influence cognitive domains, cognitive domains influence Media 1 and Media 2, or there is a mutual interaction between these variables. An example of the structural equations that underlie model I is presented in Figure 6.19.

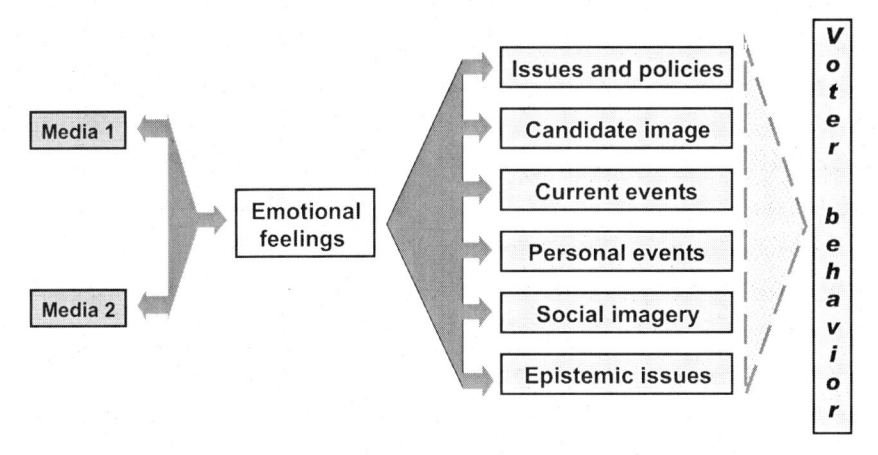

FIGURE 6.18. Structural model of voter behavior III.

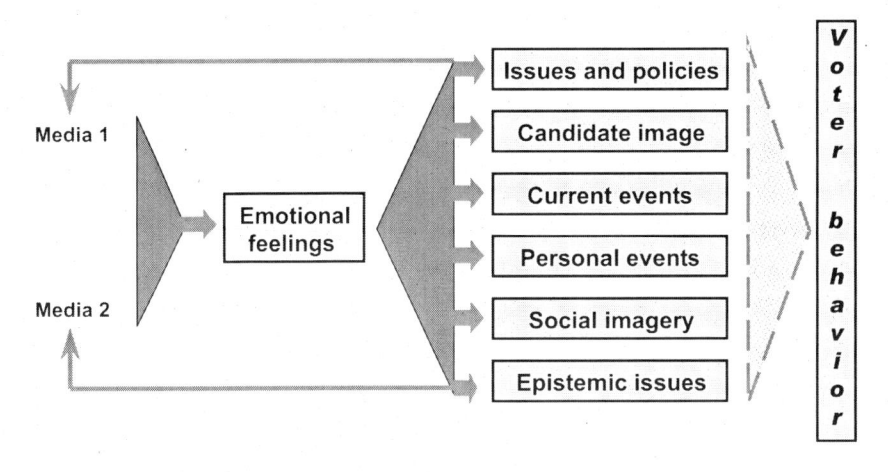

FIGURE 6.19. Structural model of voter behavior IV.

Here we see that in addition to the causal relations presented in Figure 6.16, it is assumed that a mutual and direct influence exists between the media and cognitive domains. This means that the particular shape of cognitive domains in voters' minds is the result of the direct influence of broadcast messages and emotions. On the other hand, the way the broadcast messages are perceived depends on already formed cognitive domains. That means that the media and cognitive domains reinforce one another.

The same empirical material was used for testing the models as the material that was used to analyze voter behavior according to the constructive approach. Empirical data from Poland and the United States was used for the present analysis (see "Structural Equation Models of Voter Behavior: A Constructivist Approach" in this chapter).

Structural Equation Models in the Polish Presidential Election of 2000

The fit of data for models I, II, and III for Kwaśniewski and Olechowski was much worse than in the case of model IV. It should also be stressed that model IV explains the data much better than the models including causal connections between media and cognitive domains added to the second and third model. The good fit indices ($\chi 2$) for each of the four models is presented in Table 6.5. Because model IV has the best fit (it differs significantly from the fit of the other models), only the results of path analysis for this model will be discussed in detail. Figure 6.20 presents the empirical structural equation model IV for Aleksander Kwaśniewski.

TABLE 6.5. Structural equation models' goodness-of-fit for Aleksander Kwaśniewski and Andrzej Olechowski.

	Aleksander Kwaśniewski	Andrzej Olechowski
Structural equation model I	$\chi^2 = 179.67$; $p < 0.001$	$\chi^2 = 88.98$; $p < 0.001$
Structural equation model II	$\chi^2 = 179.86$; $p < 0.001$	$\chi^2 = 89.94$; $p < 0.001$
Structural equation model III	$\chi^2 = 153.95$; $p < 0.001$	$\chi^2 = 83.59$; $p < 0.001$
Structural equation model IV	$\chi^2 = 24.89$; $p < 0.001$	$\chi^2 = 8.75$; $p = 0.188$

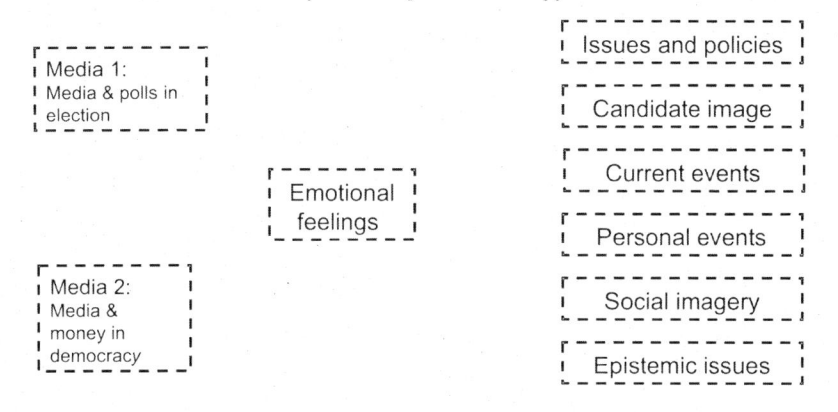

```
┌──────────────┐                              ┌─────────────────────┐
│ Media 1:     │                              │ Issues and policies │
│ Media & polls in │                          └─────────────────────┘
│ election     │                              ┌─────────────────────┐
└──────────────┘                              │  Candidate image    │
                                              └─────────────────────┘
                     ┌─────────────┐          ┌─────────────────────┐
                     │ Emotional   │          │  Current events     │
                     │  feelings   │          └─────────────────────┘
                     └─────────────┘          ┌─────────────────────┐
                                              │  Personal events    │
┌──────────────┐                              └─────────────────────┘
│ Media 2:     │                              ┌─────────────────────┐
│ Media &      │                              │  Social imagery     │
│ money in     │                              └─────────────────────┘
│ democracy    │                              ┌─────────────────────┐
└──────────────┘                              │  Epistemic issues   │
                                              └─────────────────────┘
```

$\chi^2(6) = 24.89$, $p < 0.001$; Joreskog's GFI = 0.96; Steiger's Gamma = 0.97

FIGURE 6.20. Empirical structural equation model of voter behavior IV: Aleksander Kwaśniewski.

The model's goodness-of-fit parameter ($\chi^2 = 59,89$; $p < 0.001$) in comparison to other models (see Table 6.1) allows us to treat this model as an adequate approximation of the empirical data. The model structure shows that no significant paths exist between variables. Thus it can be stated that the model structure of Kwaśniewski's electorate exhibits little variation, which means that the voters' attitudes toward Kwaśniewski are very stable and solid. Using Blumler and McQuail's (1968) terminology, the supporters of this candidate have deep-seated or "impervious" attitudes. It is interesting to note that this same conclusion was derived using a constructivist approach (Cwalina et al., 2004), and multiple regression analysis (Falkowski, Cwalina, 1999; Cwalina, Falkowski, Kaid, 2000).

The results of fitting model IV to the empirical data of Olechowski's electorate is presented in Figure 6.21. The χ^2 coefficient (8.75; $p = 0.188$) is the lowest of all obtained in analyzed models, and allows us to treat this solution as a very good fit to the empirical data. The arrows represent relevant statistical relations between particular elements of the model. A statistically standardized parameter of the path was marked above each of them. For clarity, the arrows connecting the cognitive domains with voter behavior and representing a hypothetical established connection between these variables (see Figure 6.19) were omitted.

182 A CROSS-CULTURAL THEORY OF VOTER BEHAVIOR

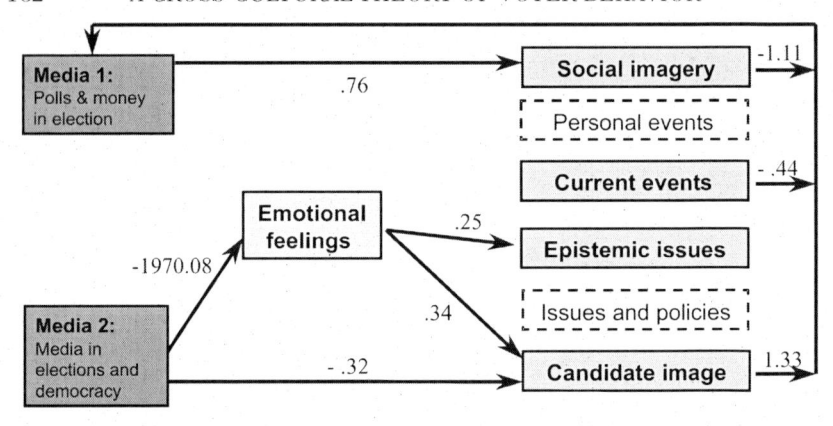

```
                                                          -1.11
 ┌─────────────┐          .76         ┌──────────────┐
 │ Media 1:    │─────────────────────▶│ Social imagery│──────▶
 │ Polls & money│                     └──────────────┘
 │ in election │                      ┌──────────────┐
 └─────────────┘                      │ Personal events│
        │                             └──────────────┘
        │        ┌──────────┐         ┌──────────────┐  -.44
        │        │ Emotional│   .25   │ Current events│──────▶
        │        │ feelings │────────▶└──────────────┘
  -1970.08      └──────────┘         ┌──────────────┐
        │                             │Epistemic issues│
 ┌─────────────┐        .34           └──────────────┘
 │ Media 2:    │                      ┌──────────────┐
 │ Media in    │                      │Issues and policies│
 │ elections and│       -.32          └──────────────┘
 │ democracy   │─────────────────────▶┌──────────────┐  1.33
 └─────────────┘                      │Candidate image│──────▶
                                      └──────────────┘
```

$\chi^2(6) = 8.75$, $p < 0.188$; Joreskog's GFI = 0.98; Steiger's Gamma = 0.99

FIGURE 6.21. Empirical structural equation model of voter behavior IV: Andrzej Olechowski.

In the case of Olechowski's supporters, Media 1 directly influences the perceived social support (social imagery) for the candidate in a positive way; that is, the perceived role of polls and money in election is higher than the wider social support Olechowski gets. On the other hand, Media 2 enhances the candidate image. One should also note that Media 2 exerts an influence on emotional feelings, which, in turn, influence the epistemic issues and candidate image. This means that an indirect influence of broadcast messages exist on cognitive domains in which emotional feelings distort the perceived messages. Furthermore, three cognitive domains—social imagery, current events, and candidate images—influence the manner in which Media 1 is perceived. As much as social imagery and current events increase the importance of the Media 1, the candidate image diminishes it.

The mutual interaction between Media and cognitive domains mediated by emotional feelings creates a picture of voters' minds consistent with the assumptions of cognitive psychology, in which it is stressed that a person "goes beyond" the perceived stimuli, constructing, on the basis of them, his or her own world as a cognitive representation of the surrounding reality (Bruner, 1973; Neisser, 1967).

Structural Equation Models in the U.S. Presidential Election of 2000

As in the case of the analyses on the Polish sample, the structural solutions for models I, II, and III for Bush and Gore do not meet the statistical requirements of good fit and were much worse than model IV in this regard. The respective goodness-of-fit indices are presented in Table 6.6. Because of the best fit of model IV (it differs significantly from the fit of the other models), only the results of the path analysis for this model will be discussed in detail.

Figure 6.22 presents the structural equation model IV for George W. Bush. Its fit to empirical data is the best from the tested models ($\chi^2 = 12,66$; $p = 0.049$; see Table 6.2).

What is characteristic here is the presence of only one positive connection between Media 2 and emotional feelings. The lack of connections between other variables means, as in Kwaśniewski's situation in Poland (see Figure 6.20), that the voters' attitudes toward Bush are very stable and impervious to any influence. The supporters of this candidate are already very confident of their decision about whom to vote for.

The structural model IV for Al Gore, presented in Figure 6.23, is more complex compared to the model for his opponent. The fit of this model to the empirical data is very good ($\chi^2 = 2.68$; $p = 0.848$; see Table 6.6).

We observe two connections in which emotional feelings exert an influence on the candidate image, and issues and policies, and two connections in which Media 2 influences current events and candi-

TABLE 6.6. Structural equation models' goodness-of-fit for George W. Bush and Al Gore.

	George W. Bush	Al Gore
Structural equation model I	$\chi^2 = 53.59$; $p = 0.003$	$\chi^2 = 56.81$; $p = 0.001$
Structural equation model II	$\chi^2 = 52.82$; $p = 0.003$	$\chi^2 = 56.80$; $p = 0.001$
Structural equation model III	$\chi^2 = 45.43$; $p = 0.01$	$\chi^2 = 54.81$; $p = 0.001$
Structural equation model IV	$\chi^2 = 12.66$; $p = 0.049$	$\chi^2 = 2.68$; $p = 0.848$

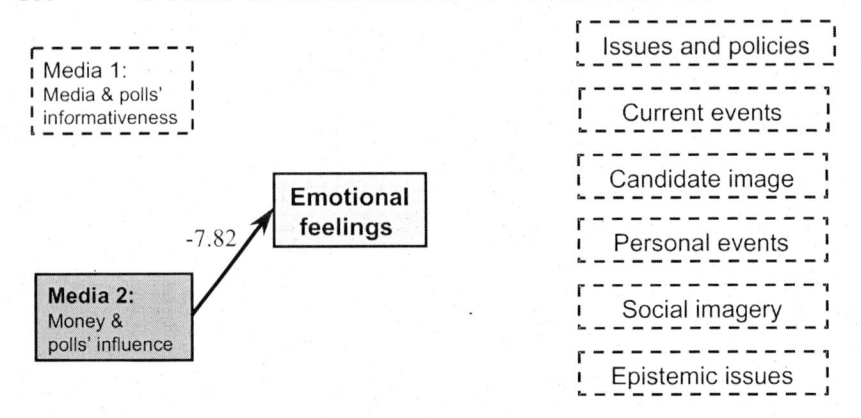

184   A CROSS-CULTURAL THEORY OF VOTER BEHAVIOR

[Media 1: Media & polls' informativeness]

[Media 2: Money & polls' influence] —7.82→ [Emotional feelings]

[Issues and policies]
[Current events]
[Candidate image]
[Personal events]
[Social imagery]
[Epistemic issues]

$\chi^2(6) = 12.66$, $p < 0.049$; Joreskog's GFI = 0.92; Steiger's Gamma = 0.97

FIGURE 6.22. Empirical structural equation model of voter behavior IV: George W. Bush.

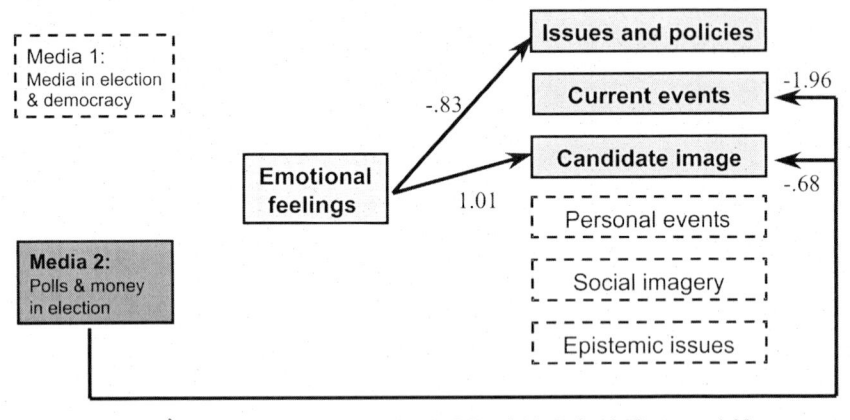

[Media 1: Media in election & democracy]

[Media 2: Polls & money in election]

[Emotional feelings] —.83→ [Issues and policies]; 1.01→ [Candidate image]

[Current events] ← −1.96
[Candidate image] ← −.68
[Personal events]
[Social imagery]
[Epistemic issues]

$\chi^2(6) = 2.68$, $p < 0.848$; Joreskog's GFI = 0.98; Steiger's Gamma = 1.00

FIGURE 6.23. Empirical structural equation model of voter behavior IV: Al Gore.

date image. The belief of his supporters in the importance of the polls and money in elections increases together with the increase of both of these cognitive domains.

The lack of influence of media on emotional feelings means that American voters present a coherent approach to voting behavior and are relatively resistant to affect. The perceived broadcast messages are not distorted by evoked emotions. Thus the voter's mind separates the emotional feelings from the messages that directly influence some of the cognitive domains. That means that the base of voter behavior is rational rather than emotional.

COMPARATIVE ANALYSIS OF MODELS OF VOTER BEHAVIOR IN ESTABLISHED AND DEVELOPING DEMOCRACIES

A comparative analysis will first be conducted separately for the constructive and realistic approach. Then the two approaches and practical implications for marketing strategies during election campaigns will be compared.

Comparative Analysis of the Structure of Voter Behavior in Poland, Slovenia, and the United States: A Constructivist Approach

The results of the research on fitting the model of structural equations to voting situations in Poland, Slovenia, and the United States allow us to draw the following conclusions. Every candidate, irrespective of the country he or she comes from, has an individualized pattern of the structure of factors influencing his or her support by voters. It demonstrates the difficulty and limitations connected with constructing universal models of voting behaviors. On the other hand, however, it shows the importance of Newman's model of voter's choice behavior (1999c; Newman, Sheth 1985), because the factors distinguished by Newman allow us to predict very well the support for individual candidates. Although not all of them are relevant to all the cases, they nevertheless offer sufficient frames for making such predictions.

In all of the countries, structural equation model III is the best-fitted model (in the majority of cases the χ^2 is not significant). It suggests that the causal relationships assumed for this model and described in it reflect well the structure of factors influencing voter decisions. The model structure is much more complex for Olechowski, Bush, and the ZLSD than for Kwaśniewski, Gore, and the LDS in Poland, the United States, and Slovenia, respectively. It means that emotional feelings toward Olechowski, Bush, and the ZSLD are directly related to changes in the media and cognitive domains, and, thus, can be relatively easily controlled.

The model structure of Kwaśniewski's, Bush's, and the LDS's electorates are less complex, which means that the voters' attitudes toward these politicians and the Slovenian party are much more stable and solid. Changing the voters' beliefs in the cognitive domains does not change the emotional feelings toward Kwaśniewski, Bush, and LDS. However, one should take into account that personal events is an important cognitive domain for Kwaśniewski and Bush, which impacts emotional feelings for Kwaśniewski and Media 2 for Bush. A significant path connects these two elements (see Figures 6.10 and 6.14). This means that the most likely way to "warm up" or "cool down" the emotional feelings toward Kwaśniewski would be to operate on personal events (see Table 6.7). How to do this is still a question, as we don't observe a significant connection between this cognitive domain and the media. One solution seems to be shifting the main emphasis in the electoral campaign to direct marketing (meetings with voters, activating volunteers, etc.). On the other hand, the influence of Media 2 for personal events domain for Bush suggests that American voters realize the influence of the media on forming in their minds ways of perceiving events from a candidate's personal life.

The other interesting observation in Poland is the so-called "underdog effect." This phenomenon describes the situation in which voters vote for the candidate who has lower social support and a lower standing in the polls. As the cognitive domain social imagery can be understood as the perceived range and amount of social support, the research results provide empirical support for this underdog effect. It

TABLE 6.7. Personal events.

I'd change my vote if the candidate I supported:

- Committed a serious crime.
- Lied about events in his or her private life.
- Was involved in a business scandal.
- Was involved in a political scandal.
- Changed his or her stand on the issues.
- Cheated on his or her tax returns.
- Became too seriously ill to work effectively.
- Had serious family trouble.
- Was caught driving drunk.
- Was a communist secret services collaborator.

can be best observed in models I and II for Olechowski, in which we notice that Media 2, media in elections and democracy, significantly influences social imagery (see Figure 6.7 and 6.9). This means that if voters are more convinced that the media influence the outcome of elections, they perceive lower social support for Olechowski. This is shown by the negative value of the path parameter. And the lower the support, the "warmer" the candidate. In other words, decreasing social imagery increases emotional feelings. In the case of Kwaśniewski's electorate, the Media 2, money and media in democracy, influences social imagery also, but in a positive way. However, no connection exists between this domain and emotional attitudes toward Kwaśniewski.

Between the United States (established democracy) and Poland and Slovenia (evolving democracies), there is an important difference in the role of the media and its influence on the election process. In the case of the United States, the media exerts an important influence on the valuation of both candidates and on forming voting preferences. In the case of post-communist countries, the influence of the media is selective and limited to the supporters of certain candidates. It can be seen in the figures by connecting Media 1 and Media 2, which are active with both candidates. In Poland and Slovenia the media is not active in each case.

Two hypotheses can be put forward to explain this situation. First, the United States has a greater independence of the media from power centers as well as a greater variety of the media. Therefore, the media can be considered as relatively independent, objective centers of observers and commentators on political life. In this way, the media perform an important function during elections (e.g. D'Alessio, Allen 2000; Negrine, 1994). Second, the media in the United States have more experience and tradition in covering election campaigns. The media are an inseparable part of the democratic system. That's why their relevance as a source of information is greater than in the case of young evolving European democracies. A characteristic feature of these democracies is the use of the media by power centers. They are not independent and are used by the competing political sides as an important element of the electoral battle. Therefore, the lack of relationships connecting Media 1 and Media 2 with cognitive domains and emotional feelings points to the limited trust of the voters from postcommunist countries in mass media.

Comparative Analysis of the Structure of Voter Behavior in Poland and the United States: A Realistic Approach

Cognitive Stability of the Electorates

The results of the research on fitting the model of structural equations according to the realistic approach to voting behavior in Poland and the United States lead us to the following conclusions. First of all, every candidate, irrespective of the country he or she comes from, has an individualized pattern of the structure of factors influencing his or her support among voters. This inference is similar to that which was derived from the analysis of voter behavior according to the constructive approach, and it demonstrates the difficulty and limitations connected with building universal models of voting behaviors (Cwalina et al., 2004).

On the other hand, an interesting structural pattern of voter behavior appears to exist that is similar in Poland and the United States. It was observed, as in the case of using a constructivist approach, that Kwaśniewski in Poland and Bush in the United States have considerably less significant paths between variables in the tested models than do their opponents (compare Figures 6.20 and 6.21 and Figures 6.22 and 6.23). The electorates of these former candidates are, then, more stable and resistant to any influence from outside broadcast messages and internal cognitive domains and affect. This means that it is more difficult to switch them to another candidate. It should be noted that Kwaśniewski was the incumbent candidate; thus his voters already had established feelings and a well-formed image that enabled them to keep a psychological distance from problems covered in such cognitive domains as issues and policies, current events, or personal events. Since the challenger Olechowski's voters were more sensitive to their own candidate than the incumbent voters were to theirs, a better fit of the model for the first one than for the second would be expected. Figure 6.24 presents the χ^2 fitness parameter for both candidates in Poland and in the United States.

It's clear that the structural equation model fits the challenger significantly better than the incumbent in Poland ($\chi^2_{difference}[1] = 16.14$, $p < .001$) and better to Bush than Gore in the United States ($\chi^2_{difference}[1] = 9.98$, $p < .01$). Therefore, it seems useful to propose that the so-called cognitive stability index of the electorate consisted

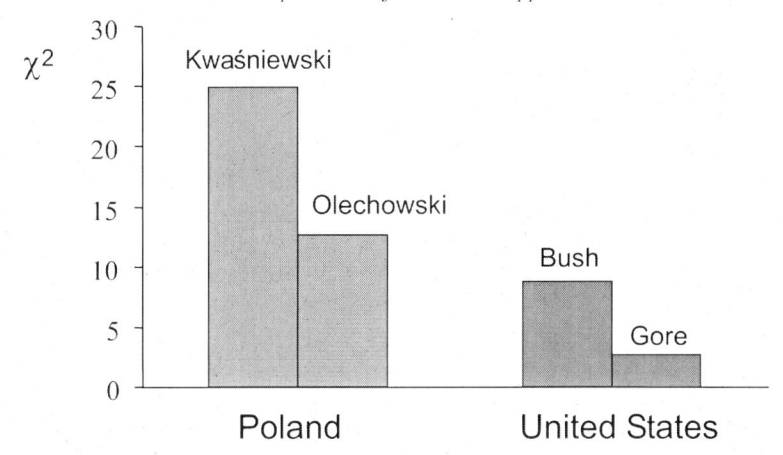

FIGURE 6.24. Goodness-of-fit parameters (χ^2) of structural equation model IV for candidates in Poland and in the United States.

of both the number of significant paths between variables of the structural equation model and the goodness-of-fit model parameter expressed by χ^2.

Because Kwaśniewski in Poland and Bush in the United States won the elections, it can be concluded that the cognitive stability index of the electorate, developed here within the framework of structural equation methodology, might be a useful sign allowing us to predict the outcome of an election. The importance of the χ^2 coefficient in such predicting is presented in Figure 6.10, which in a slightly different way presents the data of Figure 6.25.

The goodness-of-fit model parameter is much better for the winner, the stronger candidate, than for the loser, the weaker candidate, in Poland as well as in the United States.

Comparison of Realist and Constructivist Approaches

The difference between the constructivist approach and the realistic paradigm is that in the first one, emotional feelings do not precede but follow the cognitive domains, thus directly influencing voter behavior (for example, compare Figures 6.3. and 6.16). Because these same empirical data were used for both the realist and the constructivist approaches, it enables us to make a direct comparison of the tested models.

Figure 6.26 shows the fitting parameter χ^2 of the best models selected in realist and constructivist paradigms, and Table 6.8. shows the models' significance for this second paradigm. The results show that from the statistical point of view, the goodness of fit (χ^2) of the con-

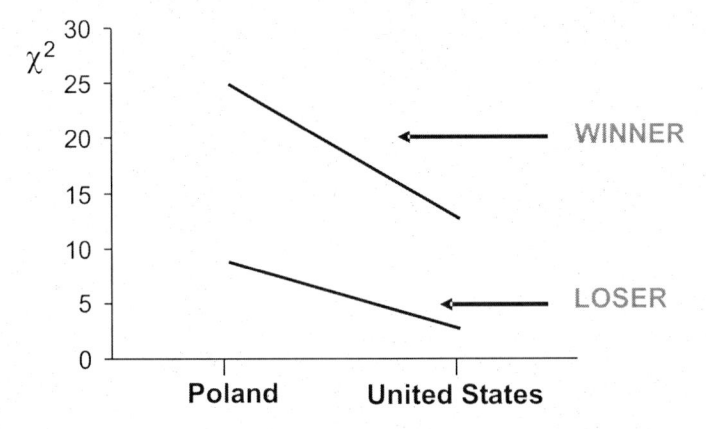

FIGURE 6.25. Goodness-of-fit parameters (χ^2) of structural equation model IV for the winner and loser in Poland and in the United States.

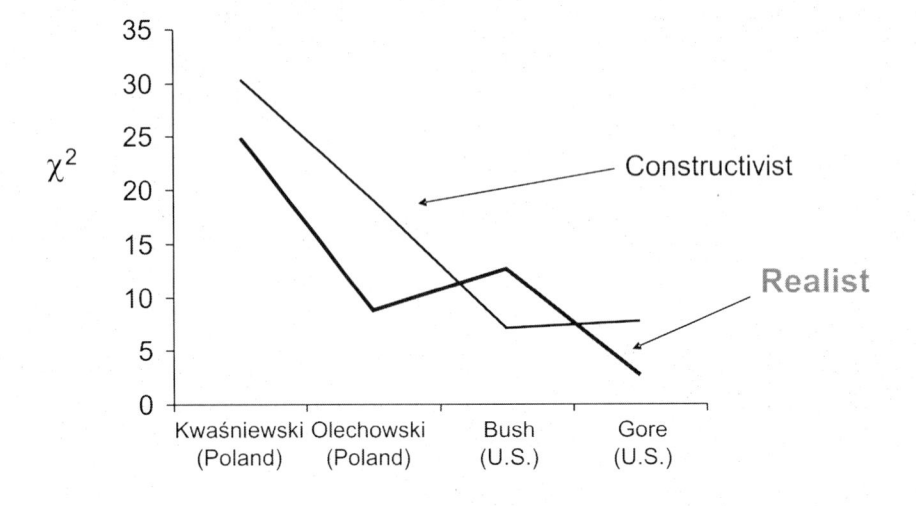

FIGURE 6.26. Constructivist and realist structural models fitting parameters χ^2.

TABLE 6.8. Structural equation constructivist models' goodness-of-fit for Poland and the United States.

United States	Poland
Bush: $\chi^2 = 7.12$; df = 8; p = 0.52	**Kwaśniewski**: $\chi^2 = 30.37$; df = 6; p < 0.001
Gore: $\chi^2 = 7.73$; df = 6; p = 0.26	**Olechowski**: $\chi^2 = 19.10$; df = 6; p < 0.005

structive model is not satisfactory for Poland, whereas it is quite acceptable for the United States. On the other hand, the realist model is satisfactory for the United States and partly satisfactory for Poland (see Tables 6.5 and 6.6).

Therefore, it seems obvious that the realistic paradigm better explains voter behavior than the constructivist one, which means that cognition of the candidate is already "colored" by affect. This is especially applicable in Poland, which means that the key factor in influencing voting behavior is evoking positive emotions toward the candidate and then providing voters with a justification for such affect. This means that some of the cognitive domains directly influencing voter behavior are already distorted by emotional feelings.

In the United States, on the other hand, it can be said that both approaches are relevant. This means that in an established democracy such as the United States, voters have already learned to analyze more carefully messages from presidential campaigns and are more resistant to the unconscious power of affect than are voters in evolving democracies, such as Poland.

It is interesting to note that this same conclusion was reached by testing the sequential model of the influence of political advertising on voting behavior in Poland and the United States (Cwalina, Falkowski, Kaid, 2005). The authors applied both the realist and constructive approaches to test whether the emotional attitude influences the candidate image or, on the contrary, the emotional attitude controls the candidate image when the voter perceives political ads. The analyses of the structural equation methodology that were used, consistent with present findings, showed that the realist approach worked better than the constructive paradigm for Poland, and both are applicable for the United States. Such a result allows us to state that Poles are more emotional and less rational than Americans in their voter behavior.

PRACTICAL IMPLICATIONS FOR MARKETING STRATEGY

The comparative analysis presented here may be an introduction to research in international marketing. Although national sovereignty does not allow for interfering in a given country's internal affairs, it does not prevent one from observing and predicting political events. Such predictions, if correct, may efficiently contribute to forming a country's policy, and adapting to the predicted changes in different spheres of life, including economic, social, and political spheres.

The presented analyses shows the importance of Newman's model of voter's choice behavior (1999c; Newman, Sheth 1985) because the cognitive domains distinguished by Newman allow us to predict very accurately the support for individual candidates. Although the model was developed within the framework of structural equation methodology specifying the causal effect relations between variables, and not all of the cognitive domains are relevant to all the cases, it, nevertheless, offers a sufficient frame for making such predictions.

The presented division into constructivist and realistic paradigms in the research on voter behavior may better demonstrate the differences between traditional and evolving democracies. From the marketing point of view, political consultants face an important challenge—to grasp the structure of the factors influencing the support for a candidate-employer. The results presented here suggest that this is very individualized and, probably, changes over time. Therefore, in conducting campaigns of various politicians, consultants must make every effort each time to understand the specificity of voter behavior toward the candidate and the role of situational factors (media and polls, current events, etc.). The technical aspects of their work (creating the image, voting segmentation) have more predictable results than the final application of the results of this work during the campaign.

The important finding was the difference in the role of media and its influence on the election process. In the case of weaker candidates, challenger Olechowski in Poland as well as Gore in the United States, the media exerts an important influence on the valuation of them both. A significant mutual influence of Media 1 and Media 2 with some of the cognitive domains (see Figures 6.21 and 6.23) was observed. On the other hand, in the case of stronger candidates, incumbents Kwaśniewski in Poland and Bush in the United States, the media is not active, that is, voters' formed cognitive domains are resistant to any broadcast messages (see Figures 6.20 and 6.22). Such a result is expressed here by the concept of cognitive stability of the electorate, and the structural equation statistics allows us to give a precise value to this stability (see "Comparative Analysis of Models of Voter Behavior in Established and Developing Democracies" in this chapter).

From the marketing point of view, political consultants can use the level of electorate cognitive stability to accurately control the media in political campaigns for their candidate. It requires them to make an effort to understand the specificity of voter behavior toward the candidate and the role of situational factors (media and polls, current events, etc.).

Moreover, the research presented here points to the important elements on which one must concentrate in order to conduct an effective electoral campaign. The models of voter behavior developed for one's own candidates may not have any application when analyzing opponents. Political opponents "activate" a distinctly different pattern of factors influencing their support. That requires a separate, individualized approach from political marketing specialists. Therefore, no universal ways of running such campaigns should be developed, because different cognitive domains of different candidates are relevant for voting preferences. The promotional campaign of candidates for state offices should therefore be developed individually for each candidate. Such an individually developed strategy can be prepared on the basis of an analysis of cause-effect relationships using the methodology of structural equations presented in this chapter.

Finally, the results presented here provide a strong test for the specificity of social cognition of the surrounding political reality. The slight advantage of the realist paradigm over the constructivist one is consistent with Zajonc's (1980) cognitive theory of affect explaining why emotions precede cognition, and Wattenberg's (1987) statement that although most of the voters know nothing about particular politicians, they still have strong feelings toward them.

Chapter 7

Constructive Mind: Political Marketing, Freedom, and Democracy

The results of the empirical research presented in Chapters 5 and 6 clearly suggest that psychological mechanisms of influencing voters can and are commonly used by political marketing specialists. They use a number of persuasion techniques and tools that allow them to influence the public opinion and successfully promote their political employers. Voters seem helpless in the face of the politicians' manipulative effort. As Konrad Lorenz (1987) observes, we are so used to the methods of propaganda existing in our society that we have developed a dangerous tolerance to empty promises and institutionalized lies. Such tolerance is particularly facilitated by the development of a constructive information society.

CONSTRUCTIVE INFORMATION SOCIETY

It is undeniable that the current social and cultural changes have led to the development of an information society, in which information becomes its fundamental resource and processing information becomes an important source of the society's gross national product (GNP). In a truly democratic manner, each member of society has the right to inform others and to be informed. The new forms of social and political life in the information society can increase people's access to democracy and administration procedures. One must then be able to transform information into knowledge, which is the task of media education (Tofler, Tofler, 1994).

Poland, similar to the other countries of the former communist bloc, open to the world and with an evolving democracy, takes advantage of the rich experiences of Western European countries and the United States. It quickly adopts the world's technological developments, including many elements of the information society.

Information technology, which is already a key element of a society's life, can be considered advantageous because it facilitates the development of cognitive structures through which one learns how to transform information into knowledge. One has to remember, however, that the world of "virtual reality" is being constructed with information. Information creates a new category of market products that can be sold to create profits. Therefore, one might be tempted to use information as a tool to achieve power and control over society. Such information often creates illusions and artificial worlds in people's minds, and the danger here lies in people's mixing fiction with reality; this threat prevents members of an information society from enjoying one of the most fundamental rights that democracy offers—the right to be broadly informed.

It is undeniable that such a vision of an information society turning quickly into reality has led to the creation of sophisticated tools that can be used to manipulate people's minds. Such visions of reality can be constructed in an individual's mind that will determine his or her preferences and attitudes, including those related to the social and political spheres. A certain construction of information can lead to increasing or decreasing people's sensitivity to certain social phenomena and controlling voting preferences during parliamentary and presidential elections.

Modern society can be seen to be implementing something that for the past decades has been the object of laboratory research in constructivist cognitive psychology. Psychology of perception, for instance, has been studying perceptual illusions. The cognitive paradigm stands often in opposition to the ecological approach in psychology which focuses not on "illusions" but on man's natural environment (Gibson, 1979). The predictive models of voter behavior presented in the previous chapter fit in very well in these psychological approaches. Constructivist cognitive psychology can interpret structural equation models of voter behavior according to the constructivist approach, but the ecological approach in psychology is a theoretical foundation of structural equation models of voter behavior according to the realistic approach (see section titled "Constructivism and Realism" in Chapter 2). Because the constructivist approach is currently very widespread not only in psychology but also in cognitive sciences in general, this chapter will seek to examine some other examples of constructivist research and its connection with the surrounding political reality.

"LABORATORY WORLD" OF COGNITIVE PSYCHOLOGY AND POLITICAL MARKETING

Some still believe that the subject of constructivist psychology is artificial stimuli, having little to do with the environment that surrounds us. However, the laws of humankind's behavior discovered in laboratories in which artificial stimuli are used can be successfully employed to control a person's behavior in the real world of politics. Therefore, the laws related to perception processes followed by memory processes will be presented here.

Constructivism in the Perception of Political Advertising

Every handbook of general or cognitive psychology offers many examples of various stimuli and their combinations that one rarely finds in the surrounding reality. Many artificial situations from the area of perception processes, which cannot be found in the natural environment, are presented as effective spectacular illusions. A number of such illusions, called perceptual illusions, are excellent illustrations of the laws of Gestalt psychology, including the law of proximity, similarity, or common fate (Wilkie, 1994). These laws, described in detail by Kurt Koffka (1935) in the first half of the previous century, show the collaboration of the mind with the sensual reception of stimuli. It means that the received stimulation is given meaning and is organized in a meaningful manner, often by the mind adding nonexistent stimuli to this stimulation and thus creating a figure that is separated from the background. Some classical examples of such a construction are presented in Figures 2.1, 2.3, and 2.4 in Chapter 2.

The laws of Gestalt psychology therefore became a foundation for formulating the constructivist approach in cognitive psychology. The laws, also called the laws of the perceptual organization, describe the functioning of people's cognitive behavior in the processes of perception, namely the ability to introduce organization, symmetry, and aesthetics to the stimulation one receives. This aesthetic is distorted when a given stimulus situation does not meet the criteria of Gestalt. What is more, Koffka (1935) claims that the aesthetic is gradable, which means that the level of positive emotions felt in the process of perception is proportional to the degree to which the situation conforms to the laws of Gestalt psychology.

It can then be stated that it was the classics of perception that introduced *implicitly* (the concept of the prototype in perception and the gradable distortion of a given prototype) which became the subject of empirical research in the field of semantic and perceptual categorization only in the 1970s following the prototypical theory of these concepts (Rosch, 1973; Posner, Keele, 1968). The theory was used in the 1980s to observe the distorted stimuli that do not conform to the laws of Gestalt psychology. Stephen Palmer, Eleanor Rosch, and Paul Chase (1981), and Irving Biederman (1987) showed how the reaction time of recognizing an increasingly distorted and degraded figure, from its full representation, or, to use the words of Gestalt psychology, its "goodness of figure" *(pragnanz),* precisely meets the laws of perceptual organization. The relationship between positive emotions and the "goodness of figure," described by Koffka, has only recently become the subject of empirical research. Robert Veryzer and Wesley Hutchinson (1998) conducted research on the perception of perceptual stimuli represented by drawn outlines of objects of everyday use, including a telephone, refrigerator, or hair dryer. The authors demonstrated that the subjects liked prototype objects the most (the goodness of figures), whereas the attractiveness of the same objects when distorted was much lower. It can then be said that the cognitive structure of a given object's category is also connected with the affective domain.

The constructivist approach was very well presented in the classical book by Ulric Neisser (1967) and in the joint publication edited by Jerome S. Bruner (1973), in which the authors analyzed in detail the psychological mechanisms of creating the surrounding reality in one's mind. According to this approach, one "goes outside" the perceived stimuli, constructing, on the basis of them, his or her own world as a cognitive representation of the surrounding reality. Although much well-conducted empirical research shows the cognitive mechanisms of creating the mind's world, these studies have been criticized as presenting a "laboratory" world, having nothing in common with the world in which one lives in on an everyday basis. Psychologists following the ecological approach to visual perception, including, among others, Edward Reed and Rebecca Jones (1982), claim that the perceptual illusions often presented in psychology handbooks or ambiguous figures can be found only in the fictitious world of laboratory research and never in the real world. They can be treated as interesting phenomena that one can watch on the computer screen, in a research lab, or in psychology handbooks, but not in everyday life.

However, given the current development of the information society, one may wonder whether this sometimes criticized "laboratory world" is not an excellent model for what is currently going on in the surrounding social reality. The fast development of the media and the ability to reach everybody with information make it very tempting to construct a certain way of perceiving the surrounding reality in one's mind. It is mainly marketing strategy managers working in business and, more recently, political consultants, who are interested in such constructing. The first group uses the achievements of modern cognitive psychology to develop methods of influencing customers, whereas the second group uses them to influence voters. The more and more sophisticated advertising used appeals to the cognitive and affection spheres, often on the level of the subconscious, the more it creates a certain image of reality in the receiver's mind. Creating such a reality follows the perceptual rules described by Gestalt psychology. Let us therefore analyze a concrete example of creating an image of a presidential candidate on the basis of visual advertising in one's mind.

In 1996 Lynda Lee Kaid (1997) conducted experimental research on the perception of advertising spots distorting the image of the candidate during the presidential campaign in the United States, in which Bill Clinton and Bob Dole were competing for the presidency. It is relatively easy to distort an image used in political advertising through modern computer technology by implementing, for instance, slow motion, superimposing of images, and top, bottom, and front shots (Cwalina, Falkowski, Rożnowski, 1999). Such manipulations have a laboratory character and are typical of the research conducted on the perception processes in the constructivist approach relative to the cognitive psychology model mentioned previously. However, unlike this research, the goal of these manipulations is to influence someone not in an artificial environment but in the real social environment. The negative affective attitude toward a candidate, created as a result of distorting his or her image, significantly influences the results of presidential elections and has consequences for the development of the state's economic and social policies. Thus, these effects are visible in a real, and not a laboratory situation.

The conclusions presented are confirmed by a number of studies on the relations between voting preferences and the emotional attitude toward a candidate, tested in a number of models of political advertising's influence on voting behaviors (including Kaid, Chanslor, 1995; Newman, Sheth, 1985; Falkowski, Cwalina, 1999; Cwalina, Falkowski, Kaid, 2000).

Kaid selected a few television spots from the presidential elections in which a visual distortion of the content describing the candidate was used. As a rule, such spots appear only in a negative campaign whose task is to reduce the appeal of the candidate among the voters. In total, as many as 70 percent of the spots distorted the image of the candidate. Clinton's campaign focused on criticizing his rival, and in 84 percent of the cases they presented a distorted picture of Dole, whereas Dole's campaign presented a distorted image of his rival half of the time.

In order to determine the influence of the distorted image of the candidate on people's evaluation of him and their voting preferences, Kaid selected four experimental groups. The first two groups watched, in sequence, two original negative portrayals of Dole and Clinton in which a distorted picture was used. Dole's spot used complex computer graphics to distort Clinton's picture by a superimposition of words consisting of big red letters. They expressed the criticism of Clinton's attitude toward taxes. It also presented a cutting from a publication, suggesting that it was published in a newspaper, presenting arguments for increasing taxes. In addition, the spot presented a growing red arrow illustrating how quickly taxes were rising. Clinton's spot presented his rival moving in slow motion among the elderly and children against the background showing a polluted environment. The spot was black and white in order to increase the viewers' negative impressions. The second and third group watched the same two spots, however, the distortion was completely removed from them. In Dole's spot the red color of the letters distorting Clinton's picture was removed and the arguments for increasing taxes were no longer presented as press cuttings. But the size of the red arrow presenting growing taxes was the same during the whole presentation of the spot. In Clinton's spot, the picture presenting Dole remained but the colors of the landscape were restored. The same verbal expression, distorted or not, was preserved in each of the candidate's spots. The influence of advertising using distortion on the evaluation of the candidate and subjects' intention to vote for him is presented in Figure 7.1.

The evaluation is the mean of twelve seven-point scales of semantic differential, developed in order to measure the candidate's image, and the intention was measured on one seven-point scale. The higher the number, the more positive the picture of the candidate or greater the intention.

The differences in the evaluation of the candidates linked with watching the distorted spots and the spots from which the distortion was removed are relevant and clearly demonstrate the negative influence of distorted stimuli in advertising on the evaluation of the rival and subjects' voting intentions. Distorted advertising not only decreases the rival's chances but it also increases the chances of the candidates whose campaign prepared these spots.

It is undeniable that the presented voting situation refers to a real social situation because the spots distorting the presented content were actually broadcast during the presidential campaign. Their influence was one of the many factors responsible for the distribution of votes in the presidential elections in the United States in 1996. The

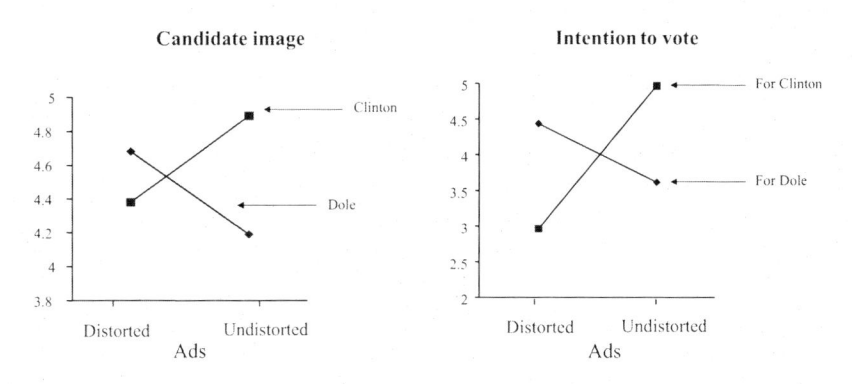

FIGURE 7.1. The effect of distorted stimuli in the ads presented by the Dole campaign on candidate vote intention. *Source:* Adapted from Kaid (1997), Table 1, p. 1088.

way of constructing them, however, had been adopted from the methodology of research on the influence of artificial perceptual stimuli and have nothing to do with the surrounding reality. Similar to proper combinations of such stimuli causing perceptual illusions in artificial situations, perceptually distorted spots create illusions about the image of the candidates. As Kaid observes, the practice of improving the candidate's own image and spoiling the image of his or her opponent by using the advanced technology of perceptual distortion is a serious problem and threat to democratic systems. The voters have the right to accurate information during political elections, and this can be controlled and blocked by specialists working for a given political side.

Constructivism in the Memory of Political Events

The situation presenting the influence of distorted perceptual stimuli in advertising on the evaluation of the candidate presented by this advertising has far-reaching consequences for people's memories of his or her image. Distorted stimuli in advertising influence people's attitude toward a candidate not only during the emission of the spot—they also cause changes in the previously remembered image. Recent research in consumer marketing on the reconstruction of memory occurring as a result of backward framing shows the way false memory about past events is created. It is worthwhile to take a closer look at some empirical research showing the changes in remembering simple perceptual stimuli as a result of distorting them in spots.

Kathryn Braun and Elizabeth Loftus (1998) conducted research on the changing of the wrapper of Suisse candy. The experimental procedure was quite simple and consisted of a few stages. In the first stage of the research the subjects evaluated the taste of the Suisse bar, which aimed to challenge a brand already existing on the market, Godiva. The experimenter passed around a few samples of the bar, each in a green wrapper. The respondents' task was to unpack the bar, taste it, and evaluate it. In the next part of the experiment, the subjects evaluated candy spots from the two companies. The first experimental group (visual) was shown a few advertisements of the Suisse bar wrapped in a blue color, that is a color different from the wrappers of the bars they had tasted at the beginning of the experiment. In the second group (verbal) advertising was descriptive and included a statement that the bars were available in blue wrappers. The third group (control) was given no information about the color of the Suisse bar wrapper.

In the last part of the research, the respondents were tested on their memory of the color of the wrappers of the bars they tasted at the beginning of the research. They were presented a color wheel divided into thirty different colors, with primary and mixed colors. The colors also included the color green that corresponded to the wrapper of the Suisse bar they had been asked to taste and the color blue representing the color in which the bar was later presented. The results of this identification are shown in Figure 7.2, showing frequency distribution of color choice in the visual, verbal, and control groups.

As one might have predicted, the control group to which the advertisements of the products were presented without any mentioning of their wrapper identified the color which was closest to the color of the Suisse bars they tasted. None of the respondents chose the color blue. In the visual group, half of the respondents chose blue. A similar result was observed in the verbal group. The results of the research presented in Figure 7.2 show that both in the visual and verbal groups, the respondents more often selected the color that was suggested to them by the advertisement of the wrapper than the color in which the

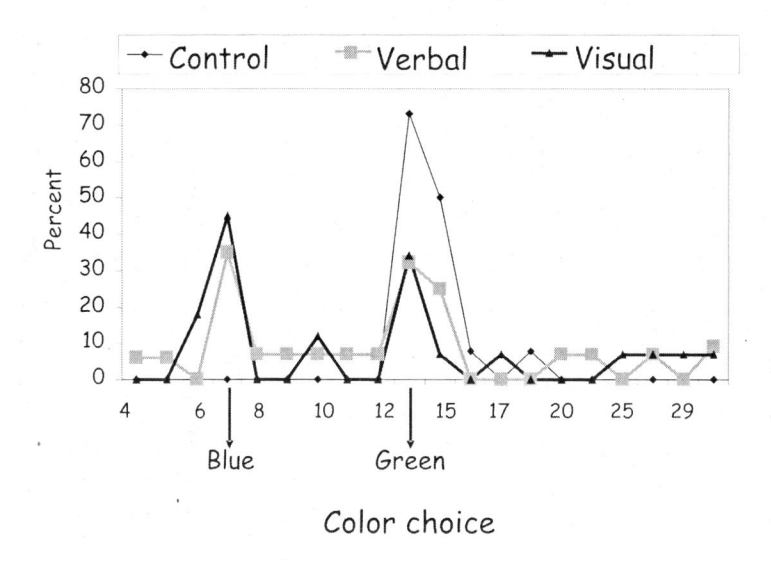

FIGURE 7.2. Frequency distribution of color memory. *Source:* Adapted from Braun and Loftus (1998).

Suisse bars were actually wrapped when they tasted them. Tulving's procedure (Tulving, 1985), used to determine the quality of the remembered events, showed that the respondents "remembered" the false blue color, that is, they reiterated and "saw" the Suisse bar wrapped in this color in their imagination. What is evident here is the advertising misinformation effect, that is, reconstructing previously recorded events in one's memory.

Although Braun and her colleagues' research is about the influence of advertising on the creation of false memory in the process of reconstructing the experience with consumer products, such a reconstruction process also occurs with people's ideas about candidates for state positions under the influence of political advertising. Many researchers, including Bruce Newman (1994), Andrew Lock and Phil Harris (1996) treat voters as consumers of political information and find analogies between voter and consumer behavior. Use of consumer marketing techniques leads to suitable "packaging" of candidates during parliamentary and presidential elections.

It can then be inferred that the distorted stimuli in Clinton's and Dole's negative advertisements and those used in Kaid's research might have distorted the voters' memory of their previous experiences with the candidates and created a false image of the candidates. From a marketing perspective, the procedure of distorting the image in the voters' memory offers a chance to make the product better or worse without any changes in its quality. The quality that is controlled in this way is an intervention into the voter's mind and fits the strategy of candidate positioning, that is, finding a clear and desirable place in the voter's mind in relation to the competition (Newman, 1994).

The history of political elections provides many examples of creating false images of candidates in the voters' memory by the strategy of distorting reality used in marketing tactics. As Newman points out (1999a,b), the first application of marketing techniques in order to create an image of the president that would not be inconsistent with reality took place under Franklin Roosevelt's presidency. The main attempt taken by his campaign advisors involved creating an image of their boss as a physically strong person. During Roosevelt's presidential campaign, specialists responsible for his image created a depiction of a man who could walk freely, whereas Roosevelt was in fact confined to a wheelchair (see Figure 3.1 in Chapter 3). The image of the president constructed in voters' minds was therefore not consistent with the reality. Due to the effects of changed stimuli, voters had false memories of Roosevelt.

The constructed image is mainly presented through the media, which can be compared to retailers. If the media is not convinced that the material provided by the campaign advisors in a certain packaging is good, then it will be hard to sell it (Newman, 1999a). Newman, like Kaid, claims that democracy is threatened by the use of increasingly sophisticated techniques in political advertising. He very clearly notices the development of a market-driven democracy, in which marketing strategies of controlling voting behaviors using falsely constructed images of reality play crucial roles. In this case, it can be stated that voters' freedom in developed democratic countries is becoming more and more limited.

However, before presenting this paradoxical relationship between freedom and democracy, it is worthwhile to take a closer look at the possibilities of resistance to voting persuasion and the empirically tested model of voter behavior in which the presented image of a candidate plays an important role. The forming of such an image on the basis of political advertising was presented in the sequential model of the influence of political advertisements describing cause-and-effect relations between image, emotions, and voters (see "Sequential Model of the Influence of Political Advertisements" in Chapter 6). This model, in the context of Miller and Krosnick's (2000) and Tverski and Kahneman's (1974) research, demonstrates how the media may limit a citizen's freedom of choice.

RESISTANCE TO VOTING MANIPULATION

Modern democratic systems cannot exist without exerting persuasive influence on their citizens. However, such persuasion is a propaganda action of the elites aimed at manipulating citizens. It poses a threat to the society as well as to the stability of democracy (see also Pratkanis, Aronson, 1992; Cwalina, Falkowski, 2005a). Therefore, learning and developing strategies to help citizens to defend themselves from the manipulations of the ruling and those fighting for power is an important challenge for not only journalists and educators but also for psychologists, sociologists, and political scientists.

Modern persuasion practices make the correct assumption that by using the same psychological principles that are used in propaganda one can also neutralize the influence of political communication on voter decisions. Therefore, the starting point for any actions aimed at protecting citizens from voting manipulation is understanding the mechanisms of persuasion. From many persuasion theories one can distinguish the theories that are very popular: the communication/persuasion process matrix model of influence developed by William J. McGuire (1985, 1989), and the elaboration likelihood model of persuasion (ELM) developed by Richard E. Petty and John T. Cacioppo (1986, 1990; Petty, Priester, 1994; Petty, Unnava, Strathman, 1991). The first one stresses that the influence of the persuasion message on the recipients' attitudes and behavior depends, above all, on such elements of the communication process as the channel through which the message is sent and the context in which it is set. Another important component of the communication process is demographic and psychographic characterization of the voters at whom a given message is directed (see "Social Psychological Approach" in Chapter 4). The second model describes psychological processes responsible for the changes in the attitude toward a presented object caused by persuasion communication. The authors of this model maintain that the processes occurring during the phase of accepting the message belong to one of the following ways of persuasion: central or peripheral.

This part will present various concepts of resistance to persuasion in more detail. Persuasion theories try to describe as precisely as possible the process and variables influencing changes in human attitudes. The results of these analyses can be used both by individuals and organizations that try to influence others, but can also be used as a way of "inoculating" oneself against such influence. However, this other side of persuasion activities has become an area of independent research on how to protect society from manipulation.

Inoculation Model

The author of the model based on "inoculating" people against persuasive actions *(inoculation model)* is William J. McGuire (1964). He based his proposal on biological analogies: a person is protected against a virus by being previously vaccinated with a small dose of the same virus. This stimulates a defense mechanism so that a person would be able to overcome a concentrated attack of viruses later. McGuire suggests that analogical resistance techniques can be used for persuasion. Therefore, to inoculate people against manipulation, they should be exposed to its weaker forms. Such an "inoculation" is possible through the use of refutational messages. Such a message first presents a possible argumentation that can be used in persuasion and then refutes it, strengthening, at the same time, the recipient's attitudes and making them resistant to future persuasion efforts.

McGuire verified his theory by making people resistant to "cultural truisms." These are beliefs that the majority of people accept uncritically, without ever thinking why they do so. Such truisms include such statements as: "One should brush one's teeth after every meal," or "Democracy is the best form of ruling" (see Aronson, Wilson, Akert, 1994). The majority of people do not ponder the rational or logical arguments behind such beliefs, and that's why they are very likely to change if the presented arguments contradict them. However, according to McGuire, such changes can be prevented if people are provided with arguments supporting the validity of their original beliefs, in other words, by providing people with counterarguments.

The inoculation model assumes that one must feel threatened in order to develop resistance to persuasive communication. Only by being threatened will a person be motivated enough to defend his or her attitudes. Therefore, the "inoculating" message should also include elements showing this manipulative threat. Persuasion prevention, according to McGuire, can also considerably weaken the manipulative actions directed at people by political marketing specialists. One could also say that the same holds true for political marketing specialists.

The theory of "inoculation" was verified empirically several times, and a direct test of this theory in relation to a political marketing effort was conducted by Michael Pfau, Henry C. Kenski, Michael Nitz, and John Sorenson (1990).

Expectancy-Value Approach

The starting point for understanding resistance relative to persuasion is also understanding man's cognitive mechanisms that participate in the transmission of the manipulative message. The theory that allows one to distinguish and analyze such mechanisms is the expectancy-value approach theory proposed by Martin Fishbein and Icek Ajzen (1981). They claim that one can specify three cognitive processes whose importance for yielding to and resisting persuasion is the greatest: message acceptance, its influence, and evaluation of the attributes of the object that it concerns. *Message acceptance* processes determine the extent to which the perceiver accepts or denies the target message. In the case of resistance to persuasion, it can be connected with such phenomena as source derogation, argument scrutiny, and biased memory search in order to find proper counter-argumentation. If the mechanism works, one can most often observe *biased assimilation* of the message (Ahluwalia, 2000). It is represented by people's tendency to consider the information that is consistent with their beliefs as correct and true and question the values that are incompatible with them.

Impact effects occur to the extent that the persuasive arguments influence recipients' beliefs relating to attributes not directly addressed by the message. For example, if information focuses on demonstrating a candidate's dishonesty, it may also make the voter think that he or she is immoral. People can then try to "immunize" themselves to negative messages by trying to limit the range of the message's influence only to those attributes that were presented there. In this way, the danger of breaking the whole structure of the attitude will be diminished. Such resistance activities can then be defined as *minimizing impact* behaviors (Ahluwalia, 2000).

The third process distinguished by Fishbein and Ajzen (1981) is the *evaluation* of attributes. The reception of new information about a candidate may make the voter evaluate again the importance of honesty for running for the president's office. In other words, the recipient will wonder whether this characteristic is really as relevant as it seemed to him. If the attempt to diminish the relative importance of some characteristics proves successful, then resistance to persuasion and attitude consistency will increase. This mechanism can be defined as *attribute weighting* (Ahluwalia, 2000).

It should be stressed that whereas assimilation processes are about accepting or rejecting information inconsistent with attitudes, the other two processes distinguished by Fishbein and Ajzen focus on beliefs and evaluations of attributes that are not present in the persuasion message but are related to it. These are the attributes that are an important part of the attitude, and in order to preserve the attitude, individuals should protect themselves against them. In this way, people who have strong attitudes about some object (for instance a candidate) will be more motivated to defend them. This aspect brings the model of value-expectancy closer to Petty's and Cacioppo's model. The mechanisms of resistance to persuasion distinguished by Fishbein and Ajzen take place outside of the recipient's awareness. These processes occur automatically.

Strategies for Resisting Persuasion

The models of resistance to persuasion try to describe not only ways of protecting oneself from such communication, but they also highlight the psychological mechanisms lying at the foundation of such efforts. Another approach is defining particular strategies that people use to make themselves resistant to manipulation.

Reviewing the literature dedicated to these problems, Julia Zuwernik Jacks and Kimberly A. Cameron (2003) distinguished seven strategies of resisting persuasion:

- *Counterarguing.* This technique comes down to a direct rebuttal of message arguments. Using this strategy allows one to directly refute the statements included in the message.
- *Attitude bolstering.* This method involves support arguing. It is about generating thoughts that are consistent with and supportive of one's original attitude without directly refuting message arguments.
- *Message distortion.* This is an approach that is connected with selectively processing or understanding a message that is inconsistent with one's attitude. One selects from it only what is acceptable; all the other elements are skipped.
- *Social validation.* This strategy is about bringing to mind beliefs or statements of others, authorities, or important representatives of the society, who share one's original attitude. In this way, one gets social "support" for his or her ideas.
- *Source derogation.* This is a way of making the sender of the message not credible. If one dismisses his competencies then the content of the message becomes valueless. As in the case of social validation, this strategy does not require analyzing argumentation.

- *Negative affect.* This tactic is connected with reacting to persuasion with anger or irritation. In most cases, it leads to a complete break in message reception.
- *Selective exposure.* This strategy allows the recipient to resist persuasion by leaving the situation or actively tuning out the persuasive message. The recipient is seeking only the messages whose content is consistent with his or her point of view. The other channels are simply eliminated.

Obviously, all of the attempts to describe persuasion resistance mechanisms as well as strategies that are used for this purpose stress that any attempt to resist manipulation can be undertaken only when one actually wants to protect oneself. In their research on factors motivating people to resist persuasion, Brad Sagarin, Robert Cialdini, William Rice, and Sherman Serna (2002) reach the following conclusion: resisting manipulation is the result of one's acquired ability to distinguish between real authorities speaking about particular issues and those who pretend to be authorities. Their conclusion is a clear message to people who try to prevent voters from falling prey to "false prophets" and make them deliberately evaluate all the politicians participating presenting themselves in different ways. They should make more effort to distinguish truth from lies and facts from illusions.

One should also mention the importance of antipersuasion education for resisting voter manipulation. It is the journalists and educators who mainly carry the burden of making society aware of the threats resulting from the old or emerging power elites' use of manipulation techniques. Psychological research and analyses offer useful directions on how such activities should be conducted.

Public journalism and special programs showing the mechanisms of constructing political advertising in adwatches can be considered as promising attempts to make citizens aware of the threats of submitting to propaganda.

Public Journalism

Public journalism is organized by the people involved in journalism, and the intellectual leader of the movement is Jay Rosen (Shepard, 1994). The movement is based on a few major principles or dogmas (Rosen, 1991; Glasser, 1999). First, citizen concerns will be solicited and voiced. Only what is important for citizens is important for journalists as well. Second, media coverage will shift from polls and strategy to issues of public policy. Press articles or television programs cannot focus purely on the competition for power or influences. Their goal is to present the consequences of implementing various programs, not from the politicians' but from citizens' perspective. Third, substantive reporting should prevail over short candidate sound bites. Only then will the citizens have a chance to understand what a political debate or conflict is all about. Fourth, partnership and solutions will be stressed over independence and professional detachment.

Adwatch Report

In 1992, during the presidential campaign in the United States, all the major television news programs presented, for the first time in history, the adwatch in which candidates' spots were analyzed according to their honesty and adherence to facts (Ansolabehere, Iyengar, Simon, 1995). The intention of such journalism is to stop candidates from using false and exaggerated statements.

In the fall of 1991, Kathleen Hall Jamieson together with her research team and CNN employees, developed a visual grammar for such programs as "adwatch" (Jamieson, 1992). Its goal was to develop some rules for presenting the critique of spots by the journalists. These techniques included a sequence of the following: (1) placing the offending commercials in a mock television screen, and then moving the screen into the background *(distancing)*, (2) attaching a new logo and a notice that this was an ad for a particular candidate *(disclaiming)*, (3) stopping the commercial to comment on its content, (4) commenting upon its content and putting print correctors on the screen *(displacing)*. The purpose of these procedures was to encourage the audience to process the content of the critique rather than the content of the ad. It was hoped that the attitudinal effect of misleading, false, highly emotional, and demagogic commercials would be minimized by the contextualizing effects of the adwatch.

The authors of the project developed a sample adwatch, supplemented it with a special guide, and distributed it with the help of the National Association of Broadcasters to all the television stations that were interested in it. As Jamieson writes, during the presidential elections in 1992, some forms of adwatch were used by CNN, ABC, NBC, and CBS.

Obviously the methods of resisting voter manipulation may contribute to diminishing the influence of persuasion, but cannot eliminate it completely. Various studies from cognitive psychology have shown that despite that a person may very well know the logical rules of reasoning, he or she does not follow them in everyday reality and gives in to fallacy (Cheng et al., 1986). Therefore, one should take a closer look at limiting citizens' freedom in democratic countries; the freedom has an internal character resulting from the constructive character of the human mind. The modeling of such character is very well demonstrated by the constructivist approach in voting behaviors.

FREEDOM IN DEMOCRATIC NATIONS: A PARADOX

The constructivist approach in voting behaviors was used not only in predictive models of voter behavior (see "Structural Equation Models of Voter Behavior: A Constructivist Approach" in Chapter 6) but also in the sequential model of voting behaviors developed by Falkowski and Cwalina (1999), and Cwalina, Falkowski, and Kaid (2000, 2005) (see "Sequential Model of the Influence of Political Advertisements" in Chapter 6). The model, tested empirically in Poland, France, Germany, and the United States, shows causal relations between the image of the candidate formed during the process of watching advertisements and the affective attitude toward the candidate and voting intentions.

Voting Behaviors

The sequential model of voting behaviors assumes that in order to determine whether political advertising has an influence on voting decisions, it is necessary to determine the links between the four components: (1) cognitive-affective elements—the image of the candidate, (2) general feelings toward the candidate, (3) intention for whom to vote, and (4) decision for whom to vote. The causal relations between the elements, in which the image influences affection that then in turn influences voting intention, are presented in Figure 6.2 in Chapter 6.

A concrete example of using this model with voting behaviors is presented in Figure 7.3, which shows cause-and-effect relationships on the basis of the analysis of structural equations. The example (see Figure 7.3) presents the influence of political advertising on the image, emotional attitude, and voting intentions for Al Gore during the presidential elections in the United States in 2000 (Cwalina, Falkowski, Kaid, 2005).

The image of the candidate analyzed with semantic differential was divided into two components obtained as a result of using factor analysis for the differential: "leadership skills" and "self-control." The goodness of fit of the empirical data is ($\chi^2 = 17.21$, $p = 0.19$, and $\chi^2/df = 1.32$).

After using regression analysis, in which the dependent variable is the emotional attitude and the independent variables are the adjectives describing the image of the candidate through semantic differential, it was possible to find out to which characteristics of the candidate the voters were most and least sensitive. Using such an analysis before and immediately after watching the spots helped researchers to observe changes in the relevance of these characteristics relative to voting preferences and thus changes in the influence of these characteristics on the voters' emotional attitude toward the candidate. A detailed presentation of such analyses and the testing of the sequential

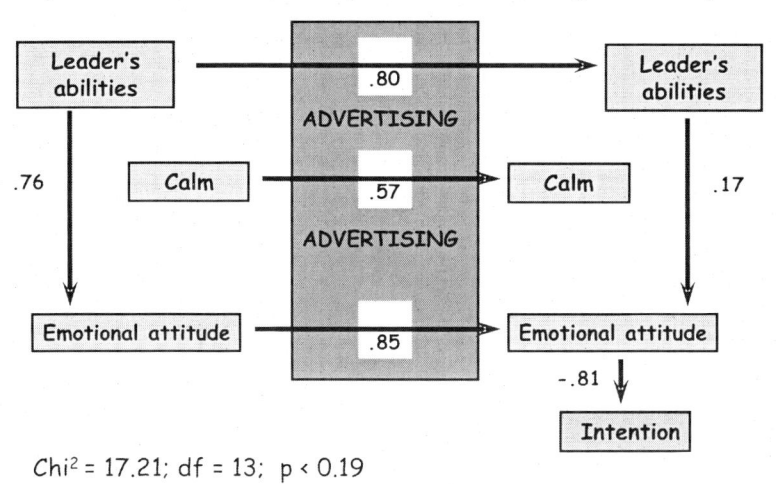

Chi² = 17.21; df = 13; p < 0.19

FIGURE 7.3. Cause-and-effect relationships in voting behaviors toward Al Gore. *Source:* Cwalina, Falkowski, Kaid (2005), p. 29.

model during parliamentary and presidential elections can be found in the previously mentioned works by Cwalina, Falkowski, and Kaid (2000, 2005).

Empirical research in the sequential model of the influence of political advertising shows the way political reality is created in the minds of the voters. However, one should remember that the example presented here is only one of the versions of the model, and one should not ignore that the emotions invoked by advertising may contribute to the formation of the candidate's image, which would mean that the direction of cause-and-effect relationships presented in Figure 6.2 in Chapter 6 should be changed. Empirical testing of such a model is presented by Cwalina, Falkowski, and Kaid. It is highly probable then that the sequential model would provide a good interpretation of the results of Kaid's (1997) research on the influence of perceptually distorted negative advertising on the evaluation of the candidate and people's voting intentions.

Additional research on the influence of the media on voting behaviors was presented by Joanne M. Miller and Jon A. Krosnick (2000). They demonstrated, on the basis of empirical research, that the evaluation of the president depends on the perceived relevance of domestic or international problems and his way of managing these problems. By highlighting the relevance of various social and economic problems such as drugs, immigration, crime, environmental pollution, and unemployment, the media causes them to be more important to the voters. In evaluating the president, voters recall the previously highlighted problems that have an important influence on the evaluation.

The authors place their research within the theoretical perspective of priming, in which a previously remembered event, that is, a multiple description of certain problems in the media, is recalled from memory and is the basis for the evaluation of the president. In light of John Anderson's (1983) model of association-memory network, one can talk about a strong correlation between the perceived situation in which the evaluation of the remembered problems takes place and spreading of activity following such stimuli as the survey questions about the president's performance or spots associated with presidential elections. This problem can also be approached from the perspective of the availability hypothesis, according to which priming provides easy access to the remembered events that are important for political evaluations. "More frequent" events, including various social problems publicized by the media are, due to the frequency of their occurrence, more available to our memory than "less frequent" events. The availability hypothesis is described by Amos Tversky and Daniel Kahneman (1974) as heuristics used by people for the evaluation of various cognitive and social situations, which may lead to illusions, and, as a consequence, to availability bias.

The media can then consciously publicize various problems in order to influence political evaluations through the psychological processes of remembering them. Miller and Krosnick, like Kaid and Newman, claim that democracy is threatened by such conduct. Intentional control of the evaluations of a politician's activities by the voters limits the voters' access to broad information and, by causing priming and heuristics, it creates the illusion of a free and conscious choice. It is worthwhile to quote the authors' words here: "According to the theory of media priming people are victims of the architecture of their minds—if a political issue is activated in people's memories by media attention to it, they presumably use the concept when asked to make political judgments—not by conscious choice, but merely because information about the issue appears automatically and effortlessly in consciousness" (Miller and Krosnick, 2000, p. 302). But, as Ulrich Beck (1992) points out, what is publicized by the media, whose task is to look reliable and credible, are only single facts extracted from the excess of various hypothetical results. The point here is that the political sphere cannot afford to ignore "well-known common views" without losing votes (Beck, 1992).

Does Freedom Constrain?

The research on voting behaviors and political judgments in light of psychological processes of perception and memory points to a certain characteristic of the development of democratic societies. The foundation of such societies is their citizens' freedom, which helps to create more and more sophisticated marketing strategies whose goal is to make the voter vote for a certain political option. We face then a paradoxical situation, because a side product of these strategies is the limitation of the voter's choice in his or her voting decisions.

The character of limiting freedom in democratic states is different from totalitarian states. In the latter, this limitation is imposed from outside. The whole legal structure, including state laws and rulings, had efficiently inhibited the freedom of citizens in East-Central Europe. The citizens were aware of the limitations imposed by the state. In democratic countries, however, these limitations come from the inside, through the creation of a certain picture of a part of reality in an individual's mind, stimulating certain behaviors. The character of such internal limitation is much more dangerous than external limitation, because one does not often realize that he or she is being limited in his or her freedom, and no formal ways to oppose these limits exist. As in totalitarian states, political organizations in democratic countries can achieve their goals through dishonest competition or falsifying the results of political elections. This falsifying, however, does not take place outside the voters but inside them, when false images and false memories of a candidate are created in their minds.

The problem of limiting voters' choice by political advertising and its threat to democracy was the subject of a boisterous debate in the Australian Parliament at the beginning of the 1990s. Ian Ward and Ian Cook (1992), describe in detail the debate during which the Australian government, reaching similar conclusions on the paradoxical relationship between freedom and democracy, suggested a ban on political advertising. The authors do not agree with the sharp criticism of this ban and state that a ban on political advertising violates the right to the freedom of thought. On the contrary, they claim that such a ban protects this right.

Freedom of expression is guaranteed by the First Amendment to the U.S. Constitution, which declares that "Congress shall make no law . . . abridging the freedom of speech, or of the press. . . ." Interpreting this provision, Justice Oliver Wendell Holmes of the Supreme Court used the analogy of a marketplace with regard to election campaigns, when considering the need for ideas to be freely disseminated in the community, the freedom of speech promotes "a free circulation of ideas from which people could pick those which seemed most likely to be true" (Ward, Cook, 1992, p. 23).

A healthy democracy means that voters are offered a number of ideas from which, based on their critical judgment, they reject those they do not accept. However, the market mechanisms allowing information to reach various voter segments permit the complete freedom in creating and broadcasting political advertising to limit the expression of political ideas rather than facilitate it. The research presented here on perception and remembering political advertisements shows that the goal of such advertising is at variance with the classical notion of freedom and democracy, according to which they should contribute to voters' conscious participation and critical reflection. Instead of stimulating critical thinking, advertising inhibits it by not conveying accurate information and by hiding and distorting that information instead.

Using the power of the media, marketing strategies in the economic and political spheres have expanded the methods of laboratory cognitive psychology into the natural social environment in democratic countries. An important point in case is Newman's book (1999a) *The Mass Marketing of Politics: Democracy in An Age of Manufactured Images*, whose very title suggests that the process of creating various images of politicians is particularly important in modern democracies. The work of Miller and Krosnick discussed previously presents practical applications of empirical research on priming, until recently conducted only in a laboratory environment.

After 1989, many countries of East-Central Europe opposed the totalitarian dictatorships and, when creating democratization processes in their societies, adopted, quite naturally, many models from well-established democracies. A rapid development of economic marketing was followed by political marketing. Television and the Internet began to be used to create economic and political realities in consumers' and voters' minds. The reality that is constructed in this way is reinforced in the form of remembered images, where political and economic brand personalities are created. It is exactly these images, equipped with a huge load of emotions, that direct the behavior of the consumer and voter. A number of empirical research projects on political elections in Poland, Hungary, Bulgaria, and Slovenia have shown that the development of democracy in these countries is proceeding in the same direction that the United States and Western Europe have been heading toward (Falkowski, Cwalina, 2004).

References

Abelson, R.P., Kinder, D.R., Peters, M.D., Fiske, S.T. (1982). Affective and semantic components in political person perception. *Journal of Personality and Social Psychology,* 42, 619-630.

Agnew, J. (1996). Mapping politics: How context counts in electoral geography. *Political Geography,* 15(2), 129-146.

Ahluwalia, R. (2000). Examination of psychological processes underlying resistance to persuasion. *Journal of Consumer Research,* 27, 217-232.

Ajzen, I. (1991). The theory of planned behavior. *Organizational Behavior and Human Decision Processes,* 50, 179-211.

Ajzen, I. (1996). *Attitudes, personality, and behavior.* Buckingham, UK: Open University Press.

Ajzen, I., Fishbein, M. (1980). *Understanding attitudes and predicting social behavior.* Englewood Cliffs, NJ: Prentice-Hall.

Anderson, J.R. (1983). *The architecture of cognition.* Cambridge, MA: Harvard University Press.

Ansolabehere, S., Iyengar, S. (1994). Riding the wave and claiming ownership over issues: The joint effects of advertising and news coverage in campaigns. *Public Opinion Quarterly,* 58, 335-357.

Ansolabehere, S., Iyengar, S., Simon, A. (1995). Evolving perspectives on the effects of campaign communication. *Research in Political Sociology,* 7, 13-31.

Argyle, M. (1983). *The psychology of interpersonal behaviour.* Harmondsworth, Middlesex, UK: Penguin Books.

Aristotle (1995). *Politics.* Oxford: Oxford Univeristy Press/World's Classics.

Aronson, E. (1992). *The Social Animal.* New York: W.H. Freeman And Company.

Aronson, E., Wilson, T.D., Akert, R.M. (1994). *Social psychology: The heart and the mind.* New York: HarperCollins College Publishers.

Atkin, C.K., Heald, G. (1976). Effects of political advertising. *Public Opinion Quarterly,* 40, 216-228.

Averill, J.R. (1980). A constructivism view of emotion. In R. Plutchik, H. Kellerman (eds.), *Emotion: Theory, research, and experience.* Vol. 1: *Theories of emotion* (pp. 305-339). San Diego, CA: Academic Press.

Bazylko, P., Fafara, P., Wysocki, P. (1991). Czarna teczka. Rzecz o sztabie wyborczym Stanisława Tymińskiego. In M. Grabowska, I. Krzemiński (eds.), *Bitwa o*

Belweder (pp. 56-68).Warszawa-Kraków, Poland: Wydawnictwo „Myśl" i Wydawnictwo Literackie.
Beck, U. (1992). *Risk society: Towards a new modernity.* London: Sage Publications.
Berelson, B., Lazarsfeld, P., McPhee, W. (1954). *Voting: A study of opinion formation in a presidential campaign.* Chicago, IL: University of Chicago Press.
Beyer, L. (1996). The making of Bibi. *Time,* 147(24), 40.
Biederman, I. (1987). Recognition-by-components: A theory of human image understanding. *Psychological Review,* 94, 115-147.
Blalock, H.M. (1960). *Social statistics.* New York: McGraw-Hill.
Blumler, J.G., Kavanagh, D. (1999). The third age of political communication: Influences and features. *Political Communication,* 16(3), 209-230.
Blumler, J.G., McQuail, D. (1968). *Television in politics.* London, UK: Faber and Faber.
Bourne Jr., L.E., Healy, A.F., Beer, F.A. (2003). Military conflict and terrorism: General psychology informs international relations. *Review of General Psychology,* 7(2), 189-202.
Braithwaite, V. (1997). Harmony and security value orientations in political evaluation. *Personality and Social Psychology Bulletin,* 23(4), 401-414.
Brams, S.J. (1976). *Paradoxes in politics: An introduction to the nonobvious in political science.* New York: Free Press.
Bransford, J. (1979). *Human cognition: Learning, understanding, and remembering.* Belmont, CA: Wadsworth Publishing Company.
Braun, K.A., Loftus, E.F. (1998). Advertising's misinformation effect. *Applied Cognitive Psychology,* 2, 569-591.
Brennan, G., Buchanan, J. (1984). Voter choice: Evaluating political alternatives. *American Behavioral Scientist,* 28(2), 185-201.
Britton, C.R., Ford, R.K. (2001). Weather and legislation: The effect of drought and flood on water laws. *The Social Science Journal,* 38, 503-514.
Bruner, J.S. (1973). *Beyond the information given. Studies in the psychology of knowing.* New York: W.W. Norton.
Buck, R. (1984). *The communication of emotion.* New York: Guilford Press.
Buck, R. (1988). *Human motivation and emotion.* New York: John Wiley & Sons.
Butler, D., Kavanagh, D. (1984). *The British general election of 1983.* London, UK: Macmillan.
Butler, D., Kavanagh, D. (1992). *The British general election of 1992.* London, UK: Macmillan.
Campbell, A., Converse, P.E., Miller, W.E., Stokes, D.E. (1960). *The American voter.* New York: John Wiley & Sons.
Campbell, A., Converse, P.E., Miller, W.E., Stokes, D.E. (1967). *Elections and the political order.* New York: John Wiley & Sons.
Campbell, J.E., Cherry, L.L., Wink, K.A. (1992). The convention bump. *American Politics Quarterly,* 20(3), 287-307.

References

Cantor, N., Mischel, W. (1979). Prototypes in person perception. In L. Berkowitz (ed.), *Advances in experimental social psychology*, Vol. 12 (pp. 3-28). New York: Academic Press.

Carmines, E.G., Gopoian, J.D. (1981). Issue coalitions, issueless campaigns: The paradox of rationality in American presidential elections. *Journal of Politics*, 43, 1170-1189.

Carmines, E.G., Kuklinski, J.H. (1990). Incentives, opportunities, and the logic of public opinion in American political representation. In J.A. Ferejohn, J.H. Kuklinski (eds.), *Information and democratic processes* (pp. 240-268). Urbana, IL: University of Illinois Press.

Chaffee, S.H., Choe, S.Y. (1980). Time of decision and media use during the Ford-Cartes campaign. *Public Opinion Quarterly*, 44, 53-69.

Chaffee, S.H., Hochheimer, J.L. (1985). The beginnings of political communication research in the United States: Origins of the "limited effects" model. In E. Rogers, F. Balle (eds.), *The media revolution in America and Western Europe* (pp. 267-296). Norwood, NJ: Ablex.

Chaffee, S.H., Rimal, R.N. (1996). Time of vote decision and openness to persuasion. In D. Mutz, P. Sniderman, R. Brody (eds.), *Political persuasion and attitude change* (pp. 267-291). Ann Arbor, MI: University of Michigan Press.

Chaffee, S.H., Zhao, X., Leshner, G. (1994). Political knowledge and the campaign media of 1992. *Communication Research*, 21(3), 305-324.

Chaiken, S., Lieberman, A., Eagly, A.H. (1989). Heuristic and systematic information processing within and beyond the persuasion context. [w:] J.S. Uleman, J.A. Bargh (red.), *Unintended thought* (pp. 212-252). New York: Guilford Press.

Chaiken, S., Stangor, C. (1987). Attitudes and attitude change. *Annual Review of Psychology*, 38, 575-630.

Cheng, P., Holyoak, K.J., Nisbett, R.E., Oliver, L.M. (1986). Pragmatic versus syntactic approaches to training deductive reasoning. *Cognitive Psychology*, 18, 293-328.

Conover, P.J., Feldman, S. (1981). The origins and meaning of liberal/conservative self-identifications. *American Journal of Political Science*, 25(4), 617-645.

Converse, P.E. (1964). The nature of belief systems in mass public. In D.E. Apter (ed.), *Ideology and discontent* (pp. 206-261). New York: The Free Press of Glencoe.

Cwalina, W. (2000). *Telewizyjna reklama polityczna: Emocje i poznanie w kształtowaniu preferencji wyborczych* [*Television political advertising: Emotions and cognition in forming voting preferences*]. Lublin, Poland: TN KUL.

Cwalina, W. (2003a). Historyczno-geograficzne uwarunkowania modeli zachowań wyborczych. Analiza porównawcza dwóch regionów Polski w kontekście wyborów prezydenckich w 2000 r [Historical and geographical determinants of voter behavior models. Comparative analysis of two Polish regions in the context of the 2000 presidential elections]. In M. Kowalski (ed.), *Przestrzeń wyborcza Polski* [*Poland's electoral space*] (pp. 87-114). Warsaw, Poland: Polish

Geographical Society Academic Branch and Institute of Geography and Spatial Organization, Polish Academy of Sciences.

Cwalina, W. (2003b). Życie polityczne w cieniu marketingu [Political life in the shadow of marketing]. In R. Szwed (ed.), *Społeczenstwo wirtualne, społeczenstwo informacyjne* [*Virtual society, informational society*] (pp.55-77). Lublin: Wydawnictwo KUL.

Cwalina, W., Falkowski, A. (1999). Decision processes in perception in the political preferences research: A comparative analysis of Poland, France, and Germany. *Journal for Mental Changes,* 5(2), 27-49.

Cwalina, W., Falkowski, A. (2000). Psychological mechanisms of political persuasion: The influence of political advertising on voting behavior. *Polish Psychological Bulletin,* 31(3), 203-222.

Cwalina, W., Falkowski, A. (2003). Advertising and the image of politicians. National elections in Poland, France, and Germany. In F. Hansen, L.B. Christensen (eds.), *Branding and advertising* (pp. 205-231). Copenhagen, Denmark: Copenhagen Business School Press.

Cwalina, W., Falkowski, A. (2005a). *Marketing polityczny: Persepektywa psychologiczna* [*Political marketing: A psychological perspective*]. Gdańsk, Poland: Gdańskie Wydawnictwo Psychologiczne.

Cwalina, W., Falkowski, A. (2005b). Towards the development of a cross-cultural model of voter behavior: Comparative analysis of Poland and the U.S. Paper presented at the I International Conference on Political Marketing 2005: "Political marketing & democracy," Kastoria, Greece, March 31-April 4, 2005.

Cwalina, W., Falkowski, A., Kaid, L.L. (2000). Role of advertising in forming the image of politicians: Comparative analysis of Poland, France, and Germany. *Media Psychology,* 2(2), 119-146.

Cwalina, W., Falkowski, A., Kaid, L.L. (2005). Advertising and the image of politicians in evolving and establishing democracies: Comparative study of the Polish and the U.S. presidential elections in 2000. *Journal of Political Marketing,* 4(2/3), 29-54.

Cwalina, W., Falkowski, A., Newman, B.I., Verčič, D. (2004). Models of voter behavior in traditional and evolving democracies: Comparative analysis of Poland, Slovenia, and U.S. *Journal of Political Marketing,* 3(2), 7-30.

Cwalina, W., Falkowski, A., Rożnowski, B. (1999). Television spots in Polish presidential elections. In L.L. Kaid (ed.), *Television and politics in evolving European democracies* (pp. 45-60). Commack, NY: Nova Science Publishers.

Däcker, M.L., Ekehammar, B., Sidanius, J. (1983). Adolescents' political rebellion and psychosocial factors in the home. *Reports from the Department of Psychology, The University of Stockholm,* No. 605.

D'Alessio, D., Allen, M. (2000). Media bias in presidential elections: A meta-analysis. *Journal of Communication,* 50(4), 133-156.

Dahl, R. (2000). *On Democracy.* New Haven, CT: Yale University Press.

Dalton, R.J., Wattenberg, M.P. (1993). The not so simple act of voting. In A. Finifter (ed.), *The state of the discipline II* (pp. 193-218). Washington, DC: The American Political Science Association.

Debord, G. (1994). The society of the spectacle. New York: Zone Books.

Denton, R.E., Woodward, G.C. (1990). *Political communication in America*. New York: Praeger.

Diamond, E., Bates, S. (1992). *The spot: The rise of political advertising on television*. Cambridge, MA: MIT Press.

Douglas, J. (1972). The verbal image: Student perceptions of political figures. *Speech Monographs*, 39, 1-15.

Downs, A. (1957). *An economic theory of democracy*. New York: Harper.

Echebarria, A., Paez, D., Valencia, J.F. (1988). Testing Ajzen and Fishbein's attitudes model: The prediction of voting. *European Journal of Social Psychology*, 18, 181-189.

Echebarria, A., Valencia, J.F. (1994). Private self-consciousness as moderator of the importance of attitude and subjective norm: The prediction of voting. *European Journal of Social Psychology*, 24, 285-293.

Ekman, P. (1992). *Telling lies: Clues to deceit in the marketplace, politics and marriage*. New York: W.W. Norton.

Election '96: Defining Mr. Right (1996). The Wirthlin Quorum Online, June 1996. Available at: http://www.wirthlin.com/publicns/quorum/wq9607.htm.

Eysenck, H.J. (1990). Biological dimensions of personality. In L.A. Pervin (ed.), *Handbook of personality: Theory and research* (pp. 244-276). New York: Guilford Press.

Falkowski, A., Cwalina, W. (1999). Methodology of constructing effective political advertising: An empirical study of the Polish presidential election in 1995. In B.I. Newman (ed.), *Handbook of political marketing* (pp. 283-304). Thousand Oaks, CA: Sage Publications.

Falkowski, A., Cwalina, W. (2002). Structural models of voter behavior in the 2000 Polish presidential election. *Journal of Political Marketing*, 1(2/3), 137-158.

Falkowski, A., Cwalina, W. (eds.) (2004). *Journal of Political Marketing*, 3(2).

Fiedler, J.A., Maxwell, R.A. (2000). Perceptual mapping and campaign. Eighth Sawtooth Software Conference on Quantitative Methods in Marketing Research. Hilton Head Island, South Carolina, March 23.

Fineman, H., Breslau, K. (2003). Arnold's Earthquake. *Newsweek*, October 20.

Fishbein, M., Ajzen, I. (1975). *Belief, attitude, intention, and behavior: An introduction to theory and research*. Reading, MA: Addison-Wesley.

Fishbein, M., Ajzen, I. (1981). Acceptance, yielding, and impact: Cognitive processes in persuasion. In R.E. Petty, T.M. Ostrom, T.C. Brock (eds.), *Cognitive responses in persuasion* (pp. 339-359). Hillsdale, NJ: Lawrence Erlbaum.

Fiske, S.T., Neuberg, S.L. (1990). A continuum of impression formation, from category-based to individuating processes: Influences of information and motivation on attention and interpretation. In M.P. Zanna (ed.), *Advances in experimental social psychology*, Vol. 23 (pp. 1-74). San Diego, CA: Academic Press.

Fiske, S.T., Pavelchak, M. (1986). Category-based versus piecemeal-based affective responses: Developments in schema-triggered affect. In R.M. Sorrentino, E.T. Higgins (eds.), *Handbook of motivation and cognition: Foundations of social behavior* (pp. 167-203). New York: Guilford Press.

Fiske, S.T., Taylor, S.E. (1991). *Social cognition*. New York: McGraw-Hill.

Forma, P. (2000). Comparing class-related opinions between MP candidates and party supporters: Evidence from Finland. *Scandinavian Political Studies*, 23(2), 115-137.

Frijda, N.H. (1988). The laws of emotion. *American Psychologist*, 43, 349-358.

Fromm, E. (1965). *Escape from freedom*. New York: Avon Books.

Gibson, J.J. (1966). *The senses considered as perceptual systems*. Boston: Houghton Mifflin.

Gibson, J.J. (1979). *The ecological approach to visual perception*. Boston: Houghton Miffin.

Glasser, T. (ed.) (1999). *The idea of public journalism*. New York: Guilford Press.

Goffman, E. (1959). *The presentation of self in everyday life*. Garden City, NY: Doubleday.

Greenberg, E.S., Page, B.I. (1995). *The struggle for democracy*. New York: HarperCollins College Publishers.

Harrison, M. (1965). Television and radio. In D. Butler, A. King (eds.), *The British general election of 1964* (pp. 156-184). London, UK: Macmillan.

Harrison, T.M., Stephen, T.D., Husson, W., Fehr, B.J. (1991). Images versus issues in the 1984 presidential election: Differences between men and women. *Human Communication Research*, 18(2), 209-227.

Hayes, B.C., McAllister, I. (1996). Marketing politics to voters: Late deciders in the 1992 British Election. *European Journal of marketing*, 30, 127-139.

Heaven, P., Stones, C., Nel, E., Huysamen, G., Louw, J. (1994). Human values and voting intention in South Africa. *British Journal of Social Psychology*, 33, 223-231.

Holbrook, A.L., Krosnick, J.A., Visser, P.S., Gardner, W.L., Cacioppo, J.T. (2001). Attitudes toward presidential candidates and political parties: Initial optimism, inertial first impressions, and focus on flaws. *American Journal of Political Science*, 45(4), 930-950.

Holbrook, T.M. (1996). *Do campaigns matter?* Thousand Oaks, CA: Sage Publications.

Holtz-Bacha, C., Kaid, L.L. (1995). Television spots in German national elections: Content and effects. In L.L. Kaid, C. Holtz-Bacha (eds.), *Political advertising in Western democracies: Parties and candidates on television*, (pp. 61-88). Thousand Oaks, CA: Sage Publications.

Huntington, S.P. (1991). *The Third Wave: Democratization in the Late Twentieth Century*. Norman, OK: University of Oklahoma Press.

Inglehart, R. (1977). *Silent revolution: Changing values and political styles among Western publics.* Princeton, NJ: Princeton University Press.
Ingram, P., Lees-Marshment, J. (2002). The anglicisation of political marketing: How Blair "out-marketed" Clinton. *Journal of Public Affairs,* 2(2), 44-56.
Jacks, J.Z., Cameron, K.A. (2003). Strategies for resisting persuasion. *Basic and Applied Social Psychology,* 25(2), 145-161.
Jamieson, K.H. (1992). *Dirty politics: Deception, distraction, and democracy.* New York: Oxford University Press.
Johnson, R.M. (1971). Market segmentation: A strategic management tool. *Journal of Marketing Research,* 8, 13-19.
Johnston, R.J., Pattie, C.J., Allsopp, J.G. (1988). *A nation dividing? The electoral map of Great Britain 1979-1987.* London, UK: Longman.
Kahle, L.R., Beatty, S.E., Homer, P. (1986). Alternative measurement approaches to consumer values: The list of values (LOV) and values and live styles (VALS). *Journal of Consumer Research,* 13, 405-409.
Kahneman, D., Slovic, P., Tversky, A. (red.) (1982). *Judgment under uncertainty: Heuristics and biases.* Cambridge, MA: Cambridge University Press.
Kaid, L.L. (1995). Measuring candidate images with semantic differentials. In K.L. Hacker (ed.), *Candidate images in presidential election* (pp. 131-134). Westport, CT: Praeger.
Kaid, L.L. (1997). Effects of television spots on images of Dole and Clinton. *American Behavioral Scientist,* 40(8), 1085-1094.
Kaid, L.L. (ed.) (1999). *Television and politics in evolving European democracies.* Commack, NY: Nova Science Publishers.
Kaid, L.L., Chanslor, M. (1995). Changing candidate images: The effects of political advertising. In K.L. Hacker (ed.), *Candidate images in presidential election* (pp. 83-97). Westport, CT: Praeger
Kaid, L.L., Gerstlé, J., Sanders, K.R. (eds.) (1986). *Mediated politics in two cultures: Presidential campaigning in the United States and France.* New York: Praeger.
Kaid, L.L., Holtz-Bacha, C. (eds.) (1995). *Political advertising in Western democracies: Parties and candidates on television.* Thousand Oaks, CA: Sage Publications.
Kaid, L.L., Nimmo, D., Sanders, K.R. (eds.) (1986). *New perspectives on political advertising.* Carbondale, IL: Southern Illinois University Press.
Key, V.O. (1966). *The responsible electorate.* Cambridge, MA: Belknap.
Kinder, D.R. (1986). Political character revisited. In R.R. Lau, D.O. Sears (eds.), *Political cognitions* (pp. 233-256). Hillsdale, NJ: Lawrence Erlbaum.
Kinsey, D.E. (1999). Political consulting: Bridging the academic and practical perspectives. In B.I. Newman (ed.), *Handbook of political marketing* (pp. 113-127). Thousand Oaks, CA: Sage Publications.
Klingemann, H.D., Wattenberg, M.P. (1992). Decaying versus developing party systems: A comparison of party images in the United States and West Germany. *British Journal of Political Science,* 22, 131-149.

Koffka, K. (1935). *Principles of Gestalt psychology.* New York: Harcourt, Brace.
Kotler, P., Kotler, N. (1999). Political marketing. Generating effective candidates, campaigns, and causes. In B.I. Newman (ed.), *Handbook of political marketing* (pp. 3-18). Thousand Oaks, CA: Sage Publications.
Kramer, M. (1996). The people choose. *Time,* 147(22), May 27. Available at: http://www.time.com/time/magazine/article/0,9171,984594-1,00.html.
Krzemiński, I. (1991). Wybrać lepszy świat. Postawy ówyborcow i kampanie wyborcze z punktu widzenia psychologa społecznego. W: M. Grabowska, I. Krzemiński (red.), *Bitwa o Belweder* (pp. 218-241). Warszawa, Poland: Kraków: Wydawnictwo „Myśl" i Wydawnictwo Literackie.
Lazarsfeld, P., Berelson, B., Gaudet, H. (1944). *The peoples choice: How the voter makes up his mind in a presidential campaign.* New York: Columbia University Press.
Lazarus, R.S. (1982). Thoughts on relations between emotion and cognition. *American Psychologist,* 37, 1019-1024.
Lazarus, R.S. (1984). On the primacy of cognition. *American Psychologist,* 39(2), 124-129.
Lazarus, R.S. (1991a). *Emotion and adaptation.* New York: Oxford University Press.
Lazarus, R.S. (1991b). Progress on a cognitive-motivational-relational theory of emotion. *American Psychologist,* 46, 819-834.
Lazarus, R.S., Kanner, A.D., Folkman, S. (1980). Emotions: A cognitive-phenomenological analysis. In R. Plutchik, H. Kellerman (eds.), *Emotion: Theory, research, and experience.* Vol. 1: *Theories of emotion* (pp.189-217). San Diego, CA: Academic Press.
Le Bon, G. (2002/1895). *The crowd: A study of the popular mind.* Mineola, NY: Dover Publications.
Leary, M. (1996). *Self-presentation.* Boulder, CO: Westview Press.
Lees-Marshment, J. (2001). The product, sales and market-oriented party: How Labour learnt to market the product, not just the presentation. *European Journal of Marketing,* 35(9/10), 1074-1084.
Lees-Marshment, J. (2003). Political marketing: How to reach that pot of gold. *Journal of Political Marketing,* 2(1), 1-32.
Lipset, S.M. (1981). *Political man: The social bases of politics.* Baltimore: Johns Hopkins University Press.
Lock, A., Harris, P. (1996). Political marketing—*vive la différence! European Journal of Marketing,* 30, 14-24.
Loehlin, J.C. (1987). *Latent variable models: An introduction to factor, path, and structural analysis.* Hillsdale, NJ: Lawrence Erlbaum.
Lorenz, K. (1987). *The waning of humaneness.* Boston: Little, Brown & Co.
Lott, B., Lott, A., Saris, R. (1993). Voter preference and behavior in the presidential election of 1988. *Journal of Psychology,* 127(1), 87-97.

Lupia, A.W., McCubbins, M.D. (1997). *The democratic dilemma: Can citizens learn what they need to know?* New York: Cambridge University Press.

Markus, G.B. (1988). The impact of personal and national economic conditions on the presidential vote: A pooled cross-sectional analysis. *American Journal of Political Science*, 32, 137-154.

Marland, A. (2003). Marketing political soap: A political marketing view of selling candidates like soap, of electioneering as a ritual, and of electoral military analogies. *Journal of Public Affairs*, 3(2), 103-115.

Marvin, C. (1994). Fresh blood, public meat: Rituals of totem regeneration in the 1992 presidential race. *Communication Research*, 21(3), 264-292.

Masterson, J.T., Biggers, T. (1986). Emotion-eliciting qualities of television campaign advertising as a predictor of voting behavior. *Psychology. A Quarterly Journal of Human Behavior*, 23(1), 13-19.

Mazzoleni, G., Roper, C.S. (1995). The presentation of Italian candidates and parties in television advertising. In L.L. Kaid, C. Holtz-Bacha (eds.), *Political advertising in Western democracies: Parties and candidates on television* (pp. 89-108). Thousand Oaks, CA: Sage Publications.

McAllister, I., Studlar, D.T. (1995). New politics and partisan alignment: Values, ideology and elites in Australia. *Party Politics*, 1(2), 197-220.

McCombs, M.E. (1981). The agenda-setting approach. In D.D. Nimmo, K.R. Sanders (eds.), *Handbook of political communication* (pp. 121-140). Beverly Hills, CA: Sage Publications.

McCombs, M.E., Shaw, D.L. (1972). The agenda-setting function of mass media. *Public Opinion Quarterly*, 36(2), 176-185.

McCrae, R.R., Costa, P.T., Jr. (1996). Toward a new generation of personality theories: Theoretical contexts for the five-factor model. In J.S. Wiggins (ed.), *The five-factor model of personality: Theoretical perspectives* (pp. 51-87). New York: Guilford Press.

McGinniss, J. (1969). *The selling of the president.* New York: Trident.

McGuire, S. (1997a). How Tony Blair won. *Newsweek*, 129(19), 14-17.

McGuire, S. (1997b). It's Tony Blair Time. *Newsweek*, 130, 16-18.

McGuire, W.J. (1964). Inducing resistance to persuasion: Some contemporary approaches. In L. Berkowitz (ed.), *Advances in experimental social psychology*, Vol. 1 (pp. 191-229). New York: Academic Press.

McGuire, W.J. (1985). Attitudes and attitude change. In G. Lindzey, E. Aronson (eds.), *The handbook of social psychology*, Vol. 2 (pp. 233-346). New York: Random House.

McGuire, W.J. (1989). Theoretical foundations of campaigns. In R.E. Rice, C.K. Atkin (eds.), *Public communication campaigns* (pp. 43-65). Newbury Park, CA: Sage Publications.

McQuail, D. (1969). *Towards a sociology of mass communications.* London, UK: Collier-Macmillan.

Miller, A.H., Gronbeck, B.E. (eds.) (1994). *Presidential campaigns and American self-images.* Boulder, CO: Westview Press.

Miller, J.M., Krosnick, J.A. (2000). News media impact on the ingredients of presidential evaluations: Politically knowledgeable citizens are guided by trusted source. *American Journal of Political Science,* 44(2), 301-315.

Miron, D., Marinescu, V., McKinnon, L.M. (1999). Romanian elections and the evolution of political television. In L.L. Kaid (ed.), *Television and politics in evolving European democracies* (pp. 85-111) Commack, NY: Nova Science Publishers.

Mondak, J.J. (1994). Cognitive heuristics, heuristic processing, and efficiency in political decision making. *Research in Micropolitics,* 4, 117-142.

Morrow, L. (1998). The reckless and the stupid. *Time,* 151(5), p. 72.

Negrine, R. (1994). *Politics and the mass media in Britain.* London, UK: Routlege.

Neisser, U. (1967). *Cognitive psychology.* New York: Appleton-Century-Crofts.

Newirt, J. (2003). *Between emotion and cognition: The generative unconscious.* New York: Other Press, LLC.

Newman, B.I. (1981). *The prediction and explanation of actual voting behavior in a presidential primary election.* Unpublished doctoral dissertation. University of Illinois at Urbana-Champaign.

Newman, B.I. (1994). *The marketing of the president: Political marketing as campaign strategy.* Thousand Oaks, CA: Sage Publications.

Newman, B.I. (1999a). *The mass marketing of politics: Democracy in an age of manufactured images.* Thousand Oaks, CA: Sage Publications.

Newman, B.I. (1999b). Politics in an age of manufactured images. *Journal of Mental Changes,* 5(2), 7-26.

Newman, B.I. (1999c). A predictive model of voter behavior: The repositioning of Bill Clinton. In B.I. Newman (ed.), *Handbook of political marketing* (pp. 259-282). Thousand Oaks, CA: Sage Publications.

Newman, B.I. (2002). Testing a predictive model of voter behavior on the 2000 U.S. presidential election. *Journal of Political Marketing,* 1(2/3), 159-173.

Newman, B.I., Sheth, J.N. (1985). A model of primary voter behavior. *Journal of Consumer Research,* 12, 178-187.

Nie, N., Verba, S., Petrocik, J. (1976). *The changing American voter.* Cambridge, MA: Harvard University Press.

Niffenegger, P.B. (1988). Strategies for success from the political marketers. *Journal of Services Marketing,* 2(3), 15-21.

Nisbett, R.E., Ross, L. (1980). *Human inference: Strategies and shortcomings of social judgment.* Englewood Cliffs, NJ: Prentice-Hall.

Noller, P., Galois, C., Hayes, A., Bohle, P. (1988). Impressions of politicians: The effect of situation and communication channel. *Australian Journal of Psychology,* 40(3), 267-280.

Osgood, C.E., Suci, G.J., Tannenbaum, P.H. (1957). *The measurement of meaning.* Urbana, IL: University of Illinois Press.

Ottati, V., Fishbein, M., Middlestadt, S.E. (1988). Determinants of voters' beliefs about the candidates' stands on the issues: The role of evaluative bias heuristics and the candidates' expressed message. *Journal of Personality and Social Psychology,* 55(4), 517-529.
Pacek, A.C., Radcliff, B. (1995). Economic voting and the welfare state: A cross-national analysis. *Journal of Politics,* 51(1), 44-61.
Page, B.I. (1977). Elections and social choice: The state of the evidence. *American Journal of Political Science,* 21(3), 639-668.
Palmer, S., Rosch, E., Chase, P. (1981). Canonical perspective and the perception of objects. In J. Long, A. Baddley (eds.), *Attention and performance,* Vol. 9 (pp. 135-151). Hillsdale, NJ: Lawrence Erlbaum.
Pattie, C., Johnston, R. (1998). The role of regional context in voting: Evidence from the 1992 British general election. *Regional Studies,* 32(3), 249-263.
Perloff, R.M., Kinsey, D. (1992). Political advertising as seen by consultants and journalists. *Journal of Advertising Research,* 32(3), 53-60.
Petrocik, J.R. (1979). Levels of issue voting: The effect of candidate-pairs in presidential elections. *American Politics Quarterly,* 7(3), 303-327.
Petrocik, J.R. (1996). Issue ownership in presidential elections, with a 1980 case study. *American Journal of Political Science,* 40(3), 825-850.
Petty, R.E., Cacioppo, J.T. (1986). *Communication and persuasion: Central and peripheral routes to attitude change.* New York: Springer Verlag.
Petty, R.E., Cacioppo, J.T. (1990). Involvement and persuasion: Tradition versus integration. *Psychological Bulletin,* 107(3), 367-374.
Petty, R.E., Priester, J.R. (1994). Mass media attitude change: Implications of the elaboration likelihood model of persuasion. In J. Bryant, D. Zillmann (eds.), *Media effects: Advances in theory and research* (pp. 91-122). Hillsdale, NJ: Lawrence Erlbaum.
Petty, R.E., Unnava, R.H., Strathman, A.J. (1991). Theories of attitude change. In T.S. Robertson, H.H. Kassarjian (eds.), *Handbook of consumer behavior* (pp. 241-280). Englewood Cliffs, NJ: Prentice-Hall.
Pfau, M., Kenski, H.C., Nitz, M., Sorenson, J. (1990). Efficacy of inoculation strategies in promoting resistance to political attack messages: Application to direct mail. *Communication Monographs,* 57, 25-43.
Plasser, F., Scheucher, C., Senft, C. (1999). Is there a European style of political marketing? A survey of political managers and consultants. In B.I. Newman (ed.), *Handbook of political marketing* (pp. 89-112). Thousand Oaks, CA: Sage Publications.
Popkin, S. (1991). *The reasoning voter: Communication and persuasion in presidential campaigns.* Chicago: University of Chicago Press.
Portrety liderów opozycji [Portraits of opposition leaders] (1997). Centrum Badania Opinii Społecznej [The Public Opinion Research Center], April 1997, BS/52/52/97.

Posner M. I., Keele S. W. (1968). On the genesis of abstract ideas. *Journal of Experimental Psychology,* 77, 353-363.
Pratkanis, A.R., Aronson, E. (1992). *Age of propaganda: The everyday use and abuse of persuasion.* New York: W.H. Freeman and Company.
Purzycki, J. (1991). *Prezydencki poker.* Warszawa, Poland: Wydawnictwo ROK Corporation.
Pye, L.W. (1972). The stages of socialization. In D.R. Reich, P.A. Dawson (eds.), *Political images and realities: Essays and readings on the concepts and substance of American politics* (pp. 103-106). Belmont, CA: Duxbury Press.
Rahn, W., Krosnick, J.A., Breuning, M. (1994). Rationalization and derivation processes in survey studies of political candidate evaluation. *American Journal of Political Science,* 38(3), 582-600.
Reed E., Jones R. (1982). *Reasons for realism: Selected essays of James J. Gibson.* Hillsdale, NJ: Lawrence Erlbaum.
Reimanis, G. (1982). Relationship of locus of control and anomie to political interest among American and Nigerian students. *Journal of Social Psychology,* 116, 289-290.
Riley, M. (1988). *Power, politics, and voting behaviour: An introduction to the sociology of politics.* London, UK: Harvester-Wheatsheaf.
Rokeach, M. (1973). *The nature of human values.* New York: The Free Press.
Rosch, E. (1973). On the internal structure of perceptual and semantic categories. In T. E. Moore (ed.), *Cognitive development and acquisition of language* (pp. 111-144). New York: Academic Press.
Rosen, J. (1991). Making journalism more public. *Communication,* 12, 267-284.
Russel, B. (1980). *The problems of philosophy.* London, UK: Oxford University Press.
Sagarin, B.J., Cialdini, R.B., Rice, W.E., Serna, S.B. (2002). Dispelling the illusion of invulnerability: The motivations and mechanisms of resistance to persuasion. *Journal of Personality and Social Psychology,* 83(3), 526-541.
Sears, D.O. (1993). Symbolic politics. In S. Iyengar, W.J. McGuire (eds.), *Explorations in political psychology* (pp. 113-149). Durham, NC: Duke University Press.
Sears, D.O. (1997). The impact of self-interest on attitudes—A symbolic politics perspective on difference between survey and experimental findings: Comment on Crano (1997). *Journal of Personality and Social Psychology,* 72(3), 492-496.
Sears, D.O., Funk, C.L. (1990). The limited effect of economic self-interest on political attitudes of mass public. *Journal of Behavioral Economics,* 19(3), 247-271.
Sears, D.O., Funk, C.L. (1991). The role of self-interest in social and political attitudes. In M. Zanna (ed.), *Advances in experimental social psychology,* Vol. 24 (pp. 1-91). Orlando, FL: Academic Press.
Sears, D.O., Funk, C.L. (1999). Evidence of the long-term persistence of adults' political predispositions. *Journal of Politics,* 61(1), 1-28.

Sears, D.O., Lau, R.R. (1983). Inducing apparently self-interested political preferences. *American Journal of Political Science,* 27(2), 223-252.
Shepard, A. (1994). The gospel of public journalism. *American Journalism Review,* 16(7), 28-34.
Singh, K., Leong, S.M., Tan, C.T., Wang, K.C. (1995). A theory of reasoned action perspective of voting behavior: Model and empirical test. *Psychology and Marketing,* 12(1), 37-51.
SRI Consulting Business Intelligence (2007). VALS FAQ. Available at: http://www.sric-bi.com/VALS/help.shtml#1.
Struthers, J., Young, A. (1989). Economics of voting: Theories and evidence. *Journal of Economic Studies,* 16(5), 3-42.
Sullivan, J.L., Aldrich, J.H., Borgida, E., Rahn, W. (1990). Candidate appraisal and human nature: Man and superman in the 1984 election. *Political Psychology,* 11(3), 459-484.
Thompson, J.B. (1994). Social theory and the media. In D. Crowley, D. Mitchell (eds.), *Communication theory today* (pp. 27-49). Cambridge, UK: Polity Press.
Toffler, A., Toffler, H. (1994). *Creating a new civilization: The politics of the Third Wave.* Atlanta, GA: Turner Publishing, Inc.
Tulving, E. (1985). Memory and consciousness. *Canadian Psychologist, 26,* 1-12.
Tversky, A., Kahneman, D. (1974). Judgment under uncertainty: Heuristics and biases. *Science,* 185, 1124-1131.
Verčič, D., Verdnik, I. (2002). Models of voter behavior: The Slovenia parliamentary elections. *Journal of Political Marketing,* 1(2/3), 123-135.
Veryzer, R.W., Hutchinson, J.W. (1998). The influence of unity and prototypicality on aesthetic responses to new product designs. *Journal of Consumer Research,* 24, 374-394.
Ward, I., Cook, I. (1992). Televised political advertising, media freedom, and democracy. *Social Alternatives,* 11, 21-26.
Warner, J. (1997). In the driver's seat. *Newsweek,* 130(15), 19-20.
Wattenberg, M.P. (1987). The hollow realignment: Partisan change in a candidate-centered era. *Public Opinion Quarterly,* 51, 58-74.
Wattenberg, M.P. (1994). *The decline of American political parties 1952-1992.* Cambridge, MA: Harvard University Press.
Wattenberg, M.P. (1995). *The rise of candidate-centered politics: Presidential elections of the 1980s.* Cambridge, MA: Harvard University Press.
Weiner, B., Graham, S., Peter, O., Zmuidinas, M. (1991). Public confession and forgiveness. *Journal of Personality,* 59(2), 281-312.
Wilkie, W.L. (1994). *Consumer behavior.* New York: John Wiley & Sons.
Wilson, T.D., Schooler, J.W. (1991). Thinking too much: Introspection can reduce the quality of preferences and decisions. *Journal of Personality and Social Psychology,* 60(2), 181-192.
Winter, D.G. (1995). Presidential psychology and governing styles: A comparative psychological analysis of the 1992 presidential candidates. In S.A. Renshon

(ed.), *The Clinton presidency: Campaigning, governing, and the psychology of leadership* (pp. 113-134). Boulder, CO: Westview.

Winter, D.G., Carlson, L.A. (1988). Using motive scores in the psychobiographical study of an individual: The case of Richard Nixon. *Journal of Personality,* 56(1), 75-103.

Wolfsfeld, G. (1992). Voters as consumers: Audience perspectives on the election broadcast. In A. Arian, M. Shamir (eds.), *The elections in Israel 1992* (pp. 235-253). Albany, NY: State University of New York Press.

Wood, D. (1982). *Power and policy in Western European democracies,* Second edition. New York: John Wiley & Sons.

Yorke, D.A., Meehan, S.A. (1986). ACORN in the political marketplace. *European Journal of Marketing,* 20(8), 63-76.

Zajonc, R.B. (1980). Feeling and thinking: Preferences need not inferences. *American Psychologist,* 35, 151-175.

Zajonc, R.B. (1984). On the primacy of affect. *American Psychologist,* 39(2), 117-123.

Zajonc, R.B., Markus, H. (1982). Affective and cognitive factors in preferences. *Journal of Consumer Research,* 9, 123-131.

Index

('i' indicates an illustration; 't' indicates a table)

A Classification of Residential Neighborhoods (ACORN), 88, 89-90
Active voter factors, 64, 65i
Activity
    ideal Polish candidate study, 42t, 44t, 45i
    Polish advertising study, 52t, 53
"Adwatch" program, 211-212
Aesthetics, 198
Affect function, 99, 101t
Affective behavior, 3-4
Affective-cognitive constructivism, 26
Affective-cognitive realism, 26
Age, 135
Aggressiveness, Polish study, 50t, 51t, 52t, 53
Ajzen, Icek
    expectancy-value model, 207-208, 209
    planned behavior theory, 108
Akert, Robin M., 54
Aldrich, John H., 40
Allsopp, Charles, 104, 105i, 107
American Dream, Clinton versus Dole, 120-125, 122t, 123t, 124t
Anchoring, 99, 100t
Anderson, John
    association-memory network model, 214
    Newman-Sheth model, 117-120, 118t, 119t, 120t

Ansolabehere, Stephen, 96
Appearance, Polish study, 41, 42t, 43, 44t, 45i
Aristotle, 7
Aronson, Elliot
    political emotions, 54
    social animal, 7
Association, 8
Attitude bolstering strategies, 209
Attitudes, 108, 109i, 109, 111
Attractiveness
    ideal Polish candidate study, 41, 42t, 43, 44t
    Polish advertising study, 51t, 52, 53
Attribute evaluation, 208
Attribute weighting, 208
Audience, 151
Australia
    freedom as constraint debate, 216
    program/issues voting, 103
Authority, Polish study, 42t, 44t, 45i
"Automatic" behavior, 1
Availability
    cognitive heuristics, 99, 100t
    "political heuristics," 99, 101t
Availability hypothesis, 214-215

Background
    campaign platform, 60
    structural equation questionnaire, 160

A Cross-Cultural Theory of Voter Behavior
© 2008 by The Haworth Press, Taylor & Francis Group. All rights reserved.
doi:10.1300/5478_10

Balance, 99, 101t
Basque Country study, 109-111, 110i, 146
Beatty, Warren, 21
Behavior, 108, 109i, 109
Behavioral control, 108, 109i, 109
Believer, Polish study, 42t, 43, 44t, 45i
Biased assimilation, 208
"Big Five," 125
Blair, Tony, 17
Blue-collar support
  Bush versus Gore, 127
  SDS supporters, 132
Blumler, Jay G., 70
Borgida, Eugene, 40
Brand leaders, marketing, 62
Bransford, John, 29, 30i
Braun, Kathryn, 202-204, 203i
Brennan, Geoffrey, 61
Breuning, Marijke, 55
Britain
  ACORN model, 88-90
  candidate-centered politics, 17
  combined predictability analysis, 143, 144
  decrease in party identification, 12, 14, 14i, 74-75
  program/issues voting, 103
  sociogeographic model, 104-108, 105i
Bruner, Jerome S.
  perception research, 28, 198
  playing cards experiment, 30-31
Buchanan, James, 61
Buck, Ross, 32-33, 34
Bulgarian political trends, 217
Bureau of Applied Social Research methodology, 9
Bush, George H. W.
  epistemic issues, 116
  political emotions study, 54
  television advertising study, 47, 48t, 48
Bush, George W.
  cognitive structural equation models, 159
  comparative constructivist analysis, 185-186

Bush, George W. *(continued)*
  comparative realist analysis, 188, 189, 189i
  constructivist realist comparison, 190i, 191t
  media's role, 192-193
  Newman-Sheth model, 125-129, 127t
  realist structural equation analysis, 183t, 183-185, 184i
  U.S. cognitive structural equation analysis, 174, 175, 175i, 176
Butler, David, 88

Cacioppo, John T., 206, 209
Calmness
  ideal Polish candidate study, 42t, 44t, 45i
  ideal Romanian candidate study, 45
Cameron, Kimberly A., 209-210
Campaign platform elements, 60
Campaign voters, 1964-1992, 13, 14i
Campaigns
  costs of, 64
  economic/political marketing, 61
Campbell, Angus, 90
Campbell, James E., 80, 81
Candidate. *See* Politician
Candidate-centered politics, 16-18
Candidate focus, 72i, 72-76
Candidate image
  evoke associations, 19
  media's role, 24
  Newman-Sheth model, 115, 117i
  Polish cognitive structural equation analysis, 165i, 166i, 167i, 168i, 169i
  Polish realist structural equation analysis, 181i, 182i
  political consultants, 22-23
  predictive models study, 138t
  Reagan versus Anderson, 118t
  realist structural equation model, 178i, 179i

Candidate image *(continued)*
  sequential model, 153-154, 154i
  structural equation models, 157i, 158i, 159i
  structural equation questionnaire, 161
  structure of, 20i, 20-22
  U.S. structural equation analysis, 175i, 176i, 184i
  visual distortion study, 201i
Candidate personality
  Bush versus Gore, 126
  term, 93
Candidate positioning
  marketing technique, 57
  Newman model, 72i
Care for others, Polish study, 42t, 43, 44t, 45i
Carmines, Edgar G., 97
Carter, Jimmy
  currents events, 115
  leadership attributes study, 38
  Niffenegger model, 70
  presidency of, 68
Cat, perception experiments, 31
Categorization, 34
Causal-effect model
  multidimensional voting, 104
  political advertising impact, 212, 213i, 213i
Central Europe
  democratization of, 5
  limitations on freedom, 2
  political trends, 217
Centre Party of Finland, elections, 86, 87i, 88
Centrum Badania Opinii Spolecznej, opinion poll, 38
Chaffee, Stephen, 11, 12
Change
  Bush versus Gore, 126
  SDS supporters, 132
Chanslor, Mike, 47-49
Charisma
  ideal Polish candidate study, 42t, 44t
  ideal political leader, 36-37
  leadership attributes, 37

Chase, Paul, 198
Cherry, Lynn L., 80, 81
Chin Tiong Tan, 54
Cialdini, Robert, 210
Citizenship, 8
Clarity, Polish study, 41, 42t, 44t
Class voting model, 10-11
Clinton, Bill
  epistemic issues, 116
  moral behavior, 36
  Newman cognitive model, 94-95
  Newman-Sheth model, 120-122, 122t, 124
  political image, 19, 21
  public image development, 38
  television advertising study, 47-48, 48t
  visual distortion study, 199, 200, 201, 204
Cognition
  Newman-Sheth domains, 114-117, 117i, 134-135
  perception, 198-199
  political marketing, 3
  political marketing epistemology, 8
  voting heuristics, 99, 100t
Cognitive constructivism, information-processing, 26, 27
Cognitive philosophy
  ecological approach, 25-26
  emotions research, 26
  and Gestalt psychology, 27-28
  information-processing approach, 25-26
  political concerns, 25
Cognitive psychology
  political marketing, 3
  voter behavior, 8
Cognitive realism, 26, 32-34
"Cognitive shortcuts," 99
Cognitive stability index
  comparative realist analysis, 188-189
  marketing strategy, 193
Colleague's influence, 9
Collective decision, 61

Color memory study, 202-204, 203i
Common fate, 27, 197
Communication/persuasion process matrix model, 206
Community, 10-11
Competence
  ideal Polish candidate study, 41, 43, 44t, 45i
  ideal political leader, 36
  leadership attributes, 37
  Polish advertising study, 52t, 53
  television advertising study, 47
Comprehensive political marketing (CPM), 76
Concentration strategy, 69
Confession, 36-37
Conover, Pamela Johnson, 103
Conscience, 47
Conscientiousness, 42t, 44t, 45i
Conservative Party
  campaign spending, 14
  decrease in, 12
  program/issues voting, 103
  social class study, 88
  sociogeographic model, 106, 107
Constantinescu, Emil, 45-46
Constructivism
  ambiguous figures, 28-29, 29i
  natural/social phenomena, 25-27
Constructivist models
  affective behaviors, 3-4
  comparative analysis, 185-187
  political marketing, 197-202
  and realist model, 189-191, 190i, 192
"Constructivist oriented laboratory of cognitive psychology," 4
Constructivist structural equation model, 156
Consumer behavior, 58
Continuity, 27
Convention stage, 72i, 80-81
Converse, Philip E., 90
Cook, Ian, 216
Correctness, Romanian study, 45

Counterarguing strategies, 209
Credibility
  ideal Polish candidate study, 41, 42t, 43, 44t
  Polish advertising study, 52t, 53
Crime, 132
Current events
  cognitive structural equation models, 157i, 158i, 159i
  cognitive structural equation questionnaire, 161
  Newman-Sheth model, 115, 117i
  Polish cognitive structural equation analysis, 165i, 166i, 167i, 168i, 169i
  Polish realist structural equation analysis, 181i, 182i
  Reagan versus Anderson, 118t
  realist structural equation model, 178i, 179i
  Slovenia cognitive structural equation analysis, 172i, 173i
  U.S. cognitive structural equation analysis, 175i, 176i
  U.S. realist structural equation analysis, 184i
Current experience, 108
Cwalina, Wojciech
  Newman-Sheth model, 134
  Polish ideal politician study, 41
  Polish political emotions study, 54

Dahl, Robert A, 7-8
Dalton, Russell J.
  partisanship, 14
  party identification model objections, 91
  sociostructural critique, 11
Davis, Gray, 116
Dealignmen indicators, 15t
Debord, Guy, 17
Deception, 16
Decision making, 102

Index

Democracies
  comparative constructivist analysis, 185-187
  limitations on freedom, 3, 215-217
  media threat, 205
  partisanship, 11, 14-15
  political marketing, 2
  political organization, 7
  right to information, 196
Democratic approach, Romanian study, 45
Democratic Party
  Bush versus Gore, 125, 126-129, 127t, 128t
  decreased members, 12, 13i
  issue ownership, 96
  U.S. cognitive structural equation analysis, 174
Demographic information, questionnaire, 162
DePaul University, 125, 174
Derivation, 55
Desert, "political heuristics," 99, 101t
Determination, Polish study, 41, 43
Dewey, Thomas, 9
Dichotomous model, 11-12
Direct mail technology, Newman model, 82
Disclaiming, 211
Displacing, 211
Distancing, 211
Dole, Bob
  Newman cognitive model, 94
  Newman-Sheth model, 120-121, 122, 123t, 124
  public image development, 38
  visual distortion study, 199, 200-201, 201i, 204
Domestic issues, 132
Donators, 64, 65i
Downs, Anthony, 95
Dukakis, Michael
  political emotions study, 54
  television advertising study, 47
Dynamism, Romanian study, 45

Eastern Europe
  candidate-centered politics, 17-18
  democratization of, 5
  limitations on freedom, 2
  political trends, 217
Echebarria Echabe, A., Basque study, 109, 110, 110i, 146
Ecological model
  cognitive philosophy, 25-27, 32-34
  structural equation model, 196-197
Economic and Social Research Council (ESRC), 104
Economic marketing
  Eastern/Central Europe, 5
  and political marketing, 60-63
Economic model combined
  predictability analysis, 145
Economic optimism, 105i, 106-107
Economy, ZLDS supporters, 133
Education
  ideal Polish candidate study, 41, 42t, 43, 44t, 45i
  LDS supporters, 130
  marketing techniques, 4
  sociodemographic model, 135
Effectiveness, Romanian study, 45
Efficacy, 135
Efficiency, Polish study, 41, 42t, 44t, 45i
Eire County study, 9
Eisenhower, Dwight D.
  leadership attributes study, 38
  polling, 67
Ekman, Paul, 16
Elaboration likelihood model (ELM), 206
Elected representatives, 7
Election laws, 83
Electoral districts, 64
Electoral rewards/punishments, 97
Elmira (NY) study, 9
Eloquence, Polish study, 41, 42t, 44t, 45i
Embarrassment, 36
Embourgeoisement, 10
Emotion, in politics, 35, 54-56

Emotional attitude, advertising impact, 213i
Emotional-cognitive constructivism, 27-32
Emotional-cognitive processes, 3
Emotional feelings
　cognitive structural equation models, 157i, 157-158, 158i, 159i
　cognitive structural equation questionnaire, 161
　comparative constructivist analysis, 185-186
　constructivist-realist comparison, 189-190, 191, 193
　Newman-Sheth model, 115, 117i
　Polish cognitive structural equation analysis, 163, 165i, 166, 166i, 168, 169i
　predictive behavior, 147, 148-149
　Reagan versus Anderson, 118t
　realist structural equation model, 177-178, 178i, 179i
　Slovenian cognitive structural equation analysis, 172i, 173i
　U.S. cognitive structural equation analysis, 175i, 176i
Emotional voters, 93
Emotions
　cognitive realism, 32-34
　"cognitive-motivational-relational theory," 31-32
　creation of, 26-27
　and perception, 31
　political marketing, 1
　role of, 26
Employers, Finnish elections, 86, 87i, 88
Endorsements
　LSD supporters, 132
　ZLDS supporters, 133
Environmental forces, 72i, 82-82
Epistemic issues
　cognitive structural equation models, 157i, 158i, 159i
　cognitive structural equation questionnaire, 161
　Newman-Sheth model, 116, 117i

Epistemic issues *(continued)*
　Polish cognitive structural equation analysis, 165i, 166i, 167i, 168i, 169i
　Polish realist structural equation analysis, 181i, 182i
　Reagan versus Anderson, 118t
　realist structural equation model, 178i, 179i
　Slovenia cognitive structural equation analysis, 172i, 173i
　U.S. cognitive structural equation analysis, 175i, 176i
　U.S. realist structural equation analysis, 184i
Epistemic value, Bush versus Gore, 126
Ethical attractiveness, Polish study, 51t, 53
Ethical norms, Polish study, 50t, 51t, 52, 53
Ethics, marketing behavior, 4
European Parliament, 89
European politics, 17-18
Euskadiko Ezkerra (EE), Basque study, 110
Eusko Alkartasuna (EA), Basque study, 110
Expectancy-value model, 207-209

Fairness, Polish study, 42t, 44t, 45i
Falkowski, Andrzef
　Polish ideal politician study, 41
　Polish political emotions study, 54
False memory, 204-205
"False prophets," 210
Family influence, 9
Farmers
　Finnish elections, 86, 87i, 88
　SDS supporters, 132
Feldman, Stanley, 103
Financial resources, 64
Finland, Parliamentary elections, 86, 87i, 88

Index

Fishbein, Martin
   expectancy-value model, 207-208, 209
   reasoned action theory, 108
Fiske, Susan T., 34
Fitness parameters
   comparative realist analysis, 188, 189i
   constructivist-realist comparison, 190i
"Floating voters," 12, 92
Ford, Gerald, 38
Forma, Pauli, 86, 87i, 88
"Fourth estate," 149
France, 17
Freedom
   media threat to, 212-215
   modern democracy, 7-8
"Fresh face," 116
Friend's influence, 9
Friendliness
   ideal Polish candidate study, 42t, 44t, 45i
   Polish advertising study, 50t, 51t, 53
Funk, Carolyn L., 102-103
Future orientation, LDS, 130

Gender, 135
General election stage, 72i, 81-82
Gestalt psychology
   constructivist foundation, 187
   illusory contour, 27, 28i
   laws of, 197, 199
   principles of, 27
"Goes outside," 198
Goffman, Erving, 17
Golik & Dabrowski advertising agency, 18
"Goodness of figure" research, 198
Goodness-of-fit parameters
   comparative realist analysis, 189i, 191t
   constructivist-realist comparison, 190i

Gopoian, J. David, 97
Gore, Al
   comparative constructivist analysis, 185
   comparative realist analysis, 188, 189i
   constructivist-realist comparison, 190i, 191t
   media's role, 192
   Newman-Sheth model, 125-129, 127t, 128t
   realist structural equation analysis, 183t, 183-185, 184i
   structural equation models, 159
   U.S. cognitive structural equation analysis, 174, 175i, 176i, 176-177
Government employment, 10
Goya, Francisco, 35
Graham, Sandra, 36
Great Britain. *See* Britain
Greenberg, Edward S., 97
Gun control, Bush versus Gore, 126

Harris, Phil
   political behavior research, 57-58
   political information consumers, 204
Hart, Gary, 69
Hayes, Bernadette, 12
Health care, Bush versus Gore, 128
Herri Batasuna (HB), Basque study, 110, 110i
Heuristics, 99
Holbrook, Thomas M., 12
Holmes, Oliver Wendell, 216
Homo politicus, 7
Honesty, Polish study, 41, 42t, 43, 44t, 45i
Hot cognitions, 33
Housing, Bush vs. Gore, 128
"Human face," 20
Humphrey, Hubert, 67
Hungary, political trends, 217
Hutchinson, Wesley, 198

Ideal politician
  Polish elections, 41, 42t, 43, 44t, 45, 45i
  political image, 35-39
  prototype, 39-40
  Reagan election, 67
  Romanian study, 45-46
Ideology, 135
Iliescu, Ion, Romanian study, 45-46
Image
  campaign platform, 60
  "ideal politician," 35
  Newman-Sheth model, 115, 117i
  Polish cognitive structural equation analysis, 165i, 166i, 167i, 168i, 169i
  political advertising, 35, 46-49, 153-154, 154i
  predictive models study, 138t
  Reagan versus Anderson, 118t
  as representation, 35, 39
  visual distortion study, 201i
Image creation specialist, 16-18
Immigrants, SDS supporters, 133
Impact, 208
Impact minimization, 208
"Impervious attitudes," 181
Income, 135
Independence, Polish study, 42t, 44t, 45i
Independent voters
  dealignment indicator, 15t
  increase in, 12, 13i, 74
Inference rules, 99
Inflation
  Bush versus Gore, 126
  LDS supporters, 132
  SDS supporters, 133
Information
  in a modern democracy, 8
  as resource, 195
Information society, 195-197
Information-processing approach, 25-27
Inoculation model, 206-207
Institute for Social Research model, 90
Integrity, 37

Intelligence, Polish study, 41, 42t, 43, 44t, 45i
Intentional determinants, 108
Intentions
  planned behavior theory, 108, 109i, 111
  visual distortion study, 201i
Interactive behaviors, 151, 152
Interest, involvement model, 135
Interest groups, 64, 65i
International Survey of Economic Attitudes (ISEA), Finnish study, 86
Israel, 17
Issue ownership, 96
Issues
  Newman-Sheth model, 114, 117i
  Polish cognitive structural equation analysis, 165i, 166i, 167i, 168i, 169i
  Polish realist structural equation analysis, 181i, 182i
  predictive models study, 138t
  Reagan versus Anderson, 118t
  realist structural equation model, 178i, 179i
  Slovenia cognitive structural equation analysis, 172i, 173i
  structural equation models, 157i, 158i, 159i
  structural equation questionnaire, 160
  U.S. cognitive structural equation analysis, 175i, 176i
  U.S. realist structural equation analysis, 184i
Iyengar, Shanto, issue presentation, 96

Jamieson, Kathleen Hall, 211-212
Job security, ZLDS supporters, 133
Johnston, Ron, 104, 105i, 107
Jones, Rebecca, 199
Jospin, Lionel, 17

Kahneman, Daniel
  availability hypothesis, 215
  cognitive heuristics, 99
Kaid, Lynda Lee
  television advertising study, 47-49, 153-154
  visual distortion study, 199-202, 201i, 204
Kant, Emanuel, 8
Kavanagh, Dennis, ACORN, 88
Keeping promises, Polish study, 50t, 51t, 53
Kennedy, John F.
  campaign of, 68-69
  leadership attributes study, 38
Key, V. O., 97
Klingermann, Hans-Dieter, 17
Koffka, Kurt
  aesthetic criteria, 198
  Gestalt law, 197
  "goodness of figure," 198
Kotler, Neil
  campaign factors, 64
  political behavior research, 57-58
  on political markets, 63
Kotler, Philip
  campaign factors, 64
  political behavior research, 57-58
  on political markets, 63
Krameer, Michael, 18
Krosnick, Jon A.
  derivation/rationalization, 55
  media impact study, 214
Krzaklewski, Marian, 41, 43, 44t
Krzemiński, Ireneusz, 18
Kwaśniewski, Aleksander
  campaign factors, 69
  cognitive structural equation analysis, 162-164, 164t, 165, 166, 167, 167i, 168, 168i
  comparative constructivist analysis, 185, 186, 187
  comparative realist analysis, 188, 189, 189i
  constructivist-realist comparison, 190i, 191t

Kwaśniewski, Aleksander *(continued)*
  emotional feelings predictor, 147-148, 148t
  media's role, 192-193
  Polish presidential candidate, 41, 42t, 43, 44t
  political advertising study, 48, 49, 50t-51t, 52t, 52-53
  predictive models study, 136-142, 138t, 139t, 140t, 141t, 142t
  realist structural equation analysis, 180i, 180-181, 181i
  structural equation models, 159
Kwei Cheong Wang, 54

"Laboratory," perception research, 198-199
"Laboratory world," marketing strategy, 199
Labour Party
  campaign spending, 14
  members decrease, 12
  program/issues voting, 103
  social class study, 88
  sociogeographic model, 106, 107
Lazarsfeld, Paul, 9
Lazarus, Richard S., 31-32
LDS. *See* Liberal Democrats of Slovenia (LDS)
Leader evaluation, 105i
Learning, 32
Leary, Mark, 36, 37
Lees-Marshment, Jennifer, 72, 76
Left Alliance, 86, 87i
Lewinsky, Monica, 36
Liberal Democrats of Slovenia (LDS)
  cognitive structural equation analysis, 170, 171t, 171-172
  comparative constructivist analysis, 185, 186
  parliamentary elections, 130-131, 131t, 132, 133t, 133-134
  structural equation models, 159
Likeability, 99, 101t

Limbaugh, Rush, 22
Lipset, Seymour, 7
Locational influence, 105i, 105-106
Lock, Andrew
  political behavior research, 57-58
  political information consumers, 204
Loftus, Elizabeth, 202-204, 203i
Lorenz, Konrad
  on deception, 16
  propaganda tolerance, 195
Lott, Albert, 54
Lott, Bernice, 54
Loyal voters, 1964-1992, 13, 14, 14i

Marketing
  cognitive strategies, 25
  ethical side of, 4
  exchange process, 59
  Newman model, 72i, 73i, 75-76
  Niffenegger research model, 67
  orientation, 63
  political image literature, 54
  term 16
  voting behavior, 8
Marketing campaign, 72i, 76-78
Marketing mix
  Newman model, 77
  Niffenegger model, 66, 66i
  strategies, 59
Marketing strategies
  campaigning essence, 63
  comparative constructivist analysis, 185-187
  constructivist-realist comparison, 192-193
  marketing mix, 59
Marketing technique, physical strength, 57
Markus, Gregory B., 97
Marland, Alex, 58
Mass communication characteristics, 149-150
Mass Marketing of Politics, The: Democracy in An Age of Manufactured Images, 4-5, 217

McAllister, Ian, 12
McGovern, George, 81
McGuire, William J., 206-207
McQuail, Denis
  mass communication, 149-150
  on undecided voters, 70
Meaning, 29-30, 30i
Media
  campaign factors, 64-65, 65i
  comparative constructivist analysis, 185-186, 187
  constructivist-realist comparison, 192-193
  education task, 185
  influence of, 9, 22, 24, 149-150, 214-215
  information society, 4
  multiplicity of, 150-151
  perceptual distortion study, 199-202
  Polish cognitive structural equation analysis, 163-169, 164t, 165i, 166-168, 166i, 167i, 168, 169i
  Polish realist structural equation analysis, 180, 181i, 182
  political communication, 151
  and political marketing, 2
  realist structural equation model, 177-180, 178i, 179i
  Slovenia cognitive structural equation analysis, 170-171, 172i, 173i
  sociogeographic model, 106-107
  structural equation models, 157, 157i, 157-158, 158i, 159i
  structural equation questionnaire, 161
  threat of, 205
  U.S. cognitive structural equation analysis, 174, 175i, 175-176, 176i
  U.S. realist structural equation analysis, 183
Media voting paradox, 12
"Mediatization," 16
Meehan, Sean A., 88, 89

Index

Memory
  association-memory network model, 214
  emotion trigger, 32
  political advertising, 202, 202-205
Message
  expectancy-value model, 208
  persuasion resistance strategies, 209
  political communication element, 151, 152-153
Miller, Joanne M., 214
Miron, Dorina, Romanian study, 45-46
Misdirection strategy, 70
Mobility, 10-11
Mondak, Jeffrey J., 99, 101t
Mondale, Walter
  political campaigns, 68, 70
  superman model, 40-41
Morality
  ideal political leader, 36-37
  television advertising study, 47

National Association of Broadcasters, 211
National Coalition Party, 86, 87i
National Election Study
  ideological voting, 103
  political emotions, 55-56
"Natural social environment," 4
Negative advertising
  campaign, strategy, 70
  Niffenegger model, 71
Negative affect, resistance strategies, 210
Negrine, Ralph, 151i, 151-153
Neighbor's influence, 9
Neisser, Ulrich, 28, 198
Netanyahu, Benjamin, 17
Newman, Bruce I.
  age of manufactured images, 17
  candidate image, 21
  candidate as product, 59
  economic/political marketing, 62

Newman, Bruce I. *(continued)*
  media threat, 205
  multidimensional voting, 104
  political behavior research, 57-58
  political consultants, 22-24
  political information consumers, 204
  political marketing model, 71-83
  psychographic segmentation, 92-95, 125
  voter choice behavior, 3, 116-117
  work of, 4-5, 217
Newman model
  constructivist-realist comparison, 192
  predictive models study, 138, 138t, 139t, 139-141, 141t, 142t
Newman-Sheth model
  basic assumption, 113-114
  Bush versus Gore, 125-129, 127t, 128t
  Clinton versus Dole, 120-125
  cognitive domains, 114-117, 117i, 134-135
  description of, 113-117, 117i
  multidimensional voting, 104
  Polish presidential election, 134-135
  predictive capacity, 136-137
  Reagan versus Anderson, 117-120, 118t, 119t
  Slovenia Parliamentary elections, 129-134, 131t, 133t, 134t
Niffenegger, Phillip B.
  model implications, 71
  political marketing model, 65-71, 66i
Nixon, Richard
  conventions study, 81
  leadership attributes study, 38
  Newman model, 75
  polling, 67
  resignation of, 36
  and undecided voters, 70
"No hidden agenda," 21
Nongovernmental organizations, 64, 65i

Objectivity, Polish study, 42t, 44t
Occupation, 135
Olechowski, Andrzej
  cognitive structural equation analysis, 162-165, 164t, 166-168, 168i, 169i
  comparative constructivist analysis, 185-187
  comparative realist analysis, 188, 189i
  constructivist-realist comparison, 190i, 191t
  media's role, 192
  nontraditional background, 16
  Polish presidential candidate, 41, 43, 44t
  predictive models study, 136-142, 138t, 139t, 140t, 141t, 142t
  realist structural equation analysis, 180i, 180, 182
  structural equation models, 159
Openness, Polish study, 41, 42t, 43, 44t, 45i
Opinion leaders, 9
"Ordinary" people," candidate image, 20
Organization, 198

Pacek, Alexander C., 98
"Package," 46
"Packaged," 16
Packaging," 58, 68, 204
Paez Rovira, D., Basque study, 109, 110i, 146
Page, Benjamin I.
  rational voter critique, 98-99
  retrospective voting, 97
  party identification model objections, 91
Palmer, Stephen, 198
Partido Nacionalista Vasco (PNV), Basque study, 110
Partido Socialista Obrero Español (PSOE), Basque study, 110

Partisanship
  decreasing influence, 11, 12, 14-15, 74-75
  political involvement model, 136
Party concept, 72i, 73i, 73-74
Party events, Slovenia, 172i, 173i
Party identification
  dealignment indicator, 15t
  decreasing influence, 12, 13i
  sociogeographic model, 105i, 106, 107
Party image, Slovenia, 172i, 173i
Party platform, 68
Patriotism
  Bush versus Gore, 126
  Romanian study, 45
Pattie, Charles, 104, 105i, 107
Pavelchak, Mark A., 34
Perception
  cognitive constructivism, 27-32, 28i, 29i, 30i
  emotion trigger, 32
  organization of, 197-198
  political advertising, 197-202
  political marketing, 1
Perceptual illusions
  "laboratory" world, 199
  laws of, 197
  political advertising study of, 196
Perceptual organization, 197-198, 199
Performance, 35
"Permanent campaign," 23
Perot, Ross
  epistemic issues, 116
  nontraditional background, 16
Personal aspects, 37
Personal events
  cognitive structural equation models, 157i, 158i, 159i
  comparative constructivist analysis, 186, 186t
  Newman-Sheth model, 116, 117i
  Polish cognitive structural equation analysis, 165i, 166i, 167i, 168i, 169i

Personal events *(continued)*
  Polish realist structural equation analysis, 181i, 182i
  predictive models study, 138t
  Reagan versus Anderson, 118t
  realist structural equation model, 178i, 179i
  structural equation questionnaire, 161
  U.S. cognitive structural equation analysis, 175i, 176i
  U.S. realist structural equation analysis, 184i
Personality
  candidate image, 20-21
  voting behavior, 92-95
Personnel, 83
Persuasion
  antidotes to, 210-212
  model of resistance, 206-209
  resistance strategies, 209-210
  techniques, 4
  theories, political manipulation, 206
Peter, Orli, 36
Petrocik, John R., 96
Petty, Richard E., 206, 209
Place, 66i, 67, 69
Planned behavior model
  combined predictability analysis, 145-146
  multidimensional voting, 104, 108-111, 109i, 110i
Plasser, Fritz, 19
"Play," 16-17
Pocketbook voting, 97-98
Poland
  candidate-centered politics, 17-18
  cognitive structural equation method, 162-173, 156i, 165i, 166i, 167i, 168i, 169i
  combined predictability analysis, 142, 143, 144, 145
  comparative constructivist analysis, 185, 186-187, 186t, 187
  comparative realist analysis, 188-189, 189i

Poland *(continued)*
  constructivist-realist comparison, 190i, 191, 191t
  emotional feelings predictor, 147-148, 148t
  ideal leader survey, 38
  information technology, 196
  marketing strategy, 192
  Polish presidential candidates, 41, 42t, 43, 44t, 45, 45i
  political advertising study, 48, 49, 50t-52t, 52-53
  political emotions study, 54
  political parties, 74
  political trends, 217
  politician's background, 16
  presidential elections model predictions, 136-142, 138t, 139t, 140t, 141t, 142t
  realist structural equation analysis, 180-182, 181i
  structural equation models, 159
Policies
  Newman-Sheth model, 114, 117i
  Polish cognitive structural equation analysis, 165i, 166i, 167i, 168i, 169i
  Polish realist structural equation analysis, 181i, 182i
  predictive models study, 138t
  Reagan versus Anderson, 118t
  realist structural equation model, 178i, 179i
  Slovenia cognitive structural equation analysis, 172i, 173i
  structural equation models, 157i, 158i, 159i
  structural equation questionnaire, 160
  U.S. cognitive structural equation analysis, 175i, 176i
  U.S. realist structural equation analysis, 184i
Political "actors"
  candidate-centered politics, 16
  social categorization, 34

Political advertising
  Bush-Clinton election, 46-49, 48t
  cognitive philosophy, 25
  false memory, 202, 204-205
  image, 35
  perceptual basis, 197-199
  perceptual distortion,
  Polish elections, 48, 49, 50t-52t
  sequential model, 153-155, 154i, 212-214, 213i
  visual distortion study, 199-202, 201i
Political campaign
  marketing foundation, 71-72
  marketing orientation, 63-65
  Newman model, 78-82
Political communication model
  elements, 151i, 151-153
Political competence, Polish study, 48, 49, 50t-51t, 52t, 52-53
Political consultants
  European, 19
  influence of, 22-23
  view of, 22
"Political heuristics," 99
Political ideology, 105i, 106
Political images, 18-24. *See also* Images
Political Information Network (PIN), 67, 70
Political institutions, 151
Political involvement model
  predictive capacity, 136-137
  predictive models study, 138-139, 140t, 140-141, 141, 142t
  variables of, 135-136
Political issues, Bush versus Gore, 126
Political marketing
  consumer behavior, 58-59
  definition of, 59, 66
  Eastern/Central Europe, 5
  and economic marketing, 60-63
  emergence of, 1
  Lees-Marshment model, 72, 76
  Newman model, 71-83, 72i
  Niffenegger model, 65-71, 66i

Political marketing *(continued)*
  psychological basis of, 3
  sociostructural research, 9
Political marketing consultants, 2
Political parties
  campaign factors, 64, 65i
  conventions study, 80-81
  decline of, 12, 13i, 14, 14i, 74-75
  economic/political marketing, 61-62
  issue specialization, 96-97
  program support, 103
  SDS supporters, 133
  sociogeographic evaluation, 105i
  structural equation questionnaire, 161
  voter identification, 90-92
Political power, Polish study, 50t, 51t
"Political products," 59
"Political scene," 16
"Political stage," the, 34
Political systems, 1
Politicians
  candidate-centered politics, 16-18
  nontraditional background, 16
  political consultants' role, 23
  as products, 59-60
  social categorization of, 34
Politics, 7
Polling
  Eisenhower campaign, 67
  Newman model, 78
Popkin, Samuel L., 100, 102
Position, Newman model, 77
Positions, campaign platform, 60
Positive image, 19
Postindustrial society, 10
Postman, Leo J., 30-31
Poverty
  Bush versus Gore, 127, 128
  LDS supporters, 130
Powell, Colin
  Newman cognitive model, 94
  Newman-Sheth model, 121, 123-124,124t, 125

Power
    ideal Polish candidate study, 41, 42t, 43, 44t, 45i
    ideal political leader, 36, 37
    Polish advertising study, 50t, 51t, 53
    political communication element, 152
Preprimary stage, 72i, 78-79
Presidential candidates, Polish survey, 41, 42t, 43, 44t, 45, 45i
Price
    economic/political marketing, 60-61
    Niffenegger model, 66i, 67, 68-69
Primary stage, 72i, 79
Product
    Newman model, 72i, 73i, 75, 77
    Niffenegger model, 66i, 67-68
Professionalism
    ideal Polish candidate study, 41, 43, 44t
    Polish advertising study, 51t, 52
Program, 60
Promotion, Niffenegger model, 66i, 67, 69-70
Prototypical theory, 198
Proximity, Gestalt psychology, 27, 197
Public journalism persuasion antidote, 210-211
Pull marketing, 77
Purzycki, Jan, 18
Push marketing, 77

Questionnaire, structural equation method, 160-163

Radcliff, Benjamin, 98
Rahn, Wendy
    derivation/rationalization, 55
    superman/everyman model, 40
Rational choice theory model, 95-96
Rational voters
    combined predictability analysis, 145
    Newman/Sheth model, 92-93
Rational voting critique, 98-100
Rationalization, 55
Reagan, Ronald
    current events, 115
    everyman model, 40, 41
    leadership attributes study, 38
    Newman-Sheth model, 117-120, 118t, 119t, 120t
    Niffenegger model, 67, 68, 70, 71
Realism, natural/social phenomena, 25-27
Realist model/s
    comparative analysis, 188-189
    and constructivist model, 189-191, 190i, 192
    political marketing, 3-4
Realist structural equation analysis
    Bush versus Gore, 183-183
    Polish presidential elections, 180-182, 181i
Realist structural equation model
    approach of, 156, 177-185
    voting behavior, 177-185
Reality, 25
Reason, Polish study, 42t, 44t
Reasoned action, 108, 109
Reed, Edward, perceptual illusions, 199
Regression analysis, 109
Reliability
    ideal Polish candidate study, 42t, 44t
    leadership attributes, 37
Representativeness, 99, 100t
Republican Party
    Bush versus Gore, 125, 126-129, 127t, 128t
    decrease in, 12, 13i
    issue ownership, 96
    Reagan versus Anderson, 117-120, 118t, 119t, 120t
    U.S. cognitive structural equation analysis, 174
Residence, 135
Responsibility, Polish study, 42t, 44t, 45i
Responsible Electorate, The, 97
Retrospective voting, 97-98
Rice, William, 210

Rimal, Rajiv, 11
Romania, presidential candidate study, 45-46
Roosevelt, Franklin D. (FDR)
　false memories, 204-205
　sociostructural research, 9
　in wheel chair, 57, 58i
Rosch, Eleanor, 198
Rosen, Jay, 210
Russell, Bertrand, 33
Russia, 18

Sagarin, Brad, 210
Salaries
　LDS supporters, 130
　SDS supporters, 133
Saris, Renee, 54
Scheucher, Christian, 19
Schooler, Jonathan W., 102
Schwarzenegger, Arnold, 116
SDS. *See* Social Democrats of Slovenia (SDS)
Sears, David O., 102-103
Selective exposure, 210
Self-control
　ideal Polish candidate study, 42t, 44t
　ideal Romanian candidate study, 45
Self-interest, 102-103
Self-presentation, 57
Selling concept, 72i, 73i, 75
Senft, Christian, 19
Sequential model
　constructivist-realist comparison, 191
　political advertising, 153-155, 154i
　political advertising impact, 212-214, 212i
Seriousness, Polish study, 42t, 44t, 45i
Serna, Sherman, 210
Service sector, 10
Sheth, Jagdis N., 92, 116-117
"Showroom" target areas, 71
Siew Meng Leong, 54
Signal-taking, 99, 101t
Similarity, Gestalt psychology, 27, 197

Simulation, 99, 100t
Sincerity, ZLDS supporters, 133
Singapore
　planned behavior theory, 109
　political emotions study, 54
Singh, Kulwant, 54
Situational contingency
　Bush versus Gore, 126
　LDS supporters, 132
　SDS supporters, 133
　term, 93
　ZLDS supporters, 131, 133
Situational voters, 93
Sleep of Reason Produces Monsters, The, 35
Slovenia
　cognitive structural equation analysis, 169-173, 171t, 172i, 173i
　combined predictability analysis, 142
　comparative constructivist analysis, 185, 186, 187
　parliamentary elections, 129-134, 131t, 133t, 134t
　political trends, 217
　structural equation models, 159, 160
Social animal, 7
Social attributes, 105i, 105-106
Social class
　British study, 88
　European Parliamentary elections, 89
　Finnish Parliamentary elections, 86, 87i, 88
　sociological approach, 85
Social cleavage voting, 9-11
Social cognition, 3
Social community, 9
Social competence, 50t, 51t
Social confidence, 52t
Social Democratic Party, Parliamentary elections, 86, 87i
Social Democrats of Slovenia (SDS)
　cognitive structural equation analysis, 170
　parliamentary elections, 130, 132-134, 133t, 134t
　structural equation models, 159

Index

Social imagery
  Bush versus Gore, 126
  Newman-Sheth model, 114, 117i
  Polish cognitive structural equation analysis, 165i, 166i, 167i, 168i, 169i
  Polish realist structural equation analysis, 181i, 182i
  predictive models study, 138t
  Reagan versus Anderson, 118t
  realist structural equation model, 178i, 179i
  Slovenia cognitive structural equation analysis, 172i, 173i
  structural equation models, 157i, 158i, 159i
  structural equation questionnaire, 160-161
  term, 93
  U.S. cognitive structural equation analysis, 175i, 176i
  U.S. realist structural equation analysis, 184i
Social performance, 17
Social psychology model
  party identification, 90-92
  social animal, 7
  voter personality, 92-95
Social reality, 3
Social validation, 209
Social variables, 104
Social voters, 93
Social-psychological model, combined predictability analysis, 143-145
Sociodemographic model,
  characteristics of, 135
  combined predictability analysis, 143
  predictive capacity, 136-137
  predictive models study, 138, 139t, 139, 140, 140t, 141t, 142t
Socioeconomic program, 54
Sociogeographic model, 104

Sociological model
  assumptions of, 85-86
  combined predictability analysis, 143
  European Parliamentary elections, 86, 88-90
  Finnish Parliamentary elections, 86, 87i, 88
Sociology, *homo politicus*, 7
Sociostructural method
  assumptions of, 9-10
  class model, 10-11
  emergence of, 9
Sociotropic voting, 97, 98
Source derogation, 209
Spain, planned behavior theory, 109-111, 110i, 146
Spatial aspects, 104
Speech, 8
Split-ticket voting, 14-15
Stereotypes, 99, 101t
Stevenson, Adlai, 67
Strategy, Newman model, 72i
Streisand, Barbara, 21
Structural equation analysis
  Bush versus Gore, 173-177, 175i, 176i
  Slovenia parliamentary elections, 169-173, 171t, 172i, 173i
Structural equation method
  Polish presidential elections, 162-173, 156i, 165i, 166i, 167i, 168i, 169i
  realist approach, 177-185, 178i, 179i
  research method, 160-162
  variable hypothesis, 156-159
Subjective norms, planned behavior theory, 108, 109i, 108, 111
Sullivan, John L., 40
Superman/everyman model, 40-41
Support groups, 60
Switch gestalt, 155
Symbols, 21
Symmetry, 198
Sympathy, 36

Taxes, ZLDS supporters, 131
Technology, 83
Television
  influence of, 150-151
  Polish election study, 48, 49, 50t-51t, 52t, 52-53
  political advertising, 46, 47
  visual distortion study, 200
Test market, 79
Thatcher, Margaret, 103
"Theater of everyday life, the," 17
Thinking, 32
Timing, 69
Totalitarian states
  freedom as constraint, 215-217
  limitations on freedom, 2
  partisanship, 11
Truman, Harry, 9
Tversky, Amos
  availability hypothesis, 215
  cognitive heuristics, 99
Tymiński, Stanislaw
  candidate-centered politics, 17-18
  nontraditional background, 16

Undecided voters
  1964-1992, 13
  increase in, 12
  political campaigns, 70-71
"Underdog effect," 186-187
Unemployment, Bush versus Gore, 128
Unions, Bush versus Gore, 127
United List of Social Democrats, (ZLSD)
  cognitive structural equation analysis, 170-171, 171t, 172-173
  comparative constructivist analysis, 185-186
  parliamentary elections, 130, 131t, 132-133, 134t
  structural equation models, 159
United States (U.S.)
  candidate-centered politics, 17

United States (U.S.) *(continued)*
  cognitive structural equation analysis, 173-177, 175i, 176i
  combined predictability analysis, 142, 143, 144
  comparative constructivist analysis, 185, 186, 187
  comparative realist analysis, 188-189, 189i
  constructivist-realist comparison, 190i, 191, 191t
  decrease in party identification, 12, 74
  freedom as constraint, 216
  marketing strategy, 192-193
  Newman model, 74
  planned behavior theory, 109
  program/issues voting, 103
  realist structural equation analysis, 183t, 183-185
  structural equation models, 159, 160
Unpredictability, 51t

Valencia Garate, J. F., Basque study, 109, 110i, 146
VALS, voter traits, 92, 95
Veryzer, Robert, 198
"Virtual reality," 196
Visual distortion study, 200, 201i
Vote-splitting, 15t
Voter segmentation
  British Parliamentary elections, 88-90
  Finnish Parliamentary elections, 86, 87i, 88
  Newman model, 72i, 76-77, 125
  Niffenegger model, 66i, 70
  political communication element, 152
  social psychology models, 90-95
  sociological approach, 85
Voting behavior
  1964-1992 elections, 12-13, 14i
  causal-effect model, 104

Voting behavior *(continued)*
  cognitive philosophy, 25
  cognitive psychology, 8-9
  cognitive/affective influences, 3-4
  cognitive-emotional elements, 147-149, 148t
  combined predictability analysis, 142-146
  comparative constructivist analysis, 185-187
  comparative realist analysis, 188-189
  constructivist-realist comparison, 189-191, 191i, 191t
  dealignment indicator, 15t
  decline in partisanship, 11, 12, 74-75
  decline in party identification, 12, 13i
  economic models, 95-103
  European Parliamentary elections, 89
  Finnish Parliamentary elections, 86, 87i
  individualization of, 16
  manipulation of, 205-206
  media influence, 149-153
  Newman-Sheth model, 104, 112-146
  planned behavior model, 104, 108-111, 109i, 110i
  Polish cognitive structural equation analysis, 162-173, 156i, 165i, 166i, 167i, 168i, 169i
  Polish realist structural equation analysis, 180-183, 181i
  political involvement model, 135-137
  political marketing epistemology, 8
  practical motives, 8
  predictive models study, 137-142, 138t, 139t, 140t, 141t, 142t
  realist structural equation model, 177-185, 178i, 179i
  resistance to manipulation, 206-212
  Slovenian cognitive structural equation analysis, 169-173, 171t, 172i, 173i

Voting behavior *(continued)*
  social psychology models, 90-95
  sociodemographic model, 135
  sociogeographic model, 104-108, 105i
  sociostructural goal, 10
  sociostructural model, 10-11
  structural equation models, 156-159, 157i, 158i, 159i
  U.S. cognitive structural equation analysis, 173-177, 175i, 176i
  U.S. realist structural equation analysis, 183t, 183-185
Voting date, 60
Voting districts, 63
Voting preference, 10

Wałęsa, Lech
  emotional feelings predictor, 147-148, 148t
  Polish presidential candidate, 41, 42t
  political advertising study, 48, 49, 50t, 51t, 52, 53
Wallace, George, 67
"Waning of humanness, the," 16
Ward, Ian, 216
"Washed out," 97
Wattenberg, Martin P.
  candidate-centered politics, 17
  candidate personality attributes, 37-38
  influence of emotions, 193
  partisanship, 14, 74
  party identification model objections, 91
  political emotions, 54
  program/issues voting, 103
  sociostructural critique, 11
  vote-splitting, 15
Weiner, Bernard, 36
Wilkie, Wendell, 9
Wilson, Timothy D.
  decision making, 102
  political emotions, 54

Wink, Kenneth A., 80, 81
Winning, 61
Wirthlin Worldwide, 1996 opinion poll, 38, 39i
Wisdom, Polish study, 42t, 44t, 45i
Women's equality, Bush versus Gore, 127
Women's rights, ZLDS supporters, 131
Wood, David, 91
Workers, Finnish elections, 86, 87i, 88

Yeltsin, Boris, 18
Yorke, D. A., 88, 89

Zajonc, Robert B., 33, 34, 193
ZLSD. *See* United List of Social Democrats, (ZLSD), parliamentary elections, 130
Zmuidinas, Mary, 36
Zuwernik, Jacks, 209-210